Dartmouth College v. Woodward

LANDMARK LAW CASES & AMERICAN SOCIETY

Julie Novkov and Victoria Woeste
Series Editors

Peter Charles Hoffer
N. E. H. Hull
Founding Series Editors

RECENT TITLES IN THE SERIES

Prigg v. Pennsylvania, H. Robert Baker
The Detroit School Busing Case, Joyce A. Baugh
Lizzie Borden on Trial, Joseph A. Conforti
The Japanese American Cases, Roger Daniels
Judging the Boy Scouts of America, Richard J. Ellis
Fighting Foreclosure, John A. Fliter and Derek S. Hoff
The Passenger Cases and the Commerce Clause, Tony A. Freyer
Discrediting the Red Scare, Robert Justin Goldstein
The Great Yazoo Lands Sale, Charles F. Hobson
The Free Press Crisis of 1800, Peter Charles Hoffer
Rutgers v. Waddington, Peter Charles Hoffer
The Woman Who Dared to Vote, N. E. H. Hull
Plessy v. Ferguson, Williamjames Hull Hoffer
Goldwater v. Carter, Joshua E. Kastenberg
The Tokyo Rose Case, Yasuhide Kawashima
Gitlow v. New York, Marc Lendler
The Unusual Story of the Pocket Veto Case, 1926–1929, Jonathan Lurie
Opposing Lincoln, Thomas C. Mackey
Medellín v. Texas, Alan Mygatt-Tauber
American by Birth, abridged ed., Carol Nackenoff and Julie Novkov
The Supreme Court and Tribal Gaming, Ralph A. Rossum
The 9/11 Terror Cases, Allan A. Ryan
Obscenity Rules, Whitney Strub
On Account of Sex, Philippa Strum
Speaking Freely, Philippa Strum
The Campaign Finance Cases, Melvin I. Urofsky
Race, Sex, and the Freedom to Marry, Peter Wallenstein
Bush v. Gore, 3rd expanded ed., Charles L. Zelden

For a complete list of titles in the series go to www.kansaspress.ku.edu.

ADAM R. NELSON

Dartmouth College v. Woodward

Colleges, Corporations, and the Common Good

UNIVERSITY PRESS OF KANSAS

© 2025 by the University Press of Kansas
All rights reserved

Published by the University Press of Kansas (Lawrence, Kansas 66045), which was organized by the Kansas Board of Regents and is operated and funded by Emporia State University, Fort Hays State University, Kansas State University, Pittsburg State University, the University of Kansas, and Wichita State University.

Library of Congress Cataloging-in-Publication Data

Names: Nelson, Adam R., author.
Title: Dartmouth College v. Woodward : colleges, corporations, and the common good / Adam R. Nelson.
Other titles: Dartmouth College vs. Woodward
Description: Lawrence : University Press of Kansas, 2025. | Series: Landmark law cases and American society | Includes bibliographical references and index.
Identifiers: LCCN 2024042514 (print) | LCCN 2024042515 (ebook) | ISBN 9780700638673 (cloth) | ISBN 9780700638680 (paperback) | ISBN 9780700638697 (ebook)
Subjects: LCSH: Dartmouth College—Trials, litigation, etc. | Woodward, William Henry, 1774-1818—Trials, litigation, etc. | Contracts—United States—Cases. | Corporation law—United States—Cases. | Constitutional law—United States—Cases. | United States. Supreme Court. | New Hampshire. Superior Court of Judicature. | BISAC: LAW / Legal History | LAW / Constitutional
Classification: LCC KF228.D36 N45 2025 (print) | LCC KF228.D36 (ebook) | DDC 346.7302—dc23/eng/20240911
LC record available at https://lccn.loc.gov/2024042514.
LC ebook record available at https://lccn.loc.gov/2024042515.

British Library Cataloguing-in-Publication Data is available.
Authorised Representative Details: Easy Access System Europe
Mustamäe tee 50, 10621 Tallinn, Estonia | gpsr.requests@easproject.com

CONTENTS

Prologue vii

Introduction 1

Part I. The Context

1. A Quest for a Charter 11

2. Incorporation ... and Ill Will 26

3. Public Support and Public Supervision 40

4. Corporations, Contracts, and the Constitution 53

5. Who Controls the College? Who Controls the Church? 67

Part II. The Case

6. *Dartmouth College v. Dartmouth University* 81

7. *Trustees of Dartmouth College v. Woodward* 93

8. Founders and First Donors 108

9. Advice from a "High Authority" 120

10. "It Is, Sir, a Small College, and Yet There Are Those Who Love It" 132

Part III. The Consequences

11. How to Win Friends and Influence Justices 149

12. The Marshall Court Decides 161

13. "New Facts" ... and New Foundations 177

14. "A University ... under the Auspices and Control of the Legislature" 190

15. Colleges, Contracts, and the Common Good 203

Conclusion 213

Relevant Cases 225

Chronology 229

Bibliographic Essay 237

Index 259

PROLOGUE

How did a dispute over the charter of a colonial-era college lead to a landmark case in American corporate law? When the US Supreme Court decided *Trustees of Dartmouth College v. Woodward* in 1819, it held that charters of incorporation were legal "contracts" and, thus, off-limits to legislative interference under the Contract Clause of the US Constitution, which states that "no state shall . . . pass any . . . law impairing the obligation of contracts." In this way, the court protected the country's private corporations from any state action that might alter, amend, adjust, abridge, or annul their charters (unless a state reserved the authority for such actions in the charter itself). Simply put, *Dartmouth* placed American corporate institutions, from colleges to churches to companies, largely beyond the scope of public supervision. Hence its landmark status.

The majority opinion was crafted by John Marshall as chief justice. Arguably his most important pronouncement in the case was his definition of corporate "personhood," a definition that had evolved since the *Institutes* of Justinian (482–565 CE) to explain how law dealt with corporations as if they were unitary individuals who held legal rights and responsibilities under the government-issued charters from which they were born. "A corporation is an artificial being, invisible, intangible, and existing only in contemplation of law," Marshall wrote. "Being the mere creature of law, it possesses only those properties which the charter of creation confers upon it, either expressly or as incidental to its very existence. These are such as are supposed best calculated to effect the object for which it was created."

The question in *Dartmouth* concerned the nature of the corporate "person" whose rights were protected by contract. Under the US Constitution, all people have certain natural rights—and citizens have further rights secured by law. But what about corporations? What rights do they have, or what rights *should* they have? As "artificial beings" created by citizens through charters, should citizens retain the authority to regulate the corporations their governments create? If so, what authority should they retain, for example, to protect the public safety, or common good, from corporate malfeasance? Over the past two centuries, these questions have come before the court many times, but the court has never deviated from its original point in *Dartmouth* that private corporations have chartered rights that lie beyond the scope of public regulation.

But what if the historical foundations on which the majority built its decision were shaky? What if the court misinterpreted the history of Dartmouth College or, specifically, the roots of its charter? What if the court embraced a false narrative that mischaracterized what had been a public college—a public corporation—as "private"? What if, as this book will suggest, the court either misunderstood the history of the corporation before it or (worse) deliberately misconstrued that history? If so, then perhaps the foundations of *Dartmouth v. Woodward*, indeed the foundations of American corporate law, would rest on dubious grounds. Of course, the justices simply could have identified another case to reach the decision they wanted to reach, but they could not have used the case of Dartmouth College, and the subsequent history of corporate law, or at least the history of corporate law applied to certain kinds of colleges, might have taken a different path.

This book explores that possibility.

INTRODUCTION

In recent years, many have debated the "public" versus "private" aims of higher education, but in the early nineteenth century no state had a more contentious—or consequential—debate than New Hampshire, where bitter antagonists battled for control of Dartmouth College, the state's only institution of advanced learning. While some insisted the college was a public institution that received public aid in exchange for public authority over its educational mission, others said the college was a strictly private institution, governed solely by its self-perpetuating board of trustees. In a struggle that concluded in 1819 with a landmark decision from the US Supreme Court on "corporate" rights, the case of Dartmouth College became a national cause célèbre, with implications not only for American higher education but also for American political culture, business development, religious institutions, and constitutional law.

Many who know vaguely of the high court's decision in *Trustees of Dartmouth College v. Woodward* are surprised to learn that it dealt with events that had occurred more than a half century earlier, when New Hampshire was still a British colony. Some are even more surprised to learn that neither side in the lawsuit—the college trustees on the one hand and the representatives of New Hampshire's state legislature on the other—was fully informed of the historical context that surrounded these events or, specifically, the *decades* of disagreement that had preceded and followed the creation of the college's disputed charter of incorporation. One important purpose of this book—especially its first section—is to review that context and recount how the arguments presented in court led to a historically ignorant, but nonetheless influential, decision. Another purpose is to reveal whose interests the court's decision ultimately served.

To begin with the basics, Dartmouth College was chartered in 1769 in Hanover, New Hampshire, by the royal governor of that colony, on behalf of the British Crown. A decade later, during the uncertain years of the revolutionary war, the college jockeyed to put itself under the jurisdiction of the new state of Vermont, but eventually it settled back under New Hampshire's territorial and legislative purview. Despite financial difficulties, the institution was reasonably stable until the early years of the nineteenth century, when a wave of spiritual revivals split the students and, ultimately, the college's president and trustees. Sectarian differences fed partisan differences—particularly during the War of 1812—until the split grew into a schism. Finally, in 1816, the New Hampshire legislature voted to amend the institution's charter and place it under public oversight.

The board of trustees contested this vote in court. It said the college was a strictly private institution governed solely by its trustees. At the state level, the board lost: the Superior Court of New Hampshire held that Dartmouth College, founded by the royal Crown with royal contributions of land, was in fact a public institution created to serve the public interest. The trustees disagreed and carried their case to the US Supreme Court on appeal. With help from *wunder*-lawyer Daniel Webster (a Dartmouth alum), the college persuaded the court that its "founder" was not actually the Crown and its "first donor" was not actually the colony. On the contrary, Webster argued (with limited historical evidence) the charter had grafted the college onto a preexistent Indian Charity School that had been moved from Connecticut to New Hampshire in exchange for the protections and privileges of the charter itself. The charter, said Webster, had made the prior "school" into a newly independent and self-governed "college."

The Indian Charity School had originated in the 1740s with Reverend Eleazar Wheelock, a Yale graduate who created the school to prepare Indian students for missionary work (and who later sought a charter for Dartmouth College). To support his school, Wheelock raised funds in the colonies and, in the mid-1760s, in England, where he sent agents to solicit donations. Among the school's English donors was William Legge, second Earl of Dartmouth, who offered to establish a board of trustees to solicit more contributions and supervise their use in the Indian school. This board collected a large sum, which sustained Wheelock's school after he moved from Connecticut to New Hampshire and then sought a charter for a college (funded by a colonial land grant) to supplement his school's work. The problem—which eventually prompted the lawsuit—was that Wheelock did not tell his English board about his college (or its land grant, or its parallel board of trustees), and when his original board found out, it explicitly prohibited any use of the *school's* money to support the *college*.

The school and college were thus distinct, but in court years later, Daniel Webster used the ambiguous language of the charter to suggest they were one and the same; that Wheelock had been the "founder" as well as the "first donor" of both; and that neither the Crown nor the colony had played a key role in *either* institution's establishment. All of Webster's arguments rested on the premise that Wheelock's "school" was legally identical with and financially inseparable from the "college." This premise was false. In fact, the school had been founded by Wheelock in collaboration with private donors, whereas the college was chartered by the Crown with help from a land grant on behalf of the public (in other words, the people of New Hampshire). Yet, when the case reached the US Supreme Court, the majority accepted Webster's narrative and ruled that Dartmouth College, under its charter and board of trustees, had no legal connection either with the colony of New Hampshire or with the state that replaced the colony after the revolution.

As far as the majority—led by chief justice John Marshall—was concerned, Dartmouth College was strictly private and therefore subject only to its own trustees' governance. Thus, when New Hampshire's legislature amended the institution's charter in 1816 to exert more public supervision over college operations, the court said the state acted beyond its authority. To reach this conclusion, the court relied on the law of corporations. Most "charitable" institutions—whether colleges or churches or joint-stock companies—were chartered as corporations, which meant they held both property and privileges under the auspices of their boards of trustees. But since the US Constitution said nothing about either "charters" or "corporations," the court had to find a way to justify its decision that Dartmouth College should be independently governed. To do so, it opted to read "charters of incorporation" as legal "contracts," which, once made for charitable purposes, could not be unmade without the consent of all parties.

Article 1, section 10, clause 1 of the US Constitution said that "no state shall ... pass any ... law impairing the obligation of contracts," and the court used this clause to rule that New Hampshire's attempt to amend Dartmouth's charter and place the college under public oversight represented an unconstitutional impairment of a private contract and, thus, a violation of private corporate rights. The court admitted that Dartmouth's charter had been crafted twenty years *before* the Constitution was ratified and that, during the colonial era, the British Parliament had possessed the power to amend charters at will. In fact, the college's original board of trustees (which included several colonial officials) knew that its property and privileges were subject to colonial (ultimately royal) oversight. Still, the Marshall Court used the subsequent constitutional protection of private contracts to say that, despite an initial land grant from the royal governor on behalf of the colony (in other words, the public), the charter made Dartmouth College a private corporation that was off-limits to legislative oversight.

———

Trustees of Dartmouth College v. Woodward had far-reaching implications not only for American college governance but also for American corporate governance in general. The basic conclusion was that private corporations had constitutionally protected rights of self-governance. What made the case important was its transformation of an institution not previously considered private into what later observers would call matter-of-factly "a private college." This book shows how the court used a dispute over college governance to reach its first major decision on corporate rights, how that decision reflected a deeper shift in American legal and political culture, and, ultimately, how it launched a new movement to guard private interests from public supervision. At its core, this case asked a simple question: Should corporate entities such as colleges (as well as churches and companies) be protected from legislative oversight, and if so, how?

To some, it seemed obvious that colleges should be subject to public supervision. If education, including higher education, was a public good, then it seemed axiomatic that legislatures, as the agents of the public interest, should have the power to oversee it. To others, however, it seemed equally self-evident that institutions of higher education should be protected from majoritarian politics—especially when majority rule took narrow partisan forms. If higher education was to serve truly public interests, critics said, then it had to be disinterested: independent of political interference. Thus, when New Hampshire's legislators seized control of Dartmouth College, they said they did so because the college trustees were driven by partisan zeal, but the college trustees countered that legislators (or legislative majorities) were partisan themselves. And yet, if trustees and legislators were equally partisan, then how could a college be governed to serve truly public ends?

The case of *Dartmouth v. Woodward* asked how colleges might be protected from partisan (or majoritarian) politics and how corporations in general should be so protected. During the colonial era, charters of incorporation were relatively uncommon, but they proliferated during the early nineteenth century, in part to encourage an expansion of charitable activities that served the public good. "Charities" were soon joined by "companies," also presumed to serve public interests. Yet, this era's profusion of corporations led some to worry they might forget their public mission and focus instead on "private" gain. And if banks and businesses, or canals and turnpike companies, started to neglect their public-service mission, then it seemed plausible that *colleges* (also chartered as charitable corporations) might do the same. Was it not the state's responsibility to regulate corporations to ensure they advanced public aims? Some thought so, but others said it was the state's responsibility to protect *corporations* from overbearing public oversight.

Herein lay the central issues of the *Dartmouth* case, which reflected the court's response to a key shift in the role of corporations during the early nineteenth century (more than it reflected a careful assessment of historical circumstances that surrounded Dartmouth's original charter in the mid-eighteenth century). Initially, corporations had been chartered to fulfill valuable public functions, and many presumed a charter meant a corporation should be the only entity to serve a specific function: they expected a corporation to enjoy a public monopoly. This expectation applied to colleges no less than canals or the "established" church (entitled by law to receive local tax revenues). But this expectation of monopoly lasted only as long as one party held the right to grant charters. As soon as new parties came to power, they granted their own charters for their own corporations. In this way, they undermined their rivals' monopolies, but they also undid any presumed link between corporations and the idea of a unified "public good."

This break marked a broader shift from a "republican commonwealth" to a "democratic marketplace" that has intrigued generations of American political and constitutional historians, especially historians of the early party system. With the ratification of the US Constitution, the Federalist Party's desire for centralized legislative authority seemed ascendant, but no sooner had principles of centralization taken constitutional form than Federalists began to lose elections to anti-Federalist opponents. With the Jeffersonian "revolution of 1800," the new Republican Party seized the electoral upper hand and started to grant charters to corporations under Republicans' control—while Federalists, once enthusiastic about centralized legislative authority, increasingly looked for alternate ways to hold on to power... and property. For the Federalists, one solution was to strengthen the independent legal rights of private corporations and to secure those rights in the courts. Put simply, Federalists shifted their attention from a legislative power to establish "public" corporations to new legal protections for corporations increasingly redefined as "private."

Dartmouth exemplified this shift. With the help of politically sympathetic justices (and savvy legal strategies), the case showed how a defense of corporate rights could protect vested interests from legislative interference. Whether this defense was ultimately a defense of private or public interests was in the eye of the beholder, for even as Federalists used the law of corporations to protect the institutions they controlled (from colleges to canals), Republicans soon learned to do the same whenever their party was not in power. The defense of private corporate rights thus became a matter of bipartisan consensus, part of the basic fabric of American constitutionalism. This consensus was *not* a continuation of the early commonwealth hope that corporations would serve the public interest. Rather, its core premise was that diverse corporations should have equal access to independent charters in a competitive market of private interests.

How did such a fundamental shift arise from a dispute over the governance of a small New England college? How did partisan and sectarian disagreements get framed as fights over institutional charters? The answer is that, in the late eighteenth and early nineteenth centuries, the dispute at Dartmouth stood in for similar disputes at virtually every other college—and, in turn, countless other "corporations," from churches to joint-stock companies—all of which rose up in defense of private chartered rights. During the colonial period, all colleges were assumed to be quasi-public corporations, yet by the 1810s and 1820s many claimed to be quasi-private. Indeed, after *Dartmouth* in 1819, every new institution of higher education had to decide whether it would be "public" or "private." The same decision faced churches and companies, most of which eventually chose to embrace private corporate rights. This book reveals the roots of that choice . . . as well as its consequences for American law and society writ large.

To understand how a college once considered "public" later came to be "private," one must understand the foundation of the American corporation, and in the case of Dartmouth one cannot understand this foundation unless one understands the complex events that preceded the institution's establishment. Indeed, the dispute over Dartmouth was at its core a dispute over a document—a charter—and the contexts from which that document arose. Histories rarely have precise origins, but scholars agree this story did not begin in 1769 (when New Hampshire's royal governor issued a charter, along with a public land grant, for a college); rather, it commenced at least a quarter century earlier, in 1744, when the minister-educator Eleazar Wheelock created an Indian Charity School in Lebanon, Connecticut, an institution later conflated with the college. To understand the *Dartmouth* case, one must start with this school and its quest for spiritual, financial, and ultimately legal support to advance its evangelical aims. From that point, all else followed.

PART I

The Context

CHAPTER I

A Quest for a Charter

Eleazar Wheelock understood the difference between "public" and "private" institutions of education. Born in Windham, Connecticut, in 1711, the man who became the first president of Dartmouth College was a great grandson of the first teacher in the first tax-funded public school in the British American colonies. His great-grandfather, Ralph Wheelock, had earned a BA from Clare Hall at Cambridge University, where he was a contemporary of John Milton and John Eliot (known for his missions among the Indians of the Massachusetts Bay Colony). Early members of the Puritan movement, Wheelock's ancestors played a prominent role in colonial affairs, including educational affairs, first in Watertown, Dedham, and Medfield, Massachusetts, and later in Connecticut, New York, Ohio, and points west. It was Ralph Wheelock's grandson, also named Ralph, who brought the family to Windham and became the father of Dartmouth's future leader.

Eleazar Wheelock earned his BA at Yale in 1733 then spent an extra year at the college to qualify for ordination in the publicly supported Congregationalist church. As the colony's official "established" church, all Congregationalist parishes were entitled to public revenues from local taxes, which meant ordained ministers had a guaranteed income. To become a minister, however, candidates had to graduate from Harvard or Yale (both subsidized by their colonies) or from Oxford, Cambridge, or another European university. Wheelock followed this path. Ordained during the summer of 1734, he was called the next year to become pastor of the Second Congregationalist Church in Lebanon, Connecticut, a few miles from his childhood home. He served this parish—with a publicly funded salary and twenty-five-acre farm (later expanded to over 150 acres, worked by himself and several enslaved laborers)—for the next three decades.

Wheelock entered the ministry at the start of the first Great

Awakening, a decade-long upheaval in the religious life of the American colonies. Led by charismatic itinerant preachers such as George Whitefield, Gilbert Tennent, and James Davenport, the "awakeners" called for a return to Puritan values of personal devotion and piety. They preached a religion of the heart, not the head, and hosted all-night tent revivals to bring the wayward into their fold. Known for their fire-and-brimstone sermons, they considered many of the ministers of the colonies' established churches an overly intellectual set of pedants who cared little about the affective dimensions of faith. They often accused politically entrenched Congregationalist leaders of private, sectarian interests that were protected by publicly sanctioned monopolies (with mandatory tax support). They wanted either to reform the established church or, alternatively, to claim a share of public resources for their *own* churches.

The awakeners directed some of their sharpest criticism at Congregationalist institutions like Yale, which became a target for evangelical revivals. Tensions at Yale mounted until 1742, when a junior minister-in-training named David Brainerd returned from a revival at the so-called Shepherd's Tent and criticized the piety of a tutor who led daily chapel services. "I believe he has no more grace than the chair I am leaning on," Brainerd joked, a remark that made its way to President Thomas Clap, who decided that, since it was Brainerd's "second offense," he should be expelled (in accordance with a statute approved two years earlier by the college trustees). It was a harsh punishment, for without a degree, Brainerd had no prospect of a ministerial appointment in the publicly funded Congregational order, but Clap—aligned with colonial officials who supported the college with annual public grants—had no patience for awakeners.

Brainerd's expulsion did not end the religious conflict at Yale, however. In response, the revivalists of the Shepherd's Tent set up their own college in New London, a few miles east. Gilbert Tennent modeled his college for "dissenters" after the original "Log College" that his father, William Tennent, had founded in New Jersey a dozen years earlier. Clap, however, petitioned the colony to close the rival school. As historian Jürgen Herbst notes, the colony "looked upon Yale as its provincial establishment and did not tolerate competitors." A new law said that "unless a college ... was duly licensed by the [colony], its teachers were subject to fines and its students (and those who housed and fed them) were to come under the provisions of [an] earlier act outlawing all but 'settled' ministers." All colleges were to be *public* colleges, subject to legislative oversight. Alternatives would not be allowed.

The aim of the new law was not merely to close the Shepherd's Tent but to secure Yale's public educational monopoly. Three years later, in 1745, this aim was accomplished when Yale got a charter of incorporation from the Connecticut assembly. Yale's charter made its trustees—all Congregationalist ministers—the autonomous "fellows" of the college and said that members of the assembly held a right, as visitors, to inspect the college, as well as its curriculum, "as often as required" and to impose rules or regulations "when they shall think proper." This right of public visitation was granted in exchange for annual grants from the colony, a deal Clap accepted. In his mind, the college and colony were mutually supportive Congregationalist institutions, which, as far as he was concerned, meant that no evangelical "tent" college should be permitted to serve the "public" in Connecticut.

Here, then, was the context that Wheelock entered when he arrived in Lebanon to begin his ministry, an ordained Congregationalist who boldly sided with the awakeners. "As an itinerant preacher himself, he initially supported the rights of itinerant preachers (or so-called 'New Lights') to preach in towns without invitation, and even to criticize local clergy," notes one biographer. Within a year, he gave more than 465 sermons to spread the revivalists' message. His message, however, was not welcomed by authorities from the church or colony, who sought to put him in his place with financial penalties. In 1743, the assembly cut his tax-funded salary, but this move only led him to look for other sources of income. Later that year, he opened a Latin preparatory school in Lebanon . . . the school that would set his work on a course to subsequent litigation.

At his school, Wheelock taught local youth as well as students from local Indian tribes. In the context of British settler colonialism, during a period when revivalists put increasing energy into missionary enterprises, his school included at least two Indian pupils supported by charitable donations. In fact, David Brainerd himself, after his dismissal from Yale, had been called by the Presbyterians' evangelical branch to missionize among the Indians: first in New York in 1742, then in Pennsylvania in 1743, and finally in New Jersey in 1744. In the meantime, "New Light" dissenters continued their quest to give awakened youth alternative (in other words, non-Congregationalist) places to prepare for religious service. The result, in 1746, was the College of New Jersey, which opened to great enthusiasm (in every sense of the word). Before long, revivalist students even left Yale to enroll.

The educational challenge to established church authority continued to spread. In 1749, for example, a dissenter in New York's colonial assembly, William Livingston (the father of future US Supreme Court justice Henry Brockholst Livingston), printed *Some Serious Thoughts on the Design of Erecting a College in the Province of New York*, and that same year, Benjamin Franklin issued *Proposals Relating to the Education* of Youth in Pennsylvania, followed in 1751 by Franklin's establishment of the nonsectarian Academy of Philadelphia (which later became the College of Philadelphia and, eventually, the University of Pennsylvania). The next year, William Smith in New York revived Livingston's proposal in his *General Idea of the College of Mirania* (1752), a fantastical vision of a future college addressed to members of the colonial assembly, with a request for aid.

In 1753, Trinity Church, the wealthiest Anglican parish in New York, offered land to fund Smith's proposed college, and in 1754 the church drafted a charter that repeated this offer (in exchange for a promise that chapel services at the college would follow the colony's established Anglican liturgy). When college planners appeared ready to accept this deal, William Livingston protested. He told a fellow Yale graduate that Anglican sectarianism would bring "priestcraft and bigotry" to New York in "less than half a century." In a series of editorials, he called instead for a college under strictly civic and secular control. Aware that "creating . . . a body politic by act of legislation, without a previous charter, is unprecedented and, indeed, an infringement on the prerogatives of the crown," he nonetheless argued for a college outside the jurisdiction of the established church.

Livingston's protests fell on deaf ears. On November 2, 1754, acting colonial governor James Delaney signed a charter, issued by the Crown, for a college under Anglican control. As historian Jürgen Herbst notes, the college, "known by the name of King's College," was duly incorporated "for the instruction of New York youths in the learned languages and liberal arts and sciences." It received the land promised by Trinity Church with a stipulation that its president would forever be a member of the Anglican communion. To confirm Anglican influence, both the archbishop of Canterbury and the First Lord Commissioner of Trade and Plantations were assigned to its self-perpetuating board of trustees and "empowered to appoint proxies to represent them at meetings." Samuel Johnson, a loyal Anglican, became King's first president.

King's claimed to serve the public, supported by the Crown and the colony's established church, but Livingston said the college represented a private—sectarian—usurpation of higher education. When the colony offered King's a share of public lottery funds, he again countered with a plan to incorporate "a rival college," an institution to be known as the Provincial College of New York, with access to public funds in exchange for public oversight but outside the church's purview. His institution would bar religious test oaths and enjoy public subsidies from an excise tax. Livingston outlined this proposal in a set of essays printed in the *New York Mercury* between November 1754 and November 1755—to no effect. King's, protected by a royal charter, said it served New York's "public interest" via a publicly funded Anglican monopoly over higher education in the colony.

In the meantime, Eleazar Wheelock continued to carry the evangelical spirit to students in Connecticut via his Lebanon school. He considered his Latin charity school a way to prepare future ministers as well as missionaries and, in the mid-1750s, looked for opportunities to place Indian youth in both roles. While it was unclear whether he ever taught any of his slaves to read or write, in 1754 his project of Indian education won the endorsement of his neighbor Joshua Moor, who gave two acres with a house and teacher in support of the venture. Wheelock's school—thereafter known as the Indian Charity School—quickly expanded to include more than fifty students from the Mohegan, Mohawk, Montauk, Narragansett, and Oneida tribes. His first Indian student had been a nineteen-year-old Mohegan named Samson Occom, who attended his school from 1743 to 1747 before he became a missionary among the

Montauks of Long Island and pursued ordination with the revivalist branch of the Presbyterian church.

Impressed by Occom's missionary success, Wheelock expanded his Indian Charity School with help from past Yale president Elisha Williams and two others—his brother-in-law Benjamin Pomeroy and his friend Samuel Moseley—who together sought to incorporate the charity school with themselves as trustees. They signed a deed of trust on July 17, 1755, for the property Moor had donated "for the foundation, use, and support of a charity school forever, for the instruction of Indians of any or all the tribes in North America, or other poor persons, in the knowledge and practice of the Protestant Christian religion, and all liberal arts and sciences as the said trustees shall think proper." They promised to support the school financially and secured £500 in private subscriptions to be paid "as soon as the school should become a body corporate." Here was a first step to charter the Indian Charity School, based on its local private donations.

Wheelock consulted William Smith Sr., a lawyer in New York (and later associate justice of the US Supreme Court), about the validity of his associates' deed of trust but was told it was defective, because it did not outline terms for the perpetuation of the board or preservation of its property. Smith told Wheelock to ask for a charter either from the colony or the Crown. But his friends hesitated, not only because a charter might limit the school's operations to Connecticut (many prospective Indian students hailed from elsewhere) but also because, with a charter from the colony, the assembly might seek to control the school (many college leaders felt that Yale's charter of 1745 had given the assembly too much authority over the institution). Also, since the colony *itself* was a "corporation," lines of authority could become ambiguous. Several associates told Wheelock that "a corporation within a corporation might be troublesome, as Yale College had sometimes been."

These early debates showed that charters of incorporation had important consequences for educational governance. On the one hand, a charter seemed to carry a risk of unwanted political influence. On the other hand, Wheelock's donors said they would not fund his enterprise until it secured "corporate" protections that put their donations under the care of an independent board of trustees—and thus, in their view, *beyond* the reach of the legislature. "If our suit for a charter be successful, the subscriptions will soon be filled up to £1,000, which, with the improvement of Mr. Moor's grant, will make a fund sufficient for the support of a master forever," Wheelock assured revivalist George Whitefield in 1756. "We have also encouragement that lands will be given as soon as we are capable of holding them and making the donors safe" via a charter to ensure that land donations could not be redirected by legislative whim. (The irony of land taken from Native peoples to fund their education was obviously lost on settler colonists.)

Some felt a charter from the Crown would provide more security than one from the colony, since Congregationalist legislators warned that Wheelock's evangelicalism threatened orthodoxy. Whitefield, eager to help, put Wheelock in touch with friends in London, who, in 1757, presented the idea of a royal charter to Lord Halifax (the head of British colonial affairs in North America), but Halifax disagreed with this approach. He thought a colonial act of incorporation would be "as authentic as any act passed in England," so Wheelock agreed to make another effort. In 1758, he repeated his request for a charter from Connecticut's assembly but again was refused. Officials said his Indian Charity School might upset other colonies. "We ... have comparatively few Indians among us," Wheelock admitted in a letter to Whitefield, and Connecticut was "not willing to do anything that ... may provoke the envy of our neighbors." New York, for example, had considered an Indian school of its own and did not want a rival.

Yet even as Connecticut blocked Wheelock's bid for a charter, a group of Congregationalists in New Hampshire began to appeal for educational reforms. In 1758, they petitioned New Hampshire's royal governor Benning Wentworth for a school, or even a *college*. They cited the "difficulties which attend the education of youth in this province by reason of our distance from any of the seats of learning" and said a college in New Hampshire could succeed "without prejudice to any other such seminary in neighboring colonies." Wentworth offered a charter on the condition that any college in New Hampshire would be affiliated with the colony's established Anglican church, under the supervision of the bishop of London (who oversaw Anglicanism in all the colonies). But this condition alarmed Congregationalists, who angled for a college under their own independent control—a nonstarter for Wentworth.

Wheelock, in Connecticut, watched these developments with interest. By 1758, his school's donor, Moor, had died, and Moor's widow had issued a new deed of trust to convey the school's landed property to Wheelock personally. Besides this land, Wheelock had two other sources of support for his school, the English Society for the Propagation of the Gospel in Foreign Parts and the Society in Scotland for Propagating Christian Knowledge, both of which made donations in 1756, 1758, and 1760. Then, in 1761, the Congregationalists in New Hampshire offered Wheelock a gift of £50 a year for the next five years (1762–67) if he moved his school north, but Governor Wentworth vetoed this pledge. Undeterred, the Congregationalists in New Hampshire reaffirmed their vote in 1762, and in 1763 the governor relented. He offered Wheelock a tract of land, plus £150, if he relocated his Indian Charity School to New Hampshire's western border, close to some of the Six Nations tribes.

Why had Wentworth changed his mind? War. During the Seven Years' War (1756–63), when the Six Nations sided with British settlers against French troops, Wentworth had chartered more than 130 new towns for defense purposes. Most were in western New Hampshire between the Connecticut River and the New York line—territory Wentworth claimed as part of his colony even as New York claimed the same land for itself. The new towns protected this region from the French (and their Indian allies), but their divided jurisdiction led to a decades-long dispute over the ownership of the so-called New Hampshire grants. To solidify his claim on this land, Wentworth promised a piece to Wheelock if he put his Indian Charity School there and brought some of his Connecticut neighbors to settle in the area. (The governor also held out the prospect of a charter, which the school needed to secure outstanding pledges.)

As these negotiations unfolded, Connecticut took note and, in 1763, made a bid to keep Wheelock's school as long as it was put under the control of the colony's established church. That year, Wheelock printed *A Plain and Faithful Narrative of the Original Design, Rise, Progress, and Present State of the Indian Charity School at Lebanon, in Connecticut* (1763), which envisioned a permanent home for a larger institution: partly "a school for reading and writing, etc." and partly "a college for the education of missionaries, schoolmasters, interpreters, &etc." Connecticut, in turn, allowed Wheelock to seek contributions for this enlarged institution "under the supervision of provincial authorities." It named six public agents to collect funds "and pay them over to the provincial treasurer" and three other agents to disburse these funds "to Wheelock for the use of his school." The aim was to bring Wheelock's institution under public supervision.

Given a choice between Connecticut and New Hampshire, it seems Wheelock preferred Connecticut, because its leaders were Congregationalist (not Anglican), and he was, at least officially, a Congregationalist minister. The unanswered question was: Could he get a charter from Connecticut when Yale opposed all competitors for public aid? When that college opened in 1701, the colonial assembly had pledged a yearly grant of £120 "in country pay" (agricultural produce), replaced in the charter of 1745 with a yearly grant of £100 "in silver money." Later, the assembly offered £200 a year, which covered approximately half the college's annual budget. In exchange, the assembly considered Yale a public corporation and claimed a right to "visit" the college and review its operations. As historian Dennis Holtschneider notes, "In frequent missives to the assembly, the corporation repeatedly characterized Yale's relation to the [colony] as having 'been founded' by the government to serve its residents."

All had seemed well until 1754, when the assembly suspended Yale's subsidy to protest the administration of President Thomas Clap, who allegedly misspent college funds. In response, Clap wrote a pamphlet, "The Religious Constitution of the College" (1754), which acknowledged that members of the assembly held "the same power over the college as they have over all other persons and estates in the colony, and a greater power as [its] constant benefactors." This power derived from British jurisprudence in the case of *Sutton's Hospital* (1612, frequently called the *Charterhouse* case, after the site of Sutton's hospital and school), which identified any chartered institution's "founder" as "he who makes the first donation of lands, funds, or other gifts and who prepares the first statutes for the government of the [institution]." The colony's annual gifts since 1701 suggested that it was Yale's "founder."

According to Clap, however, the colony was not the college's *first* donor and thus not its final authority. That honor went to a group of ten ministers who, he said, had "founded" Yale in 1699 with a donation of

{ *A Quest for a Charter* }

"forty folios" for its library. As the original donors (and named trustees) of the college, this group, Clap argued, had passed its private right of visitation down to its chosen successors in perpetuity. They, not the colony, had the authority to govern the college—or so Clap maintained. The assembly disagreed. It claimed that, based on its financial support, its *own* rights of visitation and governance superseded those of Yale's trustees, a conflict that came to a head in 1763 when the assembly demanded to review the college's books (a demand that coincided with the assembly's effort that year to put Wheelock's charity school also under its own financial and governmental control).

For his part, Clap felt that if he could focus attention on Yale's folios, then he could say the college's trustees (not the members of the assembly) were its rightful overseers. He cited Edward Coke's decision in *Sutton's Hospital* to bolster his arguments. As the dispute intensified over the next three years, he maintained in his *Annals, or History, of Yale College* (1766) that Yale's first trustees, "'by contract, became a society, or quasi-corporation, . . . two years before they had a charter,' and that, with their formal donation of books . . . they had founded the college." He added that, even though Yale's trustees had received an initial donation of six hundred acres from the colony "in the time of the sitting of the assembly in which the charter was given, and as one motive to induce the assembly to give it," the private folios, not the subsequent public land grant, marked the actual founding of the college—prior to its original charter. (A remarkably similar argument would be advanced in the *Dartmouth* case a half-century later.)

Clap held that, by virtue of its first donation of folios, Yale's private trustees superseded the colony's public governance rights. But he did not have the last word. Students in the college became increasingly unhappy with his leadership and eventually called for his resignation. When the president ignored their petition, they rebelled. They burned furniture and threatened several tutors with bodily harm. Clap sought to control the situation, but the students, when disciplined, simply left for other colleges. Faced with a mass exodus (only two of forty remained), the board of trustees finally demanded Clap's departure. He gave his final commencement speech in 1766, after which the assembly took over and once again subjected Yale to public inspection—which the board accepted in exchange for aid. These events attracted widespread interest.

Three years later, when Governor Wentworth in New Hampshire promised Eleazar Wheelock a charter if he relocated his Indian Charity School, he sought to ensure the colony's governance rights.

The central question at Yale—who controlled the college, the public assembly or private trustees?—rested on the law of corporations, which had originated in Roman civil law when the *Institutes* of Justinian outlined the "perpetual" nature of corporate governance. "The corporation, unless created for a specified term of years, had perpetual existence," observes historian Mary Frampton Beach. "It was not in any way affected by the changing hands . . . of the members, or their death, for, as long as one member lived, so did the corporation." This perpetuity of governance was crucial, because legally a corporation (corpus, or body) was considered an "invisible" or "artificial" person, intended to hold property (often landed property) forever. The question at Yale was about who gave—and therefore governed—the college's original property: the public assembly or the private trustees?

The most ancient corporate forms had lapsed during the Middle Ages but returned during the Renaissance and Reformation to structure church ownership of land. The law of corporations later evolved to allow property ownership among towns, chartered as municipal corporations, as well as joint-stock companies, chartered as business corporations (which often adopted guild-like characteristics, including bylaws and the use of corporate seals). Eventually, the early modern era settled on two forms of lay (nonchurch) corporations, namely, "civil" and "charitable" corporations. Civil corporations, "including both municipal and business corporations as well as . . . the company of surgeons in London," fell under the royal authority of the monarch. Charitable corporations, by contrast, were more independent. Under the Statute of Charitable Uses (1601), the Elizabethan law of corporations ensured that founders, as "first donors," could name "trustees" (apart from the Crown) who subsequently oversaw the use of donations in accordance with the founders' wishes.

To say that charitable corporations were more independent than civil corporations did not mean they were entirely autonomous. The monarch was still in charge. The Statute of Charitable Uses authorized the royal chancellor and his court of chancery (or court of equity) to establish commissions to see that corporations did in fact obey their founders' wishes. While this statute exempted from royal investigation "any college, hospital, or free school, which has special visitors, or governors, or overseers appointed ... by their founders," it noted that a corporation's trustees could not *also* be its visitors, lest they fail to hold themselves accountable for the appropriate use of a founder's gifts. In other words, notes historian Bruce Campbell, "where visitors were also trustees, and thus in a position to abuse the trust," a corporation was subject to investigation by royal courts. In such cases, the chancellor, as representative of the Crown, retained "visitatorial" (or "visitorial") jurisdiction.

In a few cases, notably among dissenters in New England, legal protections for corporate property derived from charters "issued by provincial legislatures without royal approval." A key example was Harvard College, founded in 1636 by "defiant" Puritans who announced their own public acts of incorporation for a college "without sending them to England for review." Harvard, in fact, was a corporation within a corporation, because the Massachusetts Bay Colony itself was a joint-stock company in which every landowner had a franchise (vote) as well as representation in the so-called General Court (which, two years before Harvard's establishment, had split into two bodies, the governor and his advisors in one, local representatives in the other). The General Court upheld the company's independent charter for the next half century, until 1686, when King James II, a Catholic, replaced it with a *royal* version to govern his short-lived "Dominion of New England."

The law of corporations saw big changes during the contentious reign of James II, which culminated in the Glorious Revolution of 1688, when Parliament challenged the king's authority—including his authority to alter charters (including the charters of colleges) at will. In a key case the previous year, Magdalen College, Oxford, had taken steps to elect a new master. James II ordered the college to elect a Catholic, but the college statutes made Catholics ineligible. The faculty (or "fellows") instead elected a Protestant, whereupon the king ordered a royal commission to look into the matter. Defiantly, the Protestant master rejected the right of the commission to visit the college, citing the fact that the bishop of Winchester (another Protestant) was the college's rightful "visitor." When the royal commission replaced the Protestant master with the bishop of Oxford (a convert to Catholicism), the fellows of the college said the Crown had violated their private corporate rights.

A year later, in 1688, with his own power in question, James II reversed course and sided with the Protestant leaders of the college, but it was too late. That fall, rebellious Parliamentarians drove the king into exile. Magdalen's case, however, paved the way for another, *Phillips v. Bury*, in 1689. This case involved Exeter College, Oxford, founded in 1314 with a large donation from William Stapleton and later chartered by Queen Elizabeth with statutes that made the bishop of Exeter its visitor. On October 16, 1689, master Arthur Bury expelled a member of the faculty named John Colmier for insubordination. Colmier appealed his expulsion, but the next year, when the bishop of Exeter attempted to investigate, Bury denied the bishop's "visitatorial" authority, whereupon the bishop removed Bury from his post. Bury, who considered himself the college's rightful governor, filed suit to reclaim his position. He asked the Court of King's Bench a simple question: Who had final authority to control the college under its charter?

In a case that subsequently played a role in the Dartmouth College litigation, three judges sided with Bury, while the chief justice, John Holt, sided with the bishop of Exeter as the college's statutory "visitor," and on appeal, the House of Lords upheld Holt's decision. His thirteen-page order became *the* rule on the authority of external visitors to govern privately endowed charitable (in other words, eleemosynary) corporations in the public interest. "There are, in law, two sorts of corporations," Holt ruled. "Those for the public government of a town, city, municipality, or the like, being for public advantage, are to be governed according to the laws of the land. . . . Of these, there are no particular private founders, and consequently no particular visitors." But, he added, "Private and particular corporations for charity—founded and endowed by private persons—are subject to the private government of those who erect them."

Private corporations such as Exeter College, founded by the donation of William Stapleton, were to be overseen by their statutorily appointed visitors. "This visitatorial power . . . is an appointment of law," Holt wrote. "It arises from the property which the founder had in the lands assigned to support the charity; and, as he is the author of the charity, the law gives him and his heirs a visitatorial power, that is, an authority to inspect the actions and regulate the behavior of the members that partake of the charity." Holt added that it was "the office of visitor, by the common law, to judge according to the statutes of the college and to expel [members] and deprive [them of their privileges] on just occasions." He concluded that visitors' decisions about charities under their supervision were "final" and "examinable in no other court whatsoever." In short, the bishop of Exeter, as statutory visitor, had the authority to remove Bury as master, because the bishop was the duly constituted external supervisor of the charity (the college) who ensured that it followed its founders' wishes.

Phillips v. Bury (1689) clearly held that charitable corporations were to be overseen by their visitors, but Holt emphasized that, in cases where a visitor was simultaneously a trustee of corporate property (as was the case with the bishop of Exeter in this case), the royal courts did, in fact, retain jurisdiction (to prevent conflicts of interest or misuse of funds). "A typical charter would incorporate the rector and scholars of a school, the master and fellows of a college, or the warden and poor of a hospital," notes historian Bruce Campbell, and such figures occasionally served as "trustees." But a charity's visitor "would be an altogether separate officer and would neither own the property nor receive any of the foundation revenues." Here was good corporate governance under Elizabethan law, in which trustees and visitors had to be separate. "Assuming an absence of collusion between the visitor and the rest of the organization, the visitor was an appropriate person to audit the corporate accounts and . . . oversee the operations to prevent fraud."

What about corporations that had no separate visitors? This question (which later played a role in the *Dartmouth* litigation) arose in the case of *Eden v. Foster* (1744), in which the board of trustees, or governors, of a charitable school in Birmingham that had no separate visitors objected to an investigation of its accounts by the royal chancellor. In this case, the court held that it retained jurisdiction (on behalf of the Crown) to guarantee the board's proper use of resources. "The court resolved that the word *governor* [or *trustee*] in a charter or private statute did not imply 'visitor,' and that, where governors received rents and profits, they should be [held] accountable for the use of receipts," Bruce Campbell explains. "Where governors and visitors were one, the chancellor—either in place of the king, or in his court of equity—had all the visitatorial power there was."

The development of the law of corporations shaped the debate over corporate jurisdiction not only at Oxford and Cambridge in this period but also in American colleges. By the mid-1760s, when President Clap said the colonial assembly in Connecticut had no authority to oversee Yale, the question arose: Who controlled the college—the public assembly or the private trustees? If the public assembly, then colonial legislators retained visitatorial power; if the private trustees (or fellows), then Clap had final say in all matters of college governance (subject to judicial review). In the case of the colony's dispute with Clap, these questions were not answered definitively. "The legislature—perhaps more for political than legal reasons—... did not formally visit the college," notes Campbell, which Clap interpreted as the colony's "acknowledgment of the independence of Yale from legislative control." But as subsequent events would show, those in other colonies saw the situation differently, and they eventually asked the courts to sort out their disagreements.

CHAPTER 2

Incorporation ... and Ill Will

In 1765, as the law of public and private corporations acquired increasing clarity abroad, Eleazar Wheelock dispatched his star pupil Samson Occom, along with minister Nathaniel Whitaker, to England to solicit contributions for his Indian Charity School. A few days after they arrived, George Whitefield introduced them to Lord Dartmouth, who in turn promised to introduce them to King George III. While a personal audience with the king apparently did not occur, the monarch pledged £200 to support Wheelock's school. Dartmouth, meanwhile, pledged fifty pounds and offered to establish a trust with its own board of trustees. Even without an official charter from the Crown or colony, Dartmouth said, this board could manage the Indian Charity School's resources. Whitaker, in exchange, promised to give the English board "all his authority under Wheelock's power" to oversee the use of its donations, which soon amounted to £5,000.

Occom and Whitaker subsequently made their way to Bath to meet with John Wentworth, son of New Hampshire's governor (and soon to become governor himself), who pledged twenty-one pounds to support Wheelock's school and, in a testimonial dated December 16, 1766, promised land if the school were "located in his province." Six weeks later, the English board of trustees was formally constituted with Lord Dartmouth as president. Wheelock then signed a new will on March 4, 1767, which named Whitaker his successor as head of the school and conveyed all lands received from Moor's widow to his English board—and, simultaneously, to a parallel American board. It was a consequential move. The initial English board had comprised the first legal entity to oversee the funds given to his Indian Charity School (the board led by Joshua Moor two decades earlier had no permanent existence); the parallel American board, all residents of Lebanon, Connecticut, was to manage the local use of the school's English donations.

Yet in 1767, the new American board had no legal powers of governance. In a letter on March 10, 1767, just six days after Wheelock revised his will, his friend William Smith Sr. (now attorney general of New York), answered two questions about his school's governance structure. The first asked whether the Indian Charity School required a charter for its American board—to protect it from colonial interference. Smith, who knew the English board had a trust but no charter, responded: "Beyond all doubt, it would be best to have a charter incorporating a number of warm friends in America, near to each other, to direct and govern the school, and some reputable friends in England for correspondents and protectors." He added: "An incorporated body will not only acquire rights maintainable by law in courts of justice but [also] command the favor of the officers of the [colonial] government, who, without that sanction, may, at such distances from the crown, oppress the undertaking a thousand ways and utterly destroy it."

Whereas the first question from Wheelock asked whether a charter of incorporation was necessary for his American board, the second asked whether a charter should be sought from the Crown or the Connecticut assembly. Smith replied, *both*: "A petition should be proffered to His Majesty, for a mandamus to the governor, council, and all subordinate officers, to pass a charter . . . under the great seal of the province; at the same time, a standing instruction should be procured [from] the governor and [the] secretary for Indian affairs to aid, countenance, and protect the corporation [members] in the execution of the powers and privileges granted to them by the charter, as they will answer to the [*word omitted*] at their peril." On both points, Smith advised Wheelock to obtain a charter from the Crown—via the colony—to protect his Indian Charity School and its entrusted assets from political interference.

The members of the English board knew nothing of Wheelock's pursuit of an independent charter for his parallel American board. When they found out, they objected vociferously. They wanted to protect their own authority to oversee the use of their funds and wondered if Wheelock and his American friends could be trusted. Why this suspicion? Because it had come to light that Wheelock, perpetually short of cash, had directed his agent Whitaker to use some of the English funds to speculate in trade in hopes of a lucrative return for the school . . . but he did not inform the English board of this business. Eventually it was discovered.

One trustee called Wheelock's actions "iniquitous"—an unauthorized use of property held in trust—and considered a complete withdrawal of the English board's support. Wheelock called it a misunderstanding. To clear the air, he agreed to remove Whitaker as his designated successor to lead the school.

After these events, relations between Wheelock and the English board soured. The board had proposed to make Lord Dartmouth its heir by a "deed of trust," but Wheelock instead wanted to put his American board in charge of all the school's funds. He asked William Smith Sr.: "Will it do to have the fund there and the school ... here? How shall I ... set matters right and not offend my noble Lord Dartmouth and the other worthy gentlemen of the [English] trust?" Smith replied that, ultimately, since the English board oversaw its own contributions, Wheelock had to follow its orders, however restrictive they might seem. "You have indeed a difficult part to act," Smith wrote, aware that donors had a right to control the use of their own gifts. "The contracted views of the [English] trustees will render the project short-lived. To oppose them will be to prevent *any good* from being done by the money they have raised. *You must join them until it is spent.*"

Others shared this view. George Whitefield reminded Wheelock that Whitaker's campaign for contributions had been predicated on the promise that all resources would be controlled by the English board, so Wheelock could not retract that promise now. "A cry was continually made by Mr. Whitaker ... 'A trust! A trust!' ... Whitaker and Occom were sent for on purpose to settle one," Whitefield noted. "An agreement was made, after solemn prayer, that monies collected should be disposed of by the mutual consent of this set of trustees—on this side of the water—and you. Upon this basis all further collections and contributions were founded. [But] you have now acted as though you were determined to [cast] this most [responsible] body aside (in whom you ought to have the utmost confidence) and [have] not complied with any of their most [sensible] requests." According to Whitefield, the English board, even without an official charter, was in charge. Wheelock, however, wanted more control over the Indian school's resources for himself and his American board.

In the meantime, the English board sent Wheelock a deed of trust dated May 31, 1768, which gave Wheelock authority to draw on the English funds to run the school. Wheelock, in turn, executed another will, dated August 23, 1768, in which he replaced Whitaker as his chosen successor with his son Ralph and conveyed the right to supervise the English funds to both the nine-member English board *and* the eight-member American board. As historian Frederick Chase explains, "All the property, and the application of it, was given to the American board, subject to a veto power in the English board." With substantial resources thus at his disposal, Wheelock revived the question that had long been on his mind, namely, whether he could secure an official charter for his school—and if so, *where* and *in whose name?* His answer, it turned out, would be as legally convoluted as it was consequential.

For a while, Wheelock had considered a location near Albany, New York, which had offered six acres near a local fort, complete with "a large new building comprised of sixteen rooms," plus "a hint of possible incorporation." William Smith Sr. thought it a good offer. "Never forget that a charter will be of the utmost consequence," Smith noted. "The Albany people wish to see your school lift up its head into a *college* or *university*, and you in the chair, directing all the parts of the instruction. I have many reasons to desire that they may not be disappointed and beg you would think of nothing more than so extensive a design." Wheelock, however, thought Connecticut a better option, except for the fact that Yale rejected all rivals. "I have been much solicited to seek an incorporation from ... [Connecticut], which I might likely obtain," he told Smith. "But, as it has a college in its bowels, I sha'n't likely obtain one as agreeable to my mind as elsewhere." He soon discovered that not only Connecticut's assembly but also his English board disliked his idea of a college.

New Hampshire seemed to be his next best choice. As early as 1763, Governor Wentworth had "relented" to a five-hundred-acre donation of land within the "New Hampshire grants," and in 1765 the school had received an offer for another two thousand acres in Thetford, on the western bank of the Connecticut River. A year later, in 1766, with Occom and Whitaker overseas, Wheelock had gotten several additional offers to relocate his school. "Colonel Willard offers to sell 18,000 acres in Sugar River for £1,500, which would be the most inviting part of that country," Wheelock told Whitefield excitedly. "Samuel Stevens, Esq., offers 2,000 acres to have it at [lot] No. 4 in New Hampshire. Colonel Chandler offers 2,000 acres to have it at the center of the town of Chester, opposite No. 4 but nine miles from the river."

In the fall of 1767, shortly after John Wentworth had returned from England (where he donated to Occom and Whitaker's campaign) to succeed his father as governor, Wheelock told him of his recent offers from Albany, his support in Connecticut, and his awareness that several of his neighbors from Lebanon had removed to western New Hampshire as settlers and wanted him to join them. "A number of new settlers on the Connecticut river in the western part of your province have lately manifested a great desire to have the school fixed among them," he reported. Wentworth, eager to make his mark in office (and then only thirty years old), promised an entire township—23,040 acres of public land—"for an endowment of the school and as a site to fix it," on the condition that Wheelock settle at least "eighty to a hundred souls on the premises within five years."

The governor specifically identified the unsettled township of Landaff—within the "New Hampshire grants"—as the best place for the school. Wheelock replied that final determination of the school's location would require his English board's approval. Yet, after Wentworth said that he, as governor, would "be a trustee" of the school (which suggested either that he wanted to join the English board or that he wanted to grant a charter on behalf of the Crown), Wheelock promised that "as soon as the place for the school shall be fixed to be in your province, I shall appoint [you] for the time being a trustee on this side of the water until a legal incorporation may be obtained." Several of Wheelock's friends worried that Wentworth did not have the authority to grant royal charters and that his post as governor precluded a role as trustee. They reminded Wheelock, moreover, that his English board opposed any charter that might weaken its control of its donations for the Indian Charity School.

Wheelock knew from his correspondence that his English board did not want a charter—or a local American board of trustees. "Their sentiments of an incorporation have been different from mine," he wrote. "They have insisted that I should conduct the whole affair without one and that my successor should be nominated and appointed by my will. Experience, they think, has fully taught them that, by means of such incorporations, such designs become jobs"—that is, ways to advance overtly private rather than public interests. While the English board resisted the idea of a local board, or a charter of incorporation, it nonetheless gave Wheelock permission to move his school north in order "to accept the offer of governor Wentworth and the gentlemen of New Hampshire," by which it apparently meant the governor's offer of land but not his offer of a charter with himself as trustee—and certainly not an offer to make the Indian Charity School into a college.

Wheelock, however, used this ambiguity to ask Wentworth for a charter, with a crucial postscript: "P.S.," he penned, "If proper to use the word *college* instead of *academy* in the charter, I shall be well pleased." It seems that Wheelock expected his Indian Charity School either to be a college, or someday to become a college, or else to be affiliated with a future college. His exact intentions were unclear, but a key question concerned which of his two boards would govern the institution. This question surfaced when Governor Wentworth asked to add the bishop of London to both the English board and the American board. Wheelock groused to friends that Wentworth had "forgotten" his own proposal to make himself the only "non-elective trustee" and now wanted the bishop to be "of the trust on both sides of the water" in order to oversee "the monies now in the hands of the trust in England"—an idea Wheelock rejected, evidently in hopes that he could make the members of his American board the sole trustees of a newly chartered institution.

But the governor went further. He suggested that, besides the bishop of London's role on both of the boards, three members of New Hampshire's colonial assembly should join him on the American board, a way to increase the likelihood of public supervision of—and support for—the institution. "The nomination of three provincial officers to be of the active, influential, conducting trust in this country I strongly recommend but do not insist on," Wentworth proposed on grounds that education was a public interest. "They will be a natural defense, honor, and security for the institution, which perhaps may be the more eligible as they cannot be supposed to be at any time other than the safest and most natural guardians of education." In exchange for a (royal) charter and land grant, Wentworth suggested that Wheelock's institution should be subject to provincial—public—oversight.

In the end, Wheelock agreed that his American board could include the governor, speaker of the assembly, and three council members, but he said these members should belong as private individuals (not ex officio public representatives), which meant they could be replaced over time by a process of attrition—under the same rules of succession that governed other members of his American board. With this concession, Wheelock asked the governor to withdraw his request for the bishop of London to serve on both the English board and the American board. He told Wentworth that since the English board controlled all the institution's funds and carried the power to name its own members, it alone could decide whether to add the bishop. In short, he maintained, the English board controlled the school and its property.

This back-and-forth indicated that both Wheelock and Wentworth believed the acts of the American board would be subject to approval by the English board whenever they concerned the use of English funds. Moreover, any chartered institution—whether a "school," "academy," or "college"—was presumed to originate with the Indian Charity School, and the power to control the use of its English funds was presumed to rest with the English board, in trust. While the use of any new monies raised in America would rest with the American board (which also had a role in the administration of the English funds, subject to a veto by the English board), the important point was that all funds were presumed to be for Wheelock's school, that is, his Indian Charity School (even if it was later called or connected to a "college").

In the summer of 1769 Wheelock sent Wentworth a draft charter for review. "I have been making some attempts to form a charter in which some proper respect may be shown to those generous benefactors in England who condescended to patronize this school," he wrote. "And I want to be informed whether you think it consistent to make the trust in England a distinct corporation, with power to hold real estate, etc., for the uses and purposes of this school." Although his English board had not seen his draft charter, Wheelock nonetheless told Wentworth two months later that it had given "unanimous preference" for a site in the "western part of your province for the site of my school." He added: "I shall appoint my son, or some suitable person or persons, in my name to wait upon you, if you please, to know your determination on a rough draft of a charter of incorporation for the academy."

Wentworth read Wheelock's charter with interest and signed it on December 13, 1769. The document opened with a history of Wheelock's establishment of his Indian Charity School, his agents' solicitation of contributions in England to support that school, his agreement to form an English board of trustees with power to oversee the use of its English funds, and the English board's permission to move the school from Connecticut to New Hampshire to benefit from Wentworth's promise of public land. It went on to say that a charter was necessary for "the safety and well-being of said seminary, and its being capable of the tenure and disposal of lands and bequests for the use of the same" and the expediency "in the infancy of said institution, or till it can be accommodated in that new country, ... that the gentlemen whom he [Wheelock] has already nominated in his last will (which he has transmitted to the aforesaid gentlemen of the trust in England) to be trustees in America, should be of the corporation now proposed."

Then came the part of the charter that eventually led to legal controversy. The next section recast the "school" as a "college" and said the aforementioned "trustees in America," named in Wheelock's "last will," comprised an independent board of trustees for an institution henceforth to be known as "Dartmouth College," subject to approval by the original English board. It went on to say: "The trustees of said college may and shall be one body, corporate and politic, in deed, action, and name, and shall be called, named, and distinguished by the name of the Trustees of Dartmouth College," an institution for the education "of youth of the Indian tribes in this land ... and also of English youth and any others." This board would include Wheelock, Wentworth, and four members of New Hampshire's colonial assembly, as well as five Connecticut residents, for a total of twelve American trustees with the power to select their successors in perpetuity.

The charter gave this American board (if approved by the English board) the authority to award such degrees "as are usually granted in either of the universities, or any other college in our realm of Great

Britain" and to do so by means of diplomas under its own seal. In line with the principles of evangelical dissenters, it stipulated that Dartmouth College was not to exclude "any person of any religious denomination whatsoever from [the] free and equal liberty and advantage of education, or from any of the liberties and privileges or immunities of the said college, on account of his or their speculative sentiments in religion." Finally, and importantly, the charter required the institution to give the English board a yearly account of its use of funds donated for the Indian Charity School—recognized as the institutional foundation of the college, which, as yet, had no independent funds, donors, or practical existence of its own.

Although it acknowledged the "example" set by the English donors and the promise of a land grant from Governor Wentworth, the charter did not list any specific donations to Dartmouth College, though it named Wheelock as "the founder of said college" as well as its president, with a right to name his successor in his will. Careful readers would have noted that Wheelock used the provisions he put into his will two years earlier as the legal basis to establish a parallel American board for his Indian Charity School, and it was apparently this board that now became the board of trustees for "Dartmouth College" under the new charter. Importantly, this board had the power to replace the president of the *college*, but it did not have the power to replace the president of the *school*, though Wheelock served in both roles (and stood to name successors for both in his will). This aspect of school and college governance would become a source of intense disagreement.

Of course, at the core of any charter were its provisions for the governance of property, and six weeks after Wentworth signed this charter, he fulfilled his promise to grant the western township of Landaff to support the enterprise. This grant—registered on January 25, 1770—was the first donation of any sort given for the use of "Dartmouth College," and while the governor felt that Landaff was the best place for the institution, he admitted that other towns had contended for this honor, not least Hanover, then unsettled but later chosen as the college's home. (Two weeks before Wentworth's grant, he encouraged New Hampshire's assembly to fund a turnpike into the western territories so "the greatest benefits may result from Dartmouth College being happily established in the province, whence many hundreds of respectable families from other colonies [may be] induced to settle in and cultivate the remotest district of this government.")

When news of Wentworth's charter and land grant reached Wheelock in Connecticut, he finally contacted Lord Dartmouth and other members of his English board about the document. It was the first they heard of Wheelock's solicitation of a charter without their approval. Writing to Dartmouth on March 12, 1770 (five days after the Boston Massacre), he blamed "the present ruffled and distempered state of the kingdom" for his decision not to consult the English board earlier and said a charter would benefit their Indian Charity School, now incorporated with a new college. "Your Lordship is doubtless sensible of the danger and difficulty, if not impracticability, of proceeding in the affairs of this school ... without a legal incorporation to secure the whole against ... the many plots and devices of bad men, especially in bad times," he observed. The charter, he said, would guard the English board's money for the school from misuse.

On the authority of the American board (previously mentioned only in Wheelock's updated will) to appoint the president of the college, he said the idea had come from the governor, based on a desire to ensure local supervision of the institution. "Governor Wentworth thought best to reject that clause in my draft of the charter which gave the honorable trust in England equal power with the trustees here to nominate and appoint the president from time to time, apprehending it would make the body too unwieldy," he told Lord Dartmouth. "But he cheerfully consented [that] I should express my gratitude and duty to your lordship by christening it after your name." Dartmouth, however, did not want a college to bear his name. On the contrary, he wanted an Indian Charity School funded and governed by himself and his fellow English trustees. As he wrote on July 30, 1770, the English board considered Wheelock's charter a ploy to seize control of their money for a wholly different institution. Wheelock, in response, said the school and the college were linked, if not the same.

What remained unclear from the charter was precisely who had "founded" Dartmouth College. Wheelock continued to assume that he needed the English board's approval to select a site for the institution as long as he intended to use that board's funds to support it. "Neither the honorable trust in England nor the charter had fixed upon a particular town or spot on which the buildings should be erected," he wrote, noting Wentworth's preference for a site on the Connecticut River. In the end, he chose Hanover, but when it was revealed that Wentworth's father (himself a former governor) had given Wheelock a five-hundred-acre plot in the vicinity for his own use, many suspected that Wheelock chose this site to enrich himself. In fact, it was not long before Wheelock owned more than a thousand acres "on the east and north" sides of Hanover, beyond which lay another two thousand acres given by private donors "for the support of Dr. Wheelock's school, on condition that it be erected in Hanover."

Wheelock moved to Hanover in the summer of 1770, settled into a small log hut, and proceeded to plan the construction of an edifice to be completed with a combination of enslaved labor (he brought at least eight enslaved people with him from Connecticut) and English funds (the only funds in his possession)—a sign that he considered the "school" and "college" to be, for all intents and purposes, linked. He made this unity explicit when he announced his arrival in a newspaper in Lebanon, Connecticut, on August 23, 1770. In a statement that blurred the different institutions' origins, he declared: "My Indian Charity School ... is now become a body corporate and politic, under the name of DARTMOUTH COLLEGE, by a most generous and royal charter, granted and amply endowed with immunities, powers, and privileges, in the opinion of good judges not inferior to any university on the Continent, by his Excellency John Wentworth, Esq., Governor of New Hampshire, whom God has raised up and commissioned for this purpose."

He continued with a description of the school and college blended under a single charter. "I hope soon to be able to support by charity a large number, not only of Indian youths in Moor's Charity School, which is connected and incorporated with the College, but also of English youths in the College, in order to their being fitted for missionaries among the Indians, etc." He informed

> the generous subscribers in the colony of Connecticut and province of Massachusetts Bay, etc., who have not yet paid their subscriptions [to Moor's School,] made in the year 1755 and following for the only

use, benefit, and support of this school (the yearly interest whereof was payable ... [as] long as the school should be continued, and the principal to become payable as soon as the school should become a body corporate and thereby capable of the tenure and disposal of land, etc.), that I suppose these subscriptions are now become payable by this incorporation.

A key question was how this blended institution would be governed. Its charter required its American board to meet within a year, and when it did on October 22, 1770, its members asked whether they controlled only the assets of Dartmouth College (the Landaff grant) or also those of the Indian Charity School (the English funds, already used to erect the first edifice). In a move that later became a source of controversy, they concluded that, while the American board controlled the land donated by Wentworth *after* the charter (subject to colonial oversight), the English board controlled all funds donated previously. They resolved that "the charter gives the trustees no right of jurisdiction but over the college" and that "the school remains still under the same patronage, authority, and jurisdiction as it was under before the charter was given." In the interest of clarity, they decided that the "Indian Charity School, connected with Dartmouth College, be constantly hereafter, and forever, called and known by the name of Moor's School."

Some members of the English board said that Wheelock blurred the distinction between the school and college in order to use the school's funds to support the college. Others said that he gave the American board control of all new funds so that, gradually, as the English funds expired, the college would replace the school. Wheelock acknowledged "the surmises ... that the charitable donations made for the use of this school ... are, in whole or part, perverted to my own, or some other ... design," but he denied any trickery. "The charter was never designed to convey the least power or control of any funds collected in Europe, nor does it convey any jurisdiction over the school to the trustees of the college," he wrote to his English board on November 9, 1770. On the contrary, "The charter means to incorporate the school *with* the college and give it possession of the donations and grants made in this province to it." But what did "it" mean: the school or the college? Which board controlled which funds, and for which purposes?

The members of the English board were unsure. They contacted Wheelock on April 25, 1771, to share their concern that Wheelock had used their funds to create a college that eventually would supersede their school. "We have lately taken into our serious consideration the affair of your charter," they wrote. "When we consider that the money collected here was given for the express purpose of creating, establishing, endowing, and maintaining an Indian Charity School and a suitable number of missionaries to be employed in the Indian country for the instruction of Indians in the Christian religion, and for no other purpose whatever, we cannot but look upon the charter you have obtained and your intention of building a college and educating English youth as going beyond the line by which both you and we are circumscribed." They added: "We think ourselves bound to adhere invariably to this original plan and must therefore insist . . . that you do not deviate from it."

The members of the English board could have claimed the charter of Dartmouth College violated their rights as trustees when it augmented the board to which they pledged their original donations and did so without their consent. But they did not advance that argument. Instead, they simply claimed that Dartmouth College was prohibited from any use of funds designated for the Indian Charity School, which they considered a legally distinct—if not separate—institution. As they put it, "The corporation of Dartmouth College, in its nature and designs, differs from the establishment of [the] school," so its governance, too, must differ. This characterization appeared to remove the English board from any jurisdiction over Dartmouth College (despite the language of the charter) and place the American board exclusively in control of that institution, subject only to the will of its donors—Governor Wentworth first among them (because all donations before the charter had been for the school).

Over the next few years, Wheelock spent down the English funds. Whether he spent them exclusively on the Indian Charity School was doubtful, but as they were depleted, his focus shifted from Indian to English students. "Wheelock had brought with him only two Indian students from Connecticut," historian Dennis Holtschneider notes, and he seemed "if not to be abandoning his plan to educate Indians, at least to be welcoming more traditional [English] students into his institutions.... Even [his first Indian pupil,] Samson Occom, suspected the institution's mission was changing. [Occom] refused to write the London trustees on Wheelock's behalf in 1770, because he [believed] the school had been converted into 'an English school.' He was particularly [upset] that Wheelock recently had turned away an Indian applicant, because the available charity funds were being used by English... students."

As the English funds disappeared, Wheelock found himself in need of money (since the college had no resources except its land grants). To supplement tuition, Holtschneider recounts, he sought more assistance from New Hampshire's assembly, which granted sixty pounds in public aid in 1771 and £500 in 1773, along with a public right to operate a ferry across the Connecticut River. He also sought help from Massachusetts's governor Thomas Hutchinson, who promised £1,000, but when this pledge was deferred for legislative consultation, nothing more was heard of it. Why not? Because the Massachusetts assembly had other matters on its mind: first in 1773 the Boston Tea Party, then in 1774 the Massachusetts Government Act, which amended (many said annulled) the charter of 1691 in order to increase the royal governor's power over the colony. The colonists were on edge, and before long New Hampshire joined Massachusetts to call for an intercolonial union to seek redress for taxes imposed by Parliament without consent.

In the half decade since Dartmouth College received its charter, times had changed. The old colonial order had begun to fray, and new "republican" principles had started to spread. In the summer of 1774, Governor Wentworth dissolved New Hampshire's increasingly rebellious assembly, but its members simply redirected their attention to the first Continental Congress, held in Philadelphia that fall. Later, a town meeting in Hanover expressed its enthusiasm for the "patriot" cause as Wheelock told Wentworth of local calls for self-government. "This part of your province is as unanimous and warm (according to its ability) for the defense of that liberty which is threatened as any part of the continent," Wheelock noted, "and, when duty calls, will be... active to [resist perceived violations of its rights]." Wentworth could take a hint. He fled to Nova Scotia and left Dartmouth College without its first (and foremost) benefactor. Little did he know that his departure would leave his "public" grants to the college in legal limbo.

CHAPTER 3

Public Support and Public Supervision

Even before Wentworth left, Wheelock had looked for new sources of public and private support for his school and college. In 1774, he contemplated a proposal to his English board to join his American board "in forming, by royal incorporation, a Society for Propagating the Gospel in America, which should furnish means [to] ... take charge of the college" and its property. He proposed "to convey to the English trustees—by will—the lands on which the college buildings stood, since [the English trustees] had supplied the means of erecting them." First in June and then again in October 1774, he requested "a draft of articles of incorporation" to put the English board in control of all the college's assets, but nothing came of this effort. Not only had ties with the mother country deteriorated, but the last of the funds held by the English board had been spent earlier that year, which, for a time, diminished that body's involvement with the institution.

In the spring of 1775, after the exhaustion of his English funds, Wheelock asked for public aid from the Continental Congress on grounds that Hanover was in danger of British and Indian attacks. He sent Nathaniel Whitaker to Philadelphia to request public resources to keep Indian students enrolled and, thus, prevent their collaboration with British forces. Congress (eager to protect the project of settler colonialism) responded in January 1776 with a grant of $500—not for Dartmouth College but rather for the Indian Charity School. Despite a follow-up request for the college that spring, Congress voted that "although the prosperity of Dartmouth College in the colony of New Hampshire is a desirable object, it is neither reasonable nor prudent to contribute to its relief or support out of the public treasury." A third request to aid the college was refused a year later, and Wheelock realized he would have to find other sources of support.

Desperate for resources, Wheelock sought to sell off Wentworth's public Landaff grant, but this effort was not without complications, because the grant lay in territory claimed not only by New Hampshire but also by New York—and, specifically, by King's College. Years earlier, that institution had sent James Jay (the father of revolutionary John Jay) to raise funds in Britain, where he procured a royal grant of twenty thousand acres in "Kingsland," just west of the Connecticut River. Later, George III made that river the boundary line between New Hampshire and New York, which meant that all the defensive towns Wentworth had chartered on the river's west bank were now at odds with New York land claims. New York, a more powerful colony, took steps to evict New Hampshire settlers from "its" land, but the king suspended all evictions until title disputes could be resolved.

Such was the state of affairs in January 1770 when Governor Wentworth gave the newly chartered Dartmouth College its Landaff grant, located within the contested region. Initially, this public grant sat unsurveyed, but in 1773 Landaff's settlers met at the college to request permanent titles from the Crown. Even before such titles could be drafted, however, the settlers learned that New York governor William Tyron had granted another ten thousand acres in the area to King's College, a move they considered outrageous. They met in Manchester in 1775 to protest Tyron's land grab, then again in 1776 to petition the Continental Congress to uphold their claims, but without success. Finally, in 1777, with the controversy still unresolved, Landaff's settlers—all linked to Dartmouth College—joined a movement to create a new and independent state: "Vermont." What followed was a series of machinations that reverberated decades later in the legal strategies that shaped the *Dartmouth* case.

Amid the military upheavals of 1778, some of the Landaff settlers called for the creation of a special Dartmouth College subdistrict along the west bank of the Connecticut River. Led by Bezaleel Woodward (in effect, the college's business manager, whose son would be the named defendant in the *Dartmouth* case four decades later), these landowners called their district New Connecticut and its main town Dartmouth (formerly Dresden, "a district ... under the immediate jurisdiction of Dartmouth College," with "special jurisdiction ... given to [Eleazar Wheelock] as its magistrate"). The district's citizens—eight hundred families who had come from Connecticut to settle near the college—drafted a municipal charter for a district of 5,670 acres (with four thousand owned by the college or the Wheelock family). Their aim was a legally autonomous town in the new state of Vermont that could protect college lands from encroachment by either New Hampshire or New York.

During the revolution, many towns sought to protect themselves via independent charters. In some cases, landowners chartered "open" (or public) corporations that welcomed newcomers as coproprietors. In other cases, they chartered "closed" (or private) corporations with perpetual control of property and no admission of new members. Dartmouth was to be a closed corporation (which some considered a haven for aristocratic privilege and thus anti-republican). "In many ways, the open-closed controversy laid the groundwork for the public-private distinction, at least with respect to corporate entities," historian Christopher Calton notes. "Both sides in the municipal corporation debate saw themselves as upholding 'republican' values," whether public interests or private rights. Some felt it was unrepublican to use charters to make (public) towns into (private) companies, but college officials in Dartmouth, unfazed by this criticism, made plans to annex both Hanover and Lebanon into their "closed" town.

As war raged around them, Wheelock and his associates used the charter of Dartmouth College to consolidate their control over landed property (so much so that subsequent legal disputes would disentangle their actions only with difficulty). As leaders of New Connecticut, they stated their intention to incorporate towns whose assets derived from the Landaff grant or from other acquisitions. "Whereas the original and great design of incorporations is to secure the rights and immunities of the people," Wheelock declared, "and whereas, for the aforesaid purposes, by the royal presents of George III, King of Great Britain, patents were made out whereby two tracts of land were incorporated in the New Hampshire Grants by the names of Hanover and Lebanon," both settlements now consented to join what essentially was a private company/college town. "We do therefore maintain, publish, and declare that we are incorporated as a distinct town," Wheelock pronounced, "a separate town by the name of Dartmouth."

Shortly after this municipal charter of incorporation, the residents of Dartmouth officially voted to leave the state of New Hampshire and join the new state of Vermont, whose constitution of 1777 conveniently included provisions for a future university. Wheelock hoped that Dartmouth College would become this institution, and in fact Vermont's legislature voted on June 15, 1778, "to take the incorporated University of Dartmouth under the patronage of this state." Wheelock thanked Vermont for its support—but he celebrated too soon. A year later, New York reasserted its control over this district, and the fate of Dartmouth (both the college and town) was cast into doubt. Its fate became even more uncertain when, on April 24, 1779, sixty-eight-year-old Wheelock died. Three weeks earlier, in a revised will, the patriarch had named his son John to succeed him as president of both Dartmouth College and the Indian Charity School ... a decision fraught with future implications.

Twenty-five-year-old John Wheelock had graduated with Dartmouth's first class and was in 1779 a lieutenant colonel in the Continental Army with no desire to become a college president. Indeed, at the annual conference of trustees in 1780, he asked to resign on grounds that he was a military officer, not a scholar, and therefore unsuited to direct students. The board, however, asked him to lead the effort to make Dartmouth into Vermont's public university, and he accepted. His first presidential act was to ask Vermont's assembly to "take this school under your friendly and charitable patronage." He said the institution preferred a connection with a state "disposed to patronize it to the utmost" (that is, one likely to follow through on pledges of public aid), whereas "if it falls into the state of New Hampshire, it will be in a state which has heretofore (as such) shown a very cool disposition toward it and probably will continue the same neglect." War-torn New Hampshire was not as generous as it had been under Governor Wentworth.

Wheelock evidently hoped that, even if "Dartmouth" could not be privately incorporated in Vermont, then perhaps its college might be considered that state's new university—"endowed with landed and other interests as the charity and pious disposition of your state, or any individuals thereof, shall induce them to liberality toward the same." Like his father, who had moved to New Hampshire in exchange for a grant of public land, John Wheelock now asked whether Vermont's "glebes"—formerly Anglican lands that were confiscated during the revolution—could be reallocated "for the only benefit, use, behoof, and support of [Dartmouth College], or the university to which [it] shall be subordinate." Aware of the importance of public aid, he specifically asked whether "Kingsland," initially granted to King's College, could be regranted to Dartmouth as soon as the latter became Vermont's state university.

All these requests fell apart in 1781, however, when the Continental Congress placed the Vermont–New Hampshire boundary at the Connecticut River, which meant that Hanover, and thus Dartmouth College, returned to New Hampshire's legislative jurisdiction. In this context, Wheelock looked back to New Hampshire for public aid (though not public authority). He did not get all the aid he wanted. The legislature gave him permission for a public lottery but denied petitions for other forms of support. And so, to meet wartime expenses, he began to sell off college lands. For example, as early as 1779 (before the Vermont–New Hampshire border had been set), he sold 140 acres in Hartford, Vermont, to Joseph Marsh: a crucial sale, for Marsh's son Charles, later a Dartmouth trustee, played a key role in the subsequent college litigation, which focused in part on property claims in this long-contested region.

———

During the revolution, college (in other words, corporate) property was often contested. The College of Philadelphia, for instance, was reincorporated as the "University of the State of Pennsylvania" (without its consent), and its endowments were seized by the state legislature to fund this new "public" institution. The legislature said it was the state's duty, "after so recent and great a revolution," to place the college under the control of "gentlemen not only of education but of known republican principles." They said it was ridiculous to suggest that "corporations, which are the creatures of society, can, under the bill of rights, plead any exemption from legislative regulation," even as critics said the new university—funded by the old college's assets, plus a public grant of $1,500 a year—signaled a "dangerous alliance" whereby the state claimed a quasi-populist right to appropriate private corporate resources with impunity.

The College of Philadelphia was not the only corporation to see its charter altered during the war. As early as 1776, the College of William and Mary had come under fire when a writer for the *Virginia Gazette* (likely Thomas Jefferson) said the college should be made accountable to "republican" legislative oversight. A year later, a new state-appointed board of visitors removed the college's loyalist president, John Camm, and replaced him with twenty-eight-year-old James Madison (a second cousin of the eponymous future president). Then, in 1779, when Jefferson became governor—and thus a public visitor of William and Mary—he severed the college's statutory connection with the Anglican church, summoned its trustees to Williamsburg, and said they could keep their seats only if they denounced the Crown and declared their allegiance to Virginia's new state constitution.

Pennsylvania and Virginia, while different in many ways, shared the view that colleges should be subject to public authority in exchange for public aid. Similarly, in 1780, when John Adams drafted Massachusetts's new state constitution, he echoed Jefferson's bills for state aid to education. "Wisdom and knowledge, as well as virtue, diffused generally among the body of the people, [are] necessary for the preservation of their rights and liberties," Adams wrote. "And, as these depend on spreading the opportunities and advantages of education in the various parts of the country and among the different orders of the people, it shall be the duty of legislatures and magistrates in all future periods of this commonwealth to cherish the interests of literature and the sciences and all seminaries of them, especially the University at Cambridge [that is, Harvard, a corporation supervised by a public board of overseers]."

Massachusetts's aid to the college did not go unnoticed. In 1783, the *Connecticut Courant and Weekly Intelligencer* published a series of articles under the penname "Parnassus" (after the Greek home of literature), which urged Yale to accept public aid in exchange for public oversight. "The president and fellows of *Harvard College* think it no [insult] that [all] their acts must have the sanction of the overseers," Parnassus noted as he gave two reasons to consider Yale a "public" corporation. First, he argued, "Public grants to Yale College amounted to about three times what it has received in private donations." Second, he added, Yale had accepted its charter from the colony in exchange for public grants of land and cash. "The existence of the college is derived from the general assembly," he noted. "It was not founded before the charter" (despite former president Clap's dubious claims about the "forty folios").

Like other states, New York also took steps to make its college "public" after the war. As historian David Humphrey explains, Britain's armies "had barely left New York" when legislator James Duane introduced An Act for Granting Certain Privileges to the College Heretofore Called King's College, for Altering the Name and Charter Thereof, and Erecting a University Within This State. The bill dubbed the new institution "Columbia College" and gave it a public board of regents to oversee a so-called University of the State of New York, to include not only Columbia but any new college founded by the regents in the future. The public regents, Humphrey explains, "had the 'full power' to make 'ordinances and bylaws' for each institution in the 'university,' to appoint its president, [to hire and fire its] faculty, and to manage its estate."

In every respect, the new University of the State of New York was a public body. Its regents included the governor, lieutenant governor, senate president, assembly speaker, attorney general, secretary of state, and two representatives from each of the state's twelve counties, as well as the mayor of New York City (ex officio) and mayor of the state capital in Albany (likewise ex officio). Its charter, however, was not entirely clear about the governance of Columbia, a subunit within the larger university. As historian Bruce Campbell observes, while some parts of the charter affirmed King's incorporation from 1754 and "exempted [the college] from any 'visitation, act, or thing' by anyone except its own trustees," other parts "specifically 'required' the regents to 'visit and inspect all the colleges, . . . and yearly to report the state of the same to the legislature.'"

These contradictions—and the question of who controlled the college assets—eventually led to a conflict between two groups of regents: "city" regents associated with Columbia and "country" regents associated with the university at large. In 1787, the city regents suggested the dissolution of the broader public university in favor of private governance for Columbia, but this suggestion was challenged by country regent Ezra L'Hommedieu, who felt that control of colleges should continue to be exercised by the public. In the end, the city regents offered a compromise whereby they gave up all claims to public aid for Columbia in exchange for a right to keep their own independent board and choose their own trustees in perpetuity. The legislature accepted this deal. It granted a new charter in 1787 that revived Columbia's original charter and reinstated its private and self-perpetuating board of trustees.

The charter of 1787 presaged a postrevolutionary order in which

American collegiate governance was caught between the public authority of the state and the private authority of trustees. Proponents of the former said that public support went hand in hand with public supervision. Proponents of the latter said that private authority over higher education was actually more "republican" than public authority; whereas legislatures were susceptible to partisanship, they held, independent trustees were better able to represent the broad public welfare. It was a noble hope, but it was tested when the University of the State of New York called for several new colleges across the state (all under public control) and, simultaneously, Vermont revived its plan for a public university of its own. Not only Columbia but also Dartmouth sensed a broader movement to exert public authority over higher education.

Two years earlier, Wheelock had told Vermont that Dartmouth would educate Vermont's youth tuition free if the state gave the college a 23,040-acre "glebe" township that had been taken from the Anglican church during the war. He solicited this land for "The Institution, Embracing Dartmouth College and Moor's Charity School," and on June 14, 1785, Vermont had granted his request. Revenue from this new township—called "Wheelock"—was designated half for Dartmouth College and half for "The President of Moor's Charity School." Yet when Vermont legislators announced this grant, advocates for a separate (independent) University of Vermont said they did not want Dartmouth to control higher education in two states. (This concern seemed justified when, during the debate over Vermont's initial constitution, Wheelock had suggested a clause to forbid public aid to "any college other than Dartmouth.")

These disputes lasted until 1787, when Vermont reversed course and rejected Wheelock's overtures—a decision that derailed his scheme to make Dartmouth the University of Vermont but did not undo Vermont's earlier grant of the Wheelock township, which remained under his control. The income from this grant eased Dartmouth's financial distress, but it did not protect the college from rivals, whether in Vermont or in other states. In 1788, for example, the *Cumberland Gazette* in Massachusetts's northern district of Maine published a draft charter for a new (public) college, which, like the proposed University of Vermont, was to have the same "advantages, privileges, immunities, franchises, and exemptions" that Harvard enjoyed. (This institution later took shape as

Bowdoin College, founded in 1794 with a charter that gave Massachusetts's legislature the power to name its president and professors and to oversee its operations.)

———

Faced with potential rivals on every side, Wheelock again looked to New Hampshire for public aid. Moreover, as head of both Dartmouth College and Moor's Indian Charity School, he wanted to be able to use whatever public aid he obtained for the benefit of *both* institutions. Thus, at the annual meeting of the board of trustees in 1788, he asked the legislature "for an act explanatory of the charter of the college, clearly designating that the president of said school is, of right, president of said college, and that he alone has a right to apply (for the purposes for which they are given) the monies collected by Dr. Whitaker and Mr. Occom, and all other monies, legacies, and bequests vested in his hands, or the hands of said college, for the purpose of promoting Christian knowledge among the Indians, he accounting to [the] trustees for their [use]."

This request, entitled "Proposals Respecting the Connection of Dartmouth College and Moor's School," sought to resolve old debates about "whether the school be not absorbed by the establishment of the college" and, more recently, whether the college trustees could use revenues derived from the Wheelock township in Vermont, including the half earmarked for "The President of Moor's Charity School." College trustee Eden Burroughs said a clarification of all these points was "absolutely necessary ... for carrying into effect the original design of the school and college, to prevent any perversion of that design." Burroughs added that he and his fellow college trustees should be allowed to borrow school funds as long as they paid the school back. There was, however, one problem with Burroughs's plan: the college trustees never asked the English board of the Indian Charity School for permission to use their money.

Nor was the English board consulted two months later when the college trustees asked the New Hampshire legislature to compensate the college for losing its original Landaff grant in a title dispute. (A survey revealed that Governor Wentworth had given private land on the mistaken assumption that it was public.) In a petition delivered on Christmas Day 1788, the college trustees asked the state for a new tract in the northwest part of the state that was roughly twice as large as the original grant. The state replied in January 1789 with a grant of forty-two thousand acres, plus a proviso that New Hampshire's legislature would join the college trustees as coequal governors of the new grant. Why this proviso? Because the legislature suspected the college trustees had misused the English board's school funds to erect the college edifice two decades earlier, and it did not want a similar misuse to befall its new public land grant.

The college trustees resented this charge. Three months later, they released a statement to defend their use of funds to support both the school and the college. "Apprehensions have arisen in the minds of some persons that monies collected in Great Britain by Messrs. Whitaker and Occom for the use of Moor's [Indian] Charity School under the direction of the Rev. Dr. Wheelock have been applied by this board to the use and benefit of Dartmouth [College]," they wrote. On the contrary, they replied, "This board has never had any control or direction of said monies, nor have they to their knowledge at any time received or applied any sum or sums thereof to the use and benefit of said college." School funds, they said, had been controlled exclusively by "the late Rev. Dr. E. Wheelock and his successor in the presidency of Moor's Charity School" (even if neither Eleazar nor John Wheelock had consulted the English board about the use of these funds).

The college trustees acknowledged that Wheelock had used school funds to support the initial construction of the college. They admitted that "on Dr. Wheelock's removal to this place in 1770, in order to accommodate the members of the school, he laid out considerable sums of the donations made in Great Britain, together with donations made to encourage the removal of the school and establishment of the college, in erecting buildings and clearing and improving lands—of which [only the building that is] now called the Old College Building remains, which said building has undergone repairs by this board since Dr. Wheelock's death." But was this use of English funds legal? To satisfy legislative critics who said they had no authority to use school resources for college purposes, the college trustees said they had overseen these repairs as *individuals*, not in their role as corporate officers.

Still, the statement went on to say, for all practical—if not legal—purposes, the school and the college fell under the control of a single president and board. As they put it: "The charter was granted (predicated on the said school and its objects) for erecting a college for these and other purposes and constituting a board of trustees capable of the [control] and disposal of lands and bequests for the use of said school and its objects, as well as those of said college." Put another way, even if school and college *funds* were separate, their *functions* were the same. This sleight-of-hand explanation would play a key role in subsequent litigation over the powers and privileges of the Dartmouth College trustees, but it did more to confuse than clarify the question, because it suggested the school and the college were one institution, financially and functionally, when in fact the governance of each was distinct.

Moreover, while the college had land, it had few liquid assets. The college trustees hoped that revenues from New Hampshire's recent grant would meet the college's expenses, but that grant—known confusingly as the "First College Grant," despite the fact that it substituted for the original Landaff grant—turned out to be less profitable than promised, and the college's debts meant that large parcels had to be sold off quickly at low prices. As early as December 10, 1789, the college had requested permission to sell part of its public grant, but the specific plot it put on the market was not surveyed for another two years. It renewed its request on December 6, 1791, then again on February 27, 1792, after which the state finally approved the sale. A few weeks later, roughly twenty thousand acres were sold to Jasper Murdoch of Norwich, Vermont, and on February 8, 1794, another ten thousand acres were sold to Samuel Franklin of New York.

Importantly, the surveys that preceded these sales yielded the first judicial decision to recognize state land grants as "contracts." In 1790, New Hampshire and New York had named commissioners to survey these lands, which included territories jointly claimed by these states. When the surveys indicated that certain land claims would shift from New York's to New Hampshire's jurisdiction, New York's governor George Clinton said that such transfers constituted a breach of contract with the current occupants. With these sales, he argued, "The rights of citizens under charters and letters-patent, which may be ranked among the highest species of contracts, may be not only impaired but extinguished, in direct violation of... the Constitution of the United States." Only after the federal courts had dismissed Clinton's protests was New

Hampshire—and, in turn, Dartmouth College—able to claim (and thus sell) these lands.

To some, Dartmouth's land grants from Vermont in 1785 and New Hampshire in 1789 seemed to bring nothing but headaches. Complaints resurfaced a decade later when a group of Vermont speculators said the state's grant from 1785—the so-called Wheelock township divided between Dartmouth College and "The President of Moor's [Indian] Charity School"—was "void," because the school did not in fact have any Indian students. The complainants said the Indian Charity School "did not exist at the time of the grant, nor at any time since, nor has any person whatever a right or power to act for it." A legislative subcommittee empaneled to investigate the matter suggested a reset whereby the school and college would exchange the Wheelock township in Vermont for a different grant in New Hampshire to be governed solely by the college, on condition that half its proceeds support the school.

It was a good offer. "This was a very fair, reasonable, and even generous offer," argues historian Frederick Chase. "If accepted, it would forthwith have cleared up every doubt [about the blended governance of the school and college and their various land grants and would have] conferred important and lasting pecuniary benefit on the college." But the offer was not accepted, because Wheelock did not want to give the college trustees authority to govern property that he controlled as president of Moor's Indian Charity School (he thought Vermont trustee Nathaniel Niles wanted to reclaim the Wheelock township for his own state). It was a missed opportunity, for the failure to clarify the financial relations between the school and the college (not to mention Wheelock's role as president of both institutions) led to further headaches, and ultimately lawsuits, in the years to come.

Before the revolution, Dartmouth College had enjoyed the founding patronage and firm protection of New Hampshire's royal governor, but with the governor ousted and the college in desperate need of cash, it needed a new source of support. It looked first to Vermont in hopes that it might become that state's publicly funded university. Its trustees essentially sought to secede from New Hampshire and situate themselves under Vermont's political jurisdiction. But that plan failed, so the college appealed once again for aid from its home state (just as colleges elsewhere had done). In each case, the motive was the same: to request public support in exchange for public service. Yet as royalism gave way to republicanism, such requests presented a crucial question: In the new political (and legal) order, to what extent might public contributions also entail public control of chartered institutions? No question would prove more consequential for the future of Dartmouth College.

CHAPTER 4

Corporations, Contracts, and the Constitution

The postrevolutionary years were economically difficult for American colleges—and for the country in general. The causes of financial trouble were complex, but one cause was postwar currency depreciation, which in turn was caused by various bank policies that allowed debtors to pay their obligations in paper notes rather than silver or gold. Some considered these paper-note policies a violation of lenders' contracts while others said they provided necessary accommodations to debtors who had no access to precious-metal currencies. Eventually, these disagreements escalated into political disputes. In 1785, for example, the Bank of North America—chartered in Philadelphia four years earlier by the state of Pennsylvania and, simultaneously, by Congress—lost the support of Pennsylvania legislators. When the bank refused to accept loan payments by installment (or, alternatively, in commodities), lawmakers revoked the bank's state charter.

Meanwhile, the bank's charter from Congress had always been open to question. Under the Articles of Confederation, the powers of Congress were limited to powers specifically granted, and the power to charter a bank was not specified. Philadelphia attorney James Wilson, who played a role in the bank's creation, noted that Congress exercised many "implied" powers (such as the power to incorporate new states under the first Northwest Ordinance) and that charters, once granted, became permanent contracts that could not be revoked without all parties' consent. He rejected the idea that legislators, as representative of "popular opinion," could annul contracts at will. "If the act for incorporating the subscribers to the Bank of North America shall be repealed in this manner," he cautioned, then "a precedent will be established for repealing, in the same manner, every other legislative charter in Pennsylvania."

The paradigmatic case was James Wilson's own alma mater, the College of Philadelphia, whose charter had been revoked (along with all its assets) six years earlier in a process driven by the same populist justifications of "public" (or "republican") legislative control. Wilson maintained that legislatures could not repeal charters without the consent of the corporation itself. "It may be asked: 'Has not the state power over her own laws?' 'May she not alter, amend, extend, restrain, or repeal them at her pleasure?'" *No*, he answered. If charters could be nullified (or "negatized") without consent, "Those acts of the state which have hitherto been considered as the sure anchors of privilege and property will become the sport of every varying gust of politics and will float wildly backward and forward on the irregular and impetuous tides of party and faction." To guard corporate "privilege and property" in perpetuity, charters had to be sacrosanct.

According to Wilson, contracts fell into two categories: "public" contracts that affected all citizens and were thus rightly subject to legislative control and "private" contracts that affected only subgroups of citizens and were therefore off-limits to majoritarian interference. "Surely it will not be pretended that, after laws of these different kinds are passed, the legislature possesses over each the same discretionary powers of repeal," he asserted. "In a law respecting the rights and properties of all citizens of the state, this power may be safely exercised by the legislature. Why? Because in this case the interest of those who make the law (the members of the assembly and their constituents) and the interest of those who are affected by the law (the members of the assembly and their constituents) is the same. . . . None can hurt another without, at the same time, hurting himself."

But a contract between a state and subgroup of citizens—say, trustees of a church or a college—could not be revoked without the consent of its direct parties. "Very different is the case with regard to a law by which the state grants privileges to a congregation or other society," Wilson maintained. "Here, two parties are instituted and two distinct interests subsist. Rules of justice, of faith, and of honor must therefore be established between them, for [otherwise], the congregation or society must always lie at the mercy of the community." He continued: "Still more different is the case with a law by which an estate [in other words, property] is vested or confirmed in an individual. If, in this case, the legislature may, at [its own] discretion and without any reason assigned, devest or destroy his estate, then a person seized of an estate ... under legislative sanction is, in truth, nothing more than a solemn tenant at will." Without secure private contracts, no property would be safe from arbitrary public seizure.

While these arguments did not save the Bank of North America, they played an important role in the development of the law of contracts two years later when, in 1787, the Constitutional Convention met in Philadelphia to devise a new structure of government. James Wilson drafted much of the document that guided the discussion. Most notably, some have said he penned article I, section 10, clause 1 of the new federal Constitution, which stated plainly that "no state shall ... pass any ... law impairing the obligation of contracts." This clause prohibited state laws that sought to alter, amend, adjust, abridge, or annul private contracts without the consent of all parties. It made the protection of private contracts a matter of federal constitutional law and thus federal judicial review.

Some have suggested the contract clause originated with Massachusetts lawyer Nathan Dane (later a chief benefactor of Harvard Law School), who a few months earlier had drafted the second Northwest Ordinance, which outlined the process whereby territories could become states and included a provision that state laws could not override prior contracts for private land. "In the just preservation of rights and property," Dane wrote, "it is understood and declared that no law ought ever to be made, or to have force in said territory, that shall, in any manner whatever, interfere with or affect private contracts, or engagements, bona fide and without fraud, previously formed." A month later, Dane's colleague Rufus King, also of Massachusetts, moved to insert the same language into article XII of the Constitution—a motion that elicited significant debate.

James Madison admitted that "inconveniences might arise" from a federal protection of contracts because it might limit state legislative powers, but he thought such inconveniences would be "overbalanced" by a general (federal) protection of private contracts. Others disagreed. George Mason, a fellow Virginian, said the clause put too many restraints on state legislatures' ability to alter private contracts if necessary. "Cases will happen that cannot be foreseen, where some kind of interference [with contracts] will be proper and essential," say, to relieve debt obligations in the event of a dire economic downturn. James Wilson, in response, offered a compromise. He suggested that even if states could not "impair" contracts already made—for example, land contracts in the West—they could pass laws to regulate *future* contracts. Thus, as outlined in article I, section 8, clause 4 of the Constitution, a federal bankruptcy law could allow future debtors to renegotiate their liabilities.

Wilson had given the law of contracts a great deal of thought. Educated in Scotland at the universities of Edinburgh and Glasgow, he was a lecturer on the "general principles of law and obligation" at the College of Philadelphia before Pennsylvania's legislature abrogated that institution's charter. According to Wilson, the freedom of contract, like the freedom of speech or the freedom of religion, was a preconstitutional right, a part of natural law that could not be legislated away under any circumstances. It came not from government but from "the people" as such; the Constitution merely affirmed this basic freedom. Indeed, the Constitution was itself a contract—a collective act of consent that gave birth to a government with sovereign power to enact and enforce laws (and in turn all other contracts) among its citizens. Wilson called the Constitution a "formal act of incorporation" for the country, one that could not be altered or amended without consent from the citizens of its constituent states.

In fact, the states, too, were corporations, which meant the "federated" government was a corporation of corporations, none of which could be undone without the consent of the people. And state governments, like the federal government, had the power to incorporate other groups, or "societies" or "bodies politic," to fulfill important social functions. "Smaller societies may be formed within a state by a part of its members," Wilson explained. "To these societies the name of *corporation* is generally appropriated." Such corporations were "deemed to be moral persons, but not in a state of natural liberty [like the people who formed the original state]; their actions are cognizable by the superior power of the state and are regulated by its laws." Thus, a "contract" in the form of a charter of incorporation for a church or a college was subordinate to a "contract" that was the constitution of the government itself (which protected all other contracts or charters).

Wilson explained that charters for churches and colleges differed from charters, or constitutions, for countries. The latter could be altered by the people's majority vote; the former could not. Wilson of course knew that churches and colleges sometimes misused or abused their rights (their privileges or property). He thus advised caution in acts of incorporation. "In too many instances, those bodies politic [for example, corporations devoted to business, religion, or education] have, in their progress, counteracted the designs of their original formation," he observed. "Monopoly, superstition, and ignorance have been the unnatural offspring of commercial, religious, and literary corporations. This is not mentioned with a view to insinuate that such establishments ought to be prevented or destroyed. I mean only to intimate that they should be erected with caution and inspected with care," for a contract once made could be unmade only with the consent of its original parties (or their chosen successors). Such parties were rarely inclined to submit to external authority.

Colleges affected by wartime laws that had usurped their chartered property and privileges were among the first to see the value of Wilson's construction. In fact, just after the Constitution was ratified, the College of Philadelphia appealed for the recovery of its assets on grounds that Pennsylvania's legislative takeover had violated its original charter. William Smith, the college's provost, gave an "Address to the General Assembly" on the rights of colleges as corporations. He cited the post-revolutionary state constitution, which explicitly protected the property of philanthropic societies "incorporated for the advancement of religion and learning," and reminded those who argued that legislatures had an inherent power to dissolve corporations "unfriendly to the genius of government" that charters of incorporation were "permanent and inviolable and could not be undone except by mutual consent." Only courts, not legislatures, could revoke corporate rights, and only when the corporation violated its charter.

During this debate, the *Pennsylvania Gazette* described "two sorts" of corporations. First were those "constituted for public government and endowed by the public." Second were those, like the College of

Philadelphia, "constituted by *private persons* ... for charities specified in the act of foundation." Public corporations were of course subject to public supervision, but "any act violating the rights of private corporations 'stood as a *monument* of *reproach* to the *laws* and *justice* of a great commonwealth.'" The paper went on to say in the language of the *Sutton's Hospital* case that, legally, "he is a FOUNDER of a *college* ... who first erects and endows it by giving it *lands* and *possessions*, ... not he who makes it a *corporation*." Thus, "If a school or college be founded by *private persons*, and the state afterwards endows it with revenues or grants of land, etc., the state cannot [*amend*], *alter*, or *abridge* any of the *laws*, *orders*, *rules*, or *privileges* of the FOUNDERS [without their consent]."

These arguments carried the day. In 1789, the Pennsylvania legislature reinstated the College of Philadelphia's original charter, as well as its property. The preamble of the restoration act said the college had been deprived of its charter "without trial by jury, legal process, or proof of misuse or forfeiture ... all of which is repugnant to justice, a violation of the constitution of this commonwealth, and dangerous in its precedent to all incorporated bodies." Subsequently, a new state constitution in 1790 reconfirmed the rights, privileges, and immunities of corporate bodies and, to align itself with the newly ratified federal Constitution, added a provision that forbade all state laws that impaired the obligations of contract. Later that year, when the college established a new professorship of law, it went to James Wilson, and in 1792, when the state rechartered the college as the "University of Pennsylvania" with an independent and self-perpetuating board of trustees, Wilson cheered.

The restoration of the College of Philadelphia in 1790 coincided with a similar restoration at the College of William and Mary, whose charter also had been revised by the revolutionary-era state without its consent. In 1779, when Governor Thomas Jefferson "republicanized" William and Mary, he abolished its (Anglican) professorship in divinity as well as its affiliated grammar school, along with the school's principal. Ten years later, in 1789, the deposed principal, John Bracken, sued for reinstatement on grounds that Jefferson and his fellow public visitors had overstepped their authority. Bracken was represented by his attorney John Taylor; the visitors were represented by future US Supreme Court chief justice John Marshall, then a thirty-five-year-old Richmond lawyer and William and Mary graduate. *Bracken v. the Visitors of William and Mary College* (1790) asked whether the (public) visitors had a chartered right to oversee the college and its associated grammar school, including a right to dismiss the school's principal.

The case hinged on the court's interpretation of the college's original charter, granted by King William III and Queen Mary II in 1693 in response to a request from Virginia's colonial assembly three years earlier. The charter carried a grant of land and named eighteen trustees with the power "to erect, found, and establish a certain place of universal study, or perpetual college." "As soon as the college was erected," notes historian J. W. Bridge, "the original trustees were to hire a president and professors and convey all college property, by deed of transfer, into their hands." After this conveyance of property, the president and professors "were to be incorporated as a body politic [a 'corporation'] with perpetual succession," and the original eighteen trustees were to become a new—public and external—board of visitors, led by a chancellor with a right of visitation and perpetual succession. This structure, with a corporation of faculty overseen by external visitors, resembled that of an Oxford college (as reaffirmed in the recent *Magdalen* and *Exeter* cases).

While it took a while to put William and Mary into operation, the president and professors, as the corporation, drafted a set of college statutes in 1728–29, subject to public review by the visitors and the chancellor. Unfortunately, the president and professors often disagreed with the chancellor about institutional management. For example, in 1766 (just as the question of college governance came to a head at Yale), President James Horrocks denounced Chancellor Richard Terrick's self-declared power to "arbitrarily change statutes and narrowly construct the conduct of the professors." Two years later, in 1768, Horrocks said the king, not the chancellor, was actually the "supreme visitor of the college," and the professors agreed. Ultimately, everyone seemed to agree that "fundamental change in the constitution of the college could be accomplished only by the crown," the institution's founder and first donor—but change was delayed by the revolution.

Despite the Declaration of Independence in 1776, the president and professors said the king was still in charge, but others said the war cut all ties between the college and Crown. This debate surfaced in the case of

Attorney General ex rel. Bishop of London v. College of William and Mary (1790), wherein the president and professors sued to retain a prerevolutionary grant for the education of Indian students—Robert Boyle's gift of 1691, overseen by the bishop of London—even though Boyle's will had not explicitly named the college as heir to his bequest. After the revolution, London's attorney general said the college was "no longer a corporation with respect to this country [England]," so the president and professors had no further claim to Boyle's gift. The court agreed. It found that, since England no longer recognized the college—and since the college no longer had Indian students—Boyle's endowment could be legally redirected to other institutions.

This decision aligned with the public visitors' claims in *Bracken v. the Visitors of William and Mary College*, litigated the same year. Just as England's courts said the college had lost any link with its royal founders, so Thomas Jefferson and his fellow visitors said the college was no longer subject to English law and was thus unconstrained by any statutes laid down by its original corporation or its successors (the president and professors). In 1779, Jefferson's famous Bill No. 80 for Amending the Constitution of the College of William and Mary and Substituting More Certain Revenues for Its Support had argued that, henceforth, the college's public visitors should not "be restrained ... by the royal prerogative, the laws of the kingdom of England ... or the canons or constitution of the English Church as enjoined in the said charter." While the visitors might opt to retain certain statutes created by the original trustees, they did so at their own discretion.

The key question in *Bracken v. the Visitors of William and Mary College* was whether the postrevolutionary public visitors could ignore or even nullify the statute that had created Bracken's contract as head of the grammar school. Was the college a civil (public) corporation, in which case its visitors could amend its charter and statutes? Or was it a charitable (private) corporation, in which case the college would sit beyond public visitatorial authority, governed by its president and professors and reviewable only in court? The charter stated clearly that William and Mary, "being founded and endowed with lands and revenues of the [the king on behalf of the] public, and intended for the[ir] sole use and improvement and no wise in nature of a private grant ... is, of right, subject to the public direction and may by them be altered and amended until such form be devised as will render the institution publicly advantageous in proportion as it is publicly expensive." The visitors therefore argued that William and Mary was a civil (public) corporation, not a charitable (private) one. But was it?

In 1790, Bracken's case went to court. John Marshall, who represented the public visitors, noted that William and Mary's original charter had made no reference to a grammar school (established later, under the college's statutes). He therefore reasoned that abolition of the grammar school fell within the visitors' broad authority to oversee the institution. "Their power of legislation ... extended to the modification of the schools in any manner they should deem proper," he argued, "provided they did not depart from the great outlines marked in the charter, which are divinity, philosophy, and the languages." Yet while Jefferson had cast the visitors as corporate overseers who represented the public interest, Marshall took a different, and unexpected, tack—one that echoed the English law of corporations applied to endowed colleges. He cast the visitors not as supervisors of a civil (public) corporation but as trustees of a charitable (private) corporation.

It was a risky argument, because William and Mary had been founded with support from a royal land grant and had received various other public resources from the colonial assembly. For that reason, Edmund Pendleton of the court of appeals said William and Mary "had a public, not a private, foundation." Only if the College of William and Mary was public, said Pendleton, would its visitors be empowered to say how the college—and its grammar school—should be governed. Marshall, however, looked to *Philips v. Bury* (decided a year after William and Mary's charter was granted in 1693) and *King v. Bishop of Ely* (1765) to say that in colleges that were private corporations, a duly appointed visitor was "a judge without appeal." He asserted that William and Mary, *despite* its original public foundation, was a private corporation subject to its visitors' authority, not as public overseers, but as trustees responsible for its use of private assets.

During oral arguments, Bridge finds, Pendleton actually interrupted Marshall to stipulate that "the court would not have jurisdiction if the college were a 'private eleemosynary institution,'" as long as there were no violations of the original charter (and there were no such violations in this case) and no fears that its corporate trustees (its president and professors) were the same as its visitors (and they were not). This reminder, observes Bridge, caused Marshall to proceed with caution: "Admitting the college was founded on [public] donations from the king and the [colonial] government, Marshall insisted on the authority of *Philips v. Bury* and other English cases that the college was 'private' anyway. The crucial point was that William and Mary had appointed visitors to superintend [what Marshall construed as] their [private] charity. Once these [visitors] were appointed, the corporation was in the same class with 'private eleemosynary' corporations founded by individuals, and the Virginia court could have no jurisdiction over removals within the visitors' power."

Bracken's lawyer, John Taylor, seized on Marshall's (mis)characterization of William and Mary as "private" donors (who chartered the college's original trustees, who in turn appointed the president and professors as their successors) and noted that it was not until three decades later that a public board of visitors had been constituted. Before that point, Taylor asserted, the public visitors literally had "no existence, let alone authority." The visitors' authority was granted not by the charter but rather by statutes written by the president and professors as the rightful trustees of the king and queen's donation. None of the statutes had given the visitors authority to close the grammar school—the creation of which had been requested by William and Mary as part of their original gift. Moreover, he added, royal acts of incorporation were never private but always public acts.

Marshall and Taylor offered different interpretations of the college's foundations and, in turn, its visitors' authority to oversee its operations. Bridge remarks that the "critical question" was "whether the visitors were bound by the original statutes, or whether they had complete discretion to change them." According to Marshall, the college resembled a private charitable (eleemosynary) corporation whose trustees (its president and professors) were subject to public visitatorial control. Taylor said the college resembled a public corporation whose visitors (as representatives of the public) were subject to judicial review. To make this case, Taylor cited *Bentley v. Bishop of Ely* (1729), "in which a visitor abused his authority by expelling a master of a college," and *King v. Bishop of*

Chester (1747), *Green v. Rutherford* (1750), and *St. John's College v. Todington* (1757), in which the courts said visitors controlled eleemosynary corporations except when they failed to abide by the corporation's original charter or statutes.

Taylor made a strong case that Jefferson and his fellow visitors overreached when they fired Bracken as head of William and Mary's grammar school, but in the end the court decided for the visitors, and Bracken's request for reinstatement was denied. Why? According to Bridge, it was because both Marshall and Taylor had at different points characterized the institution as a "public" corporation, which meant its visitors, as representatives of the public interest, did have the authority to alter its statutes. Here was Taylor's "fatal error" as Bracken's advocate. "Taylor was confident that [William and Mary] was a public corporation," Bridge notes, but he forgot that public corporations (unlike private corporations) were susceptible to charter alterations, either by their visitors or by the legislature. The court thus decided that William and Mary's visitors had the authority to close its grammar school, and Virginia's court of appeals could not overrule this action.

Marshall won this case, and his victory may have influenced his subsequent view of the law of corporations. In particular, his characterization of the College of William and Mary as a private corporation, despite the fact that it was founded with a public (royal) grant, as well as his characterization of the college's visitors as responsible for its proper use of private assets (here too despite the fact that its original assets were public), would resurface three decades later in his majority opinion in the *Dartmouth* case. Even though Marshall represented the public visitors in *Bracken*, he cast them in the guise of private trustees with sole authority to govern the college. No longer subject to English law (which might have stressed the public foundation of the college by the Crown), the visitors reigned supreme, and courts were powerless to constrain them as long as they did not violate the operational terms of the charter. Marshall's take on this case foreshadowed the approach he would take in *Dartmouth* three decades later.

———

Not long after he argued this case, Marshall took up a related suit that involved the charter of Liberty Hall Academy, which Virginia's legislature had attempted to amend without its trustees' consent. In 1796, the academy's trustees asked the legislature to change its name to "Washington Academy" (to honor a gift from George Washington). The legislature, however, unilaterally imposed the name "Washington College" on the institution and required it to reorganize its curriculum, remove several tutors, and, crucially, replace several ministers on its board with members of the legislature. The aim was to subject the school to public control so it would serve public interests. Yet as historian Silas Lee McCormick explains, the school's trustees, represented by Marshall, called public control "an unjustifiable infringement of the rights of the corporation of Liberty Hall and an instance of tyrannical imposition in the legislature."

Two years later, the legislature's acts were repealed, but this case of state imposition was not unique. Other states, too, sought to exert more authority over chartered institutions of higher education. In 1792, for example, the Yale corporation had consented to revise its charter to add the governor, lieutenant governor, and six legislators to its board of trustees in exchange for half the income from a surplus in the state treasury. Yale president Timothy Dwight worried that state aid might lead to state control of the college, or even the possibility of state takeover, but Connecticut judge Zephaniah Swift assured the college in his *System of Laws of the State of Connecticut* (1795) that Yale was a "private" corporation and that, although the legislature admittedly had the authority to abnegate "corporations of a public nature," it could not alter or amend "corporations of a private nature."

Dwight eventually accepted the new composition of Yale's board of trustees and in 1796 asked the state to continue its annual subsidies—in part to help the college fend off a new rival, Williams College, founded in western Massachusetts three years earlier with a substantial private donation. Along with its private endowment, Williams's charter provided for annual state grants of £300 for up to four years, as well as the proceeds of a state lottery. In exchange, the legislature reserved a right to select the college's original trustees and summon them at will to report on college affairs. As historian Mary Frampton Beach notes, this reserve clause in Williams's charter also "permitted the [legislative] amendment of the charter and/or the appointment of a [public] board of overseers." Thus, while the college was founded with an ostensibly independent board to oversee its use of private and public funds, the state retained considerable influence on grounds that Williams, like Harvard, should be subject to public oversight.

Dartmouth College also welcomed closer ties with its state in this period. While President Wheelock had rejected New Hampshire's offer in 1799 to give the college more land if he agreed to consolidate the governance of the college and the Indian Charity School, nonetheless, as historian Frederick Chase explains, "The interests of the college were kept in various other ways before the legislature of New Hampshire in the hope of an enlargement of its resources." In November 1804, for example, the board of trustees petitioned the legislature to review the college's finances, and "in order that they may be fully and fairly known" invited a committee "to visit the college, at the expense of the trustees, and fully investigate its concerns." The legislature, in turn, named a state "board of visitation" to review the college's books.

When this visit did not take place, the college trustees repeated their request. In a petition dated June 5, 1805, they cast Dartmouth College in distinctly "public" terms and claimed that its financial health was a matter of "common concern to the citizens" of the state. They said they, as "trustees actuated by no personal interest, consider themselves bound to attend to the concerns of the seminary only as it is an object of public importance." The legislature subsequently pledged $900 a year from the proceeds of a new bank tax. When Governor John Langdon vetoed the bank tax on grounds that depositors were presumed to hold private contracts that could not be "impaired" by a tax, Dartmouth's trustees shifted tactics and sought to win Langdon's favor with a plan to include "certain state officers" on their board (as Harvard, Yale, and other colleges had done).

In exchange for the inclusion of the speaker of the house, president of the senate, chief justice of the Superior Court, and members of the governor's council on a proposed joint board of Dartmouth College and Moor's Indian Charity School (accompanied by a drafted Act More Effectually to Define and Improve the Charitable Establishment Known by the Name of Moor's Charity School, and the Powers and Duties of the President Thereof, and to Constitute a Board to Assist in Directing the Expenditures of the Funds of Said School), a legislative subcommittee recommended a further grant of land ("six miles square") for the college. Passed on January 12, 1807, by a vote of 88 to 60, this agreement prompted what became known as the "Second College Grant," which supplemented the "First College Grant" of 1789 that had replaced the original Landaff grant of 1770.

However, less than a year later, Wheelock questioned the legitimacy of the new "joint" board of trustees. Specifically, he doubted whether this board with its legislative representatives superseded his authority to govern resources designated for Moor's Indian Charity School—notably the rents from the "Wheelock" township in Vermont, wherein he shared authority with that state. When a set of six legislators reviewed Dartmouth's governance structure, it found in Wheelock's favor that Moor's Indian Charity School, even "before ... the incorporation of Dartmouth College, ha[d] been considered as capable of taking, holding, and conveying real property and doing all the acts and things which might be done by a body corporate." New Hampshire thus amended its recent grant to give President Wheelock a veto on the joint board, at least as far as its governance concerned the management of the Indian Charity School.

This amended grant passed on December 21, 1808, over the strenuous objections of the Dartmouth College trustees, who had long sought to control both the college and the school and who ultimately wanted to consolidate both institutions' assets under one board. The amendment of 1808, however, exposed a rift between Wheelock and the college trustees. Whereas the trustees had worked hard to secure a second land grant in exchange for public representation on a joint board (and had consented to alter both institutions' governance structures to accomplish that aim, just as other colleges had agreed to public supervision in exchange for public support), Wheelock as president of Dartmouth College and sole trustee of Moor's Indian Charity School refused to share power with either the state legislature *or* the college trustees. This conflict over corporate property and privileges did not bode well for the future.

CHAPTER 5

Who Controls the College? Who Controls the Church?

Why did Wheelock refuse to share power with Dartmouth College's board of trustees? The reasons started with religion and, specifically, a conflict over control of the college church. By 1808, the president and trustees had parted ways on questions of faith. These differences had widened during the so-called Second Great Awakening as successive disagreements between evangelicals and conservatives swept the college. To understand the source of these disagreements—and others that followed—one must begin with Dartmouth's first revival in 1770 (just after Eleazar Wheelock's arrival in Hanover), which culminated in the establishment of the evangelical Church of Christ at Dartmouth College, a parish known as "the college church," which two years later united with Presbyterian churches in Lyme, Orford, Norwich, Piermont, and Pomfret to form the self-proclaimed Grafton Presbytery.

A second revival had occurred four years later, in 1774, when Eleazar Wheelock led his students in another show of religious enthusiasm. Then, after Wheelock's death in 1779, the college church appointed his son-in-law Sylvanus Ripley as pastor, and Ripley made his mark with yet another revival. A sense of spiritual renewal continued for over a year until a particularly active (some called it aggressive) campaign to sustain the evangelical movement split the college church and led to a dispute over control of the college, the church, and the corporate powers (and property) of each. Among the leaders of this latest revival was trustee Eden Burroughs, pastor of Hanover's town church (not to be confused with the college church), who said that, if the Grafton Presbytery that oversaw the comparatively moderate college church did not enforce piety among its parishioners, including students, then he would do so himself.

This dispute—a key part of the sectarian conflicts that eventually shaped the *Dartmouth* litigation—came to a head in 1784 when a majority of townspeople rejected Burroughs's strict evangelicalism and invited Ripley to replace him as the head of Hanover's town church. Ripley accepted, then merged the town church with the college church into a single corporation of New Hampshire's (public) Congregationalist "established" church. (After the revolution, Congregationalists had replaced Anglicans as New Hampshire's established church.) Burroughs, in turn, was exiled across the Connecticut River to lead a different parish in Hartford, Vermont, while the new "town-and-college church" worshipped in Dartmouth's chapel and—importantly—claimed a right to public revenues from Hanover's tax for established churches (revenue that Burroughs's old town church formerly had received).

Despite the departure of Burroughs, some of his town-church followers continued to gather in Hanover's local "meeting house" (and refused to let town-and-college parishioners enter). They also filed protests to say they should not be taxed for the support of the new town-and-college church, a claim repeated year after year. Eventually, their protests succeeded, and Burroughs's followers were exempted from the mandatory church tax. But the joint town-and-college church still received the revenue from Hanover's tax, and when Sylvanus Ripley died in 1787, his successor John Smith, a professor at the college, similarly benefited from this public income. Smith, however, was a reluctant minister. As he aged, he asked to be relieved from pastoral duties so he could focus on his professorial responsibilities. A replacement was sought in 1796, then again in 1802 and 1803, but it was not until 1804 that a seemingly acceptable minister emerged . . . only to exacerbate the religious conflicts at the college.

That year, the Reverend Roswell Shurtleff, a friend of Dartmouth trustee (and Wheelock critic) Nathaniel Niles of Vermont who had graduated with Dartmouth's class of 1799 and had tutored in the college, was chosen for the Phillips Professorship of Divinity—a position endowed by John Phillips (who also had endowed his eponymous academies in Andover, Massachusetts, in 1778, and Exeter, New Hampshire, in 1781). Phillips had made his first donation to Dartmouth in 1780, and in 1789, as John Wheelock negotiated with New Hampshire's legislature for its "First College Grant" (to replace the Landaff property), he gave a further gift "to support a professor of divinity." Over the next decade, Phillips's donations, plus income from various land acquisitions, enabled the college to fund Shurtleff's position.

Shurtleff was recruited against the wishes of John Wheelock, who feared that his forceful revivalism would appeal only to a narrow subset of impassioned students and therefore would divide the already quarrel-prone town-and-college church. Wheelock suspected that Shurtleff wanted to make the college more "sectarian" (in violation of its original charter), and he was not mistaken. As soon as Shurtleff assumed his post, he led a series of late-night camp meetings to "reawaken the spiritual life of the college." Some called him "superstitious, enthusiastic, a methodist, etc.," but he appealed to earnest undergraduates eager to demonstrate their religious commitments. "With professor Shurtleff," one remarked, "I am highly pleased. His instructions are enlightening, weighty, and evangelical" . . . just as Wheelock feared.

In contrast to Wheelock, the college trustees wanted Shurtleff to reunite the town-and-college church with the town church and move the parish back into Hanover's local meeting house. Shurtleff welcomed this project, but Wheelock preferred his old friend John Smith as pastor of both churches. This disagreement festered until 1805, when Shurtleff's followers in town started to call themselves "The Congregation in the Vicinity of Dartmouth College" and said he should be their pastor "so far as may be consistent, and not interfere, with his duties as Professor of Divinity for Dartmouth College." They continued to occupy the meeting house, in which they claimed "partial ownership" (since Eleazar Wheelock had relied on their contributions to build it). Wheelock, meanwhile, said that Shurtleff's worship services at the meeting house in town constituted a "misuse" of funds designated for his Phillips Professorship at the college.

The debate over religion in Hanover reflected a larger debate over the control of established churches as public corporations. Since the colonial era, New Hampshire's towns had been required by law to support their local parishes with taxes. No one, "under pretense of being of a different persuasion," could be "excused from paying toward the support of the settled minister." Yet not everyone accepted this policy.

Particularly after the antiestablishment revivals of the First Great Awakening, some refused to pay church taxes. As early as 1764, for example, Baptists declined to fund the local parish in Newton (until town officials seized Baptist property "for overdue taxes"). Then, in 1769, the year Dartmouth was chartered, Baptists took over Newton's town council and exempted themselves from church taxes on grounds of private religious freedom (only for New Hampshire's assembly to override their action).

Disputes over mandatory church taxes—and the control of established churches as public corporations—escalated after the revolution. In 1782, for example, after future New Hampshire governor William Plumer became a Baptist, he wrote an editorial for the *New Hampshire Gazette* in which he decried church taxes. He later served eight one-year terms in the state legislature, including as speaker of the house and president of the senate. Then, in 1791, when he represented fellow religious dissenters in a convention to rewrite New Hampshire's postrevolutionary constitution, he recommended a repeal of church taxes on grounds that "public" corporations such as the state's established church should be subject to legislative control. His repeal failed, but in 1798, when the Superior Court of New Hampshire held in the case of *Kelley v. Bean* that a Congregationalist pastor could not be taxed for the support of his own congregation, Plumer saw a path toward more general exemption from church taxes.

Either all churches should be exempt, Plumer argued, or *all* should be considered public corporations and thus eligible to receive tax revenues. Other dissenters endorsed this view, and over the next decade, various sects petitioned for charters of incorporation so they could share in local church taxes. In the case of *Muzzy v. Wilkins* (1803), the superior court ruled that Presbyterians, together with other Protestant groups, were "equally good for the purposes of civil society, because they all inculcate the principles of benevolence, philanthropy, and the moral virtues." At the same time, the court upheld the practice of mandatory religious taxes—now among diverse sects—on grounds that "public instruction in religion and morality . . . is . . . a civil, not a spiritual, institution," so the state had the authority "to provide for it at the expense of the whole."

In subsequent years, more churches petitioned for the right to serve the public interest as civil (public) corporations: Baptists in 1804,

Unitarians in 1805, and Methodists in 1807 (though Congregationalists still retained their status as the state's established church). "Once dissenting churches served the public by addressing broadly accepted Christian values, they, too, were accorded [charters of incorporation]," historian Mark Douglass McGarvie notes. Indeed, as historian Gordon Wood adds, because legislatures during the early republic "were often unwilling to raise taxes to pay for all that the governmental leaders desired to do, states were forced to fall back on the traditional (premodern) practice of enlisting private wealth to carry out public ends." The result was an increased use of charters to advance ostensibly "public" ends— even if some were unsure whether nonestablished churches should be considered public or private corporations.

This process of "general incorporation," or "corporatization," had important consequences not only for churches but also for colleges, often considered similarly quasi-public/quasi-private entities. At first, colleges had espoused a public role in exchange for public aid (together with the political legitimacy that public aid bestowed). But later, as they saw the extent to which public charters entailed public control, they started to ask whether their public service could be recognized even under the guise of private incorporation. By the first decade of the nineteenth century, as more college leaders (mainly conservative) resisted the supervision of state legislatures (increasingly revivalist), they began to argue that colleges as private corporations were equally able to advance the "public interest" or "common good."

William Plumer reflected this shift. In 1800, he ran for the US Senate on the conservative Federalist ticket, but in 1808 he switched parties. He threw his support behind the Republicans on grounds of religious liberty (he was tired of the Congregationalist-Federalist stranglehold on New Hampshire's tax-supported churches) and endorsed Republicans' calls for a separation of church and state. Put simply, he expanded his platform from a general exemption from religious taxes to a wholesale call for religious *disestablishment*. "While not so consistently liberal as Jefferson," historian Eldon Johnson observes, "Plumer pressed religious liberty with such fervor that he provoked violent recriminations" from Congregationalist-Federalists who sought to retain the corporate privileges (and property) of New Hampshire's established church ... and college.

In 1808, as the community of Hanover—and in turn Dartmouth College—began to split over the issue of taxes for established churches, Plumer (who had no higher education) asked whether a college associated with a particular church should receive public aid. He and his fellow Baptist-Republicans thought not, and they looked to Virginia's example for support. Before the revolution, Virginia's established church had been Anglican, but as early as 1774 its colonial assembly had received petitions from sects that opposed mandatory taxes for that church. "We ask no ecclesiastical establishment for ourselves," Presbyterians remarked. "Neither can we approve of them when granted to others." A dozen years later, in 1786, Thomas Jefferson adopted this argument in his famous Act for Establishing Religious Freedom, which outlawed church taxes altogether.

Many considered Jefferson's bill a victory for religious disestablishment, but for some it did not go far enough. Presbyterians and Baptists asserted that religious disestablishment should allow the state to seize "glebe" lands from the old established Anglican—now Episcopal—church. Although the Episcopalians' ownership of these lands had been confirmed in an Incorporation Act of 1784, that act was cast into doubt after 1798, when the state barred church incorporation altogether. Four years later, in 1802, the state required the Episcopalian clergy to give up glebes under their control at death. Shocked by this "usurpation" of property, the clergy sued. In the case of *Turpin v. Lockett* (1804), they said the glebes were private corporate property for which they and their successors were trustees in perpetuity. The state countered that Anglican claims to land in Virginia had been nullified by the revolution, so lands seemingly deemed private (under the Incorporation Act of 1784) were in fact public.

Virginia judges Spencer Roane and Henry St. George Tucker upheld the state's right to seize Episcopalian glebes and based their decision on the fact that, while private gifts of property would indeed be exempt from legislative seizure, the glebes were "derived, in most cases, from public [royal] grants" to an officially established church. As historian Bruce Campbell notes, the question in *Turpin v. Lockett* was not whether to respect church property but, rather, "in whom the property in question is vested." Roane said that glebes initially granted by the Crown "did not belong to the church, but to the government." Tucker—who recently had reviewed corporate law in his edition of William Blackstone's four-volume *Commentaries on the Laws of England* (1803, originally published in 1765–70)—acknowledged the "fundamental principle of our constitution that private property shall be sacred and inviolable" but argued that "glebes, as such, were never private property."

This decision might have gone the other way had the eighty-two-year-old chief judge Edmund Pendleton, "a staunch Episcopalian," not died a day before his opinion was to be read. Tucker, his successor, "quietly signaled his approval" of glebe confiscation "in order to secure his election as a justice by the [Republican] legislature." Among those irked by Tucker's decision was US Supreme Court justice Bushrod Washington, a Virginia lawyer who, a year before he took his seat on the high court in 1798, had strongly defended the "vested rights of parishes and their property." Also upset was his fellow Virginian on the court, John Marshall, who similarly opposed confiscation. During the 1790s, some of Marshall's own land had been seized by the state despite a federal treaty with its original title holder, Lord Fairfax, an issue subsequently resolved in *Martin v. Hunter's Lessee* (1816), which ruled that federal treaties outweighed state laws under the supremacy clause of article V of the Constitution.

The son of an Episcopal vestryman, Marshall had stood up for the clergy's property rights. Indeed, he voted for the Incorporation Act of 1784 when he was a Virginia legislator. That act had converted Anglican churches, once public corporations under common law (with no formal charters but the "'presumed' consent of the crown"), into private corporations. It also converted glebes (originally "grants from the King of England") into private lands under perpetual church ownership. But the court in *Turpin v. Lockett* undid this act. Tucker's decision cited Henry VIII's dissolution of the Catholic monasteries to justify the state's power to dissolve formerly established churches as corporations. "Where the legislature creates an artificial person and endows that artificial person with certain rights and privileges," he wrote, the legislature retained the power to alter or amend those rights and privileges—or even to annul the (public) corporations it created and reassign their property to other public ends.

By 1800, many states, particularly in the South, had begun to move away from churches as common-law corporations (recognized as public corporations) to offer churches new charters of incorporation, recognized as private contracts and thus protected from legislative control. Rights formerly held by churches as common-law corporations—to make bylaws, disburse funds, bring lawsuits, and so on—were now passed on to churches recast as private corporations able to hold property on their own. Slowly but surely, legislatures that once denied charters to nonestablished "dissenter" churches now granted charters under general incorporation laws that allowed nearly *all* religious bodies to become privately incorporated. (Virginia, however, retained its prohibition against private religious incorporation until 2002, when this prohibition was declared unconstitutional in *Falwell v. Miller*.)

Even as Virginia's seizure of Episcopal glebe lands was upheld, questions persisted about when—or whether—state legislatures could seize properties granted to *public* corporations. This question would play a pivotal role in the *Dartmouth* litigation, but a decade earlier it surfaced in a particularly important case on corporate rights in higher education in the South. In *Trustees of the University of North Carolina v. Foy* (1805), the so-called Court of Conference in North Carolina said the legislature could not revoke the university's chartered right to income from confiscated glebes—a right that had been granted in the state's constitution. The original constitution of 1776 had promised that "all useful learning shall be duly encouraged and promoted in one or more universities," and thirteen years later, the charter of the University of North Carolina in 1789 said that institution would be "supported by public funds."

Since the charter did not specify any particular source of "public funds," a subsequent act four days later filled this gap. It vested in the university's trustees "all monies due and owing to the public of North Carolina ... for arrearages" (that is, uncollected payments) as well as "all the property that has heretofore or shall hereafter escheat to the state" (that is, unclaimed lands). Five years later, in 1794, the legislature further granted the university revenue from confiscated glebe lands. With these sources of revenue—arrearages, escheats, and glebes—designated in perpetuity and deemed "exempt from all kind of public taxation," the University of North Carolina became, according to one historian, "potentially one of the most richly endowed institutions of learning in the American union."

Yet the reassignment of confiscated glebes created enemies for the university. In 1800, the legislature repealed its funding act of 1789 and urged any citizen whose lands had been seized to repossess them from the university. The university, in response, brought this issue to court. As a publicly chartered institution with a perpetual right to constitutionally guaranteed property, it said its terms of incorporation, once granted, could not be revoked without its consent. The court agreed. Judge Francis Locke cited Blackstone's *Commentaries* on corporations "formed for the advancement of religion, learning, commerce, or other beneficial purposes." The University of North Carolina's charter, he proclaimed, "stood on higher ground" than most other civil (public) corporations, because it was protected by the state's constitution itself. Hence, the only way for the legislature to seize the university's property was to amend the constitution.

As this case unfolded in the South, the question of legislative control over both public and private corporations also unfolded in the North. In the case of *Wales v. Stetson* (1806), for example, Massachusetts's high court said the state could not pass laws that impaired the charter of a private corporation—although state oversight could be written into a corporation's initial charter. As Judge Theophilus Parsons observed: "Rights legally vested in . . . any corporation cannot be controlled or destroyed by any subsequent statute, unless a power for that purpose be reserved to the legislature in the act of incorporation." Parsons added, however, that if legislatures reserved a power of amendment, then courts should interpret such powers narrowly to include only those *expressly* stated, a stipulation that led Massachusetts's legislature to reserve for itself the broadest possible right to alter or amend the charters it granted.

Perhaps nowhere was the question of legislative power over corporations more fraught in this period than it was at Harvard, whose leaders had long prided themselves on close ties with the state. Indeed, for more than a quarter century, Massachusetts's constitution had required Harvard to include the governor, lieutenant governor, and members of both legislative chambers among its public board of overseers. But after the partisan conflicts that accompanied the Republican Party's rise to power of the early nineteenth century, the connection between the college and the state came under fire. In the state elections of 1810, Federalists lost their legislative majority and, in response, looked for ways to retain their control of the college (and its property). Days before they left office, they used a lame-duck session to pack Harvard's board of overseers with copartisans: fifteen ministers and fifteen laymen, all Federalists.

Federalist legislators stressed that Harvard's overseers had accepted this change willingly, but Republicans (perhaps aware of the recent decision in *University of North Carolina v. Foy*) said the college's governance structure had been specified in Massachusetts's constitution. As one Republican wrote, "The essence of every contract, charter, or constitution is the primary ground on which their inviolability and legitimacy are to be preserved, and every attempt to alter, change, or weaken their fundamental basis is considered—not only in law, but in equity—as an unjustifiable act." Indeed, the Republicans noted, just as North Carolina's relationship with its university was constitutionally established, so was Massachusetts's relationship with *its* university. Could an ostensibly public corporation be usurped by "a minority party" that had been voted from power? Republicans said no, but Federalists said that Harvard, despite the explicit terms of the state constitution, was not in fact a public corporation.

———

To support their argument, the Federalists asked Theophilus Parsons to review Harvard's charter. Parsons, a "fellow" of the college since 1806, knew that, in 1636, it had been founded by the Massachusetts Bay Colony with a public grant of £400 (a gift from John Harvard came two years later); that, in 1642, it had welcomed legislation whereby "the governor, deputy-governor, president of the college, magistrates, teaching elders, etc.," became a public board of overseers to supervise its use of endowed properties, "subject to the will of the donors"; that, in 1650, it had revised its charter to create a board of "resident" fellows, the so-called Harvard corporation, with the president and professors; and that, in 1673, Massachusetts's legislative body had enlarged the corporation with "nonresident" fellows, a step taken without the consent of the original fellows and subsequently disputed.

This governance structure had been in place until the revolution, when the initial charter and statutes were supplemented by Massachusetts's new state constitution of 1780, wherein the composition of the board of fellows stayed the same, but the membership of the board of overseers changed, with the old colonial governor, deputy governor, and magistrates replaced by the new state governor, lieutenant governor, and council, who thereafter held a right of public visitation and power to veto the fellows. And perhaps most crucially, Massachusetts's constitution had included a reserve clause that stated: "Nothing herein shall be construed to prevent the legislature of this commonwealth from making such alterations in the government of said university as shall be conducive to its advantage, and the interests of the republic of letters, in as full a manner as might have been done by the legislature of the late province of the Massachusetts Bay."

Three decades later, in 1810, the question was: Did a Federalist lame-duck state legislature have the authority to pack Harvard's board of overseers with copartisans? Parsons thought so. While the legislature could not alter the membership of the board without its consent, Harvard's overseers—all Federalists—*had*, in fact, consented to an enlargement of their number, and once installed the new overseers could not be deprived of their governance rights. Parsons said it was "difficult to conceive by what legitimate authority the legislature could afterwards deprive those new visitors of the rights of visitation thus lawfully vested in them." He concluded not only that Federalists had the power to alter the composition of Harvard's board (with its consent) but also that a subsequently elected Republican majority had no right to adjust the new board without consent.

In the wake of Parson's opinion, Republicans decided that Massachusetts's legislature, now under their control, should charter a "rival" institution of higher education with its own (Republican) board of overseers. For starters, professor of medicine Benjamin Waterhouse noted that Harvard's medical school—in cahoots with the state medical society—often refused to license Republican physicians. He thus proposed in 1811 to charter a new College of Physicians in Boston and urged the legislature's Republican majority to fund it on grounds that "two literary and scientific bodies produce more than double the advantage of one." The legislature agreed, but a year later, Federalists, determined to retain control over medical practice in the city, answered Waterhouse's proposal with a plan for a new Massachusetts General Hospital, its privileges extended first and foremost to graduates of Harvard.

Republicans agreed to incorporate this new hospital—and give it a provisional state grant of land worth $20,000—if they could reserve a legislative right to amend its charter and revise its board of visitors to include the governor, lieutenant governor, speaker of the house, chaplains of both houses, and twelve self-perpetuating laymen, all from their own party. Federalists consented and got their charter. Then, a year later, when the legislature returned to Federalist control, members of that party repealed their predecessors' reserve clause and restricted the powers of the hospital's Republican-dominated board of visitors. Over time, as the board's composition shifted, Federalists recast the hospital as a private charity governed by an independent board. Massachusetts General Hospital—like Harvard College—asserted that public functions were best served by private corporations.

This view was increasingly common, as demonstrated by a similar debate in New Hampshire, which had chartered a Dartmouth-affiliated medical school in Hanover and had given it a public grant of land and cash for construction. The school opened in 1811, but it "cost more than [New Hampshire's] appropriation," so professor of medicine Nathan Smith offered to pay the excess from private resources. The state let Smith rent out rooms in the school to recoup his contribution, but Smith considered himself a financial partner in the institution and wanted more. When the state rejected his request for a public-private partnership, he went to Yale, which had created a medical school of its own, also with public aid. Even after Smith left, however, an important question lingered: Were colleges like Harvard, Yale, and Dartmouth—all partly funded by their states, but with separate boards of trustees—public or private corporations? After decades of mounting dispute, this question soon found its way to court.

PART II

The Case

CHAPTER 6

Dartmouth College v. Dartmouth University

Even as Dartmouth's medical school got underway, tensions over control of the college took a turn in 1811 when Professor Shurtleff sought permission to preach to both of Hanover's two churches. President Wheelock denied this request on grounds that dual pulpits would distract Shurtleff from his responsibilities in the college and thus violate the requirements of his Phillips Professorship. The college trustees, however, overruled Wheelock and, in a strongly worded statement, brought their disagreements with the president into the open. "The trustees have labored to restore the harmony which formerly prevailed in this institution, without success," they wrote, "and with reluctance, they express their apprehension that, if the present state of things is suffered to remain any great length of time, the college will be essentially injured." Here, in a sense, was the match that lit the legal fuse at Dartmouth: a fuse that eventually ignited a constitutional bomb.

The board of trustees not only permitted Shurtleff to preach in both churches but pushed to limit Wheelock's authority to govern religious affairs on campus. It gave "certain powers of discipline to a majority of the executive officers of the college [the faculty] instead of leaving [those powers] solely in the hands of the president"—a move Wheelock considered an "invasion of his rights." He asked the legislature to investigate the matter on the assumption that Dartmouth was a public corporation and the legislature its rightful visitor, with a check on the board's actions. In response, the legislature pledged to examine "the funds, the government, and [the] education of the college and school." This examination never took place, but a year later, in 1812, ten of twelve members of the Federalist-dominated board reasserted their power to control the use of college property, notably the funds of the Phillips Professorship.

Meanwhile, that summer, the declaration of war between the United States and Britain opened a new front in this era's partisan conflicts.

Federalist antipathy toward "Madison's War" spread to such an extent that, in the elections of 1812 and 1813, the Federalist Party seized legislative control in both Massachusetts and New Hampshire. Then, in 1814, Federalists across New England gathered in Connecticut for the (secessionist) Hartford Convention—but they pressed their antiwar position too far, and that year Republicans took back legislative majorities in both Massachusetts and New Hampshire, where Republican candidate for governor William Plumer had won in 1812, lost in 1813, and won again in 1814. In each campaign, he cast his Federalist-Congregationalist opponents as politically disloyal, religiously oppressive, and socially aristocratic—all traits he associated with Federalist graduates of Dartmouth College.

Partisan conflicts in New Hampshire extended beyond the college and the chambers of government to affect the state courts (and hence the judges soon to hear the *Dartmouth* case). When the Federalists briefly regained power in 1813, they abruptly passed a law to abolish the superior court and fire its justices, whom they accused of Republican sympathies. This extraconstitutional coup led to "grave complications," historian John Major Shirley notes. "Some of the old judges held the act void" and served out their individual terms, even as new Federalist judges were appointed in their place. With two courts in operation side by side, "The result was scandal and disturbance." Yet, with such a brazen assault on the judiciary, the Federalists in New Hampshire again pushed too far. In 1814, when Plumer retook the governorship and his party reclaimed the legislature, they reversed the Federalists' acts.

Plumer immediately sought to restore the old court, but he was not immune to partisanship himself. His loyalties came through in his interactions with Dartmouth College, where he and his fellow Republicans consistently sided with President Wheelock against the college's predominantly Federalist-Congregationalist trustees. Ever since their dispute over the use of funds designated for Moor's Indian Charity School—and their subsequent disagreement over the use of resources for the Phillips Professorship—the president and trustees had split over partisan as well as sectarian differences. And the governor, already wary of an increased number of private corporations that had been chartered in New Hampshire, worried that Dartmouth's trustees saw themselves as private more than public actors. He was not wrong.

During the war, the conflict at Dartmouth between the president and trustees grew more and more tense. Wheelock repeated his request for a state audit of the governance of the Phillips trust, but the board rejected the legislature's claim of "visitatorial" powers. Instead, the board took further steps to restrict Wheelock's presidential role. In early November 1814, the board pronounced his teaching "ineffective" and put other professors in charge of his senior-year course on moral philosophy. Shortly thereafter, the *Boston Repertory* reported that "difficulties of a serious and unpleasant nature" might lead Dartmouth's board to seek a new president. Wheelock, furious, said any effort to remove him would violate the institution's charter, which gave him, as president, a voice in all professorial appointments, including his own. He said his appeal for a legislative audit was in the public's interest, whereas the board represented only private interests.

Tensions reached new heights in May 1815, when President Wheelock publicly criticized the board's Federalist-Congregationalist majority and claimed it had used the college to advance partisan ends and, specifically, to assert private authority over Hanover's established church via its mobilization of Professor Shurtleff and manipulation of the Phillips trust. He sent copies of his *Sketches of the History of Dartmouth College and Moors' Charity School, with a Particular Account of Some Late Remarkable Proceedings of the Board of Trustees, from the Year 1779 to the Year 1815* to New Hampshire's legislature, with five hundred additional copies distributed among the public. Why did he publish this pamphlet? According to editors at the *Boston Repertory*, it was because Dartmouth's trustees had plotted his dismissal, and he wanted to defend himself.

To print this pamphlet, Wheelock chose a strategic ally: Dartmouth graduate and Congregationalist pastor Elijah Parish, whose Federalist bona fides he thought would appeal to friends on the board. Wheelock and Parish were longtime associates (Parish's family had been members of the Wheelock congregation in Lebanon, Connecticut), and Wheelock had tried repeatedly to place him on Dartmouth's faculty (the board gave him an honorary degree in 1807). Parish combined the *Sketches* with *A Candid and Analytical Review of the Sketches of the History of Dartmouth College and Moors' Charity School*, which claimed the board had attempted to rule the college without public oversight, in violation of its charter.

"This *imperium in imperio*, this independent government in an independent state," he wrote, "may soon become an organized aristocracy, extending its influence with hallowed pretension under a sectarian banner to give a tone to government and manage the state," he wrote. "Is there no power to control them?"

Parish called on the legislature to check the board's "independent" power and claim its proper role as public visitor. "We, with all possible respect, call on the legislature of the state to cast an eye to our university," he wrote as he warned that Dartmouth's trustees sought to control all the institution's privileges and property. "While the college was poor, there was little need of legislative interference, because there were few temptations to pervert the funds or render the college the engine of party. But having become rich and powerful, unless legislators turn their attentions to the governors of the college, the governors of the college will turn their attentions to the legislators—[and thus] will ... rule the state." Parish saw a Federalist-Congregationalist scheme to "seize ... every seminary in the country which shall have any influence on the education and opinions of the rising generation."

Aside from Parish, the most outspoken defender of Wheelock's presidency was Isaac Hill, the Republican editor of the *New Hampshire Patriot*, who called on New Hampshire's legislature to protect Dartmouth College from sectarian takeover on grounds that it was a public institution founded to serve public interests. "The institution has been liberally patronized by the state, and each individual has a concern in it," he asserted. "If a majority of the legislature are not already willing dopes to the present board," he added, then "something will be done, as well to relieve the venerable Wheelock from his disagreeable dilemma as to [steer] the government of the college [from] a course no less destructive to the interests of the institution than to the intentions of its liberal founders and its generous patron, the state of New Hampshire." Only President Wheelock could block the Federalist-Congregationalists' scheme. "It seems ... there is but one barrier in the way of the consummation of their wishes," Hill wrote. "The president lives."

Wheelock agreed. In the summer of 1815, he again petitioned the legislature, as "guardian of the state's institutions," to examine the board's administrative machinations. He said the board had "forsaken" the college's "original principles"; had "violated the charter by prostrating the rights which it expressly invests in the presidential office"; and had "applied property to purposes wholly alien from the intention of the donors [notably John Phillips]." He said the legislature held "by the Constitution and the very nature of sovereignty in all countries, the sacred right, with your duty and responsibility to God, to visit and oversee the literary establishments where the manners and feelings of the young are formed, ... to restrain from injustice and rectify abuses in their management; and, if necessary, to reduce them to their primitive principles or so modify their powers as to make them subservient to the public welfare."

Wheelock's petition asked the legislature to augment the board of trustees with six new legislatively appointed members "in order to drown out" the Federalist-Congregationalists. If the legislature acted, then he promised "to give a large part of his [individual] estate to the college"—but if not, he said he might resign as president and take his (substantial) resources with him. It was a dramatic threat, and it did not go unanswered. The board replied in the *Concord Gazette* with a request for readers to "suspend judgment 'until a plain statement of facts, accompanied with proper evidence'" could be provided. In the meantime, the legislature voted 123 to 50 to empanel a Committee to Investigate the Concerns of Dartmouth College and Moor's Charity School Generally, and the Acts and Proceedings of the Trustees.

This committee was to meet in Hanover with both Wheelock and the board of trustees. In preparation, Wheelock asked the renowned Boston attorney Daniel Webster for legal assistance, but Webster declined for reasons that became clear in a letter written by trustee Thomas Thompson (who had tutored Webster in law). Thompson, a US senator whose own law tutor had been Theophilus Parsons, noted that Webster, a Federalist, had a "strong desire" to "put down a certain Mr. W[heelock]," a man he considered a danger to Dartmouth, and in fact to all "private" corporations. Indeed, as Webster wrote to Vermont resident Josiah Dunham (a former teacher at Moor's Indian Charity School, originally from Lebanon, Connecticut, who had taken Wheelock's side in the dispute), "I am not quite as convinced as you are that the president is altogether right and the trustees altogether wrong." According to Webster, the college was a private corporation, subject only to its trustees' authority—though, as it turned out, he knew little of the institution's legal origins.

Even as the legislative committee prepared to meet in Hanover, the board of trustees continued to plot Wheelock's departure, a move some considered premature. Jeremiah Mason, who later served as the college's legal counsel, urged the board to wait until the committee had met. He worried that a preemptive dismissal would alienate the college from the public. "I have felt considerable anxiety for the issue of the matter so much in public discussion relative to Dartmouth College," wrote Mason in August 1815 to his cousin Charles Marsh, a trustee who lived in Vermont (where his father had bought land from the college many years before). "I am led to believe an intention is entertained by some members of the board of ending all difficulty with the president by removing him from office. I greatly fear that such a measure, adopted under present circumstances ... would have a very unhappy effect on the public mind."

Mason asked the board to let the legislature complete its review on grounds that it had "visitatorial" authority to oversee the college. "The legislature has, I think, for certain purposes, a right to inquire into alleged mismanagement of such an institution—a visitatorial power that rests in the state," he observed. Why not let the state exercise its supervisory rights under the charter? Why not reinforce the view that Dartmouth College served the public? "I feel much confidence that a very decisive course against the president by the trustees at the present time would create an unpleasant sensation in the public mind," Mason reasoned. "I see no danger in delay but fear much in too great haste." The board, however, did not want to wait—in part because it did not believe the legislature had any public visitatorial authority.

The day after Mason sent his letter, the legislative committee met in Wheelock's home, despite the trustees' request to convene at the meeting house in town. Wheelock presented six charges against the board: that its integration of the college and town churches had subjected a "public institution to inconvenience and degradation, by means of private interference"; that it had misused funds given for the Phillips Professorship by "paying for village preaching"; that it had spent college funds "to an amount unnecessary and extravagant"; that it had refused to direct "any of the funds of which they have control to the instruction of Indians"; that it had "diverted the funds of the college for the support of Union Academy" (the preparatory school that replaced the Indian

Charity School); and that it had interfered with "the power of the president, as granted by the charter, in the education of the students, and also with his rights as an executive officer."

On the second day of the investigation, the board presented its rebuttal, which asserted that all decisions about the use of college funds had been made with the personal approval, or at least acquiescence, of Wheelock himself. The board denied that it diverted Dartmouth College funds away from the Phillips Professorship or toward Union Academy instead of to Indian students (of whom none were enrolled). It also denied any interference with the president's executive rights. At the same time, it claimed a preeminent right to govern the college according to its own interpretation of the charter and rejected the idea that a legislative committee had "visitatorial power" to review its decisions. It was a bold defense—and the board did not wait for the state to consider its merits. Eleven days later, after Wheelock refused to withdraw his criticisms of the board in exchange for lifetime protection as president, it dismissed him from his post.

The board said Wheelock had failed to respect its authority. He "insists on claims which the charter by no fair construction does allow—claims which, in their operation, would deprive the corporation of all its powers," the board announced. "He claims a right to exercise the whole executive authority of the college, which the charter has expressly committed to 'the Trustees, with the President, Tutors, and Professors by them appointed.' He also seems to claim a right to control the corporation in the appointment of executive officers, inasmuch as he has reproached them with great severity for choosing men who do not in all respects meet his wishes." Further, they added, Wheelock had slandered the board's members in his *Sketches*, which they called a "gross and unprovoked libel."

The board acknowledged that its decision to remove Wheelock superseded the legislative inquiry but said it had used its chartered power in the public interest to protect the corporate rights of the college and the rights of incorporated bodies in general. "Cases sometimes occur when it becomes expedient that corporate bodies—whatever confidence they may feel respecting the rectitude and propriety of their own measures—should explain the grounds of them to the public," it maintained. "Such an explanation becomes peculiarly important when the concerns committed to their care are dependent on public opinion for their prosperity and success." The board said it "would gladly have avoided this painful crisis" but had acted within its authority to protect corporate rights.

In the New Hampshire elections of 1816, the conflict at Dartmouth became a campaign issue. Particularly after the board of trustees appointed Francis Brown, a thirty-one-year-old Federalist, to replace Wheelock as president of the college, Republican leader William Plumer made the crisis a centerpiece of his candidacy for governor. During his previous terms in 1812 and 1814, he encouraged the legislature to reserve a right to amend charters of incorporation to protect "the public interest." Now, he extended that position to say that, since Dartmouth had a public mission, its charter too should be subject to amendment. "When the government of our college applies to the people, or the legislature, for aid, they represent the college as a *public institution*," he noted as he called for a fresh legislative review of Dartmouth's charter to reinforce the state's visitatorial rights.

Plumer seemed to have the public on his side. He was selected by a margin of 2,269 votes in an election cycle that saw the largest number of ballots cast in New Hampshire to date. During the campaign, Isaac Hill told his readers that a college under Republican control would be able to increase the pipeline of Republican candidates for office. As he put it, "The future governance of D[artmouth] College," if "judiciously managed, will be a means of perpetuating the Republican majority in the state." It was not clear, however, whether the party needed the college to achieve that goal: in 1816, Plumer clinched the governor's office by a margin seven times larger than his Federalist predecessor's advantage, and Republicans again seized both houses of the legislature—a dominance they maintained for the next forty years.

After his reelection, Plumer made public oversight at Dartmouth a central theme of his inaugural address. "The charter of that college was granted December 13, 1769, by John Wentworth, under the authority of the British king," he recollected. "As it emanated from royalty, it contained ... principles congenial to monarchy." Not only did it require all officers to declare an "oath of allegiance to the British king," but it created a board with powers of perpetual succession, a form of corporate aristocracy that Plumer called "hostile to the spirit and genius of free government." For this reason, he noted, many states (Pennsylvania, New York, Massachusetts, Connecticut, Virginia, and others) had adjusted the charters of their colleges and other corporations after the revolution to make them more amendable to new "republican" forms of public oversight.

Plumer sent a copy of his inaugural address to his friend Thomas Jefferson in Virginia, a fellow Republican then engaged in his own quest for public higher education in his state. Jefferson applauded Plumer's speech and told him its focus on public control of colleges was "replete with sound principles, and truly republican." "The idea that institutions established for the use of the nation cannot be touched or modified, even to make them answer their end . . . is most absurd," he wrote. "Yet our lawyers and priests generally inculcate this doctrine and suppose that preceding generations held the earth more freely than we do; [that they] had a right to impose laws on us, unalterable by ourselves; and that we, in like manner, can make laws and impose burdens on future generations, which they will have no right to alter; in fine, that the earth belongs to the dead, not the living."

Here was the crux of the dispute. The board of trustees said that Dartmouth's charter was not subject to any future alteration except by its trustees, while Plumer and Wheelock said it was. In his inaugural address, notes Shirley, "Governor Plumer lifted the college question out of a morass of ill-considered ranting and put it on a plane where it could be discussed sanely." Plumer said the state had the authority to amend the charter of the college, just as it had the authority to amend that of a town or any other "public" entity. "The college was, after all, formed for the public good, not for the benefit or emolument of its trustees, and the right to amend and improve acts of incorporation of this nature has been exercised by all governments, both monarchical and republican." Of course, the college trustees disagreed. They said Plumer's call to amend the charter would endanger all private corporations and their vested right to govern themselves.

Alarmed by Plumer's appeal to alter Dartmouth's charter, the college trustees proposed a legal alternative. Would it not be preferable, they asked, for the legislature to establish an entirely new and separate—"public"—college under its own control? Daniel Webster had recommended this option in a letter to Dartmouth's new president Francis Brown just two days before Plumer's election. "It is a favorite idea with some to create a new college," Webster noted as he looked for ways to steer the legislature away from its attempt to amend Dartmouth's charter. "Would it not be well if this idea could be encouraged... to let the ill humors work off in that direction? Suppose a proposition should be made for a committee to report at the next session upon the expediency of making a new college at Concord, and what donations, etc., could be obtained for such an object."

Webster's letter included a draft resolution to create a public college (and, by implication, to confirm that Dartmouth was private): "*Resolved*, that a joint committee of both houses be appointed to take into consideration the expediency of establishing a seminary of learning in some part of this state, to be called the University of New Hampshire, and to ascertain what endowment for such institution could be obtained from private donation and, also, what grants of land or money could be properly and conveniently made to the same by the state." He urged the legislature to prepare a charter with a board of trustees supervised by a public board of overseers, not unlike Harvard's structure. "Perhaps," he added, "if something of this sort should be brought forward by somebody who has been favorably inclined to Dr. W[heelock] but who should wish to prevent violent measures, it might do good."

Instead of a new university, however, Plumer moved forward with his plan to bring Dartmouth more firmly under public control. When he received the final report of the legislature's investigatory committee, he was pleased to find that it recommended a change in the charter. It argued that most of the college's difficulties had been "aggravated [by], if they did not originate from, some radical defect in the charter" and concluded that, ultimately, "the interests of the state do not require the legislature to act any further than by amending the charter" through an expansion of its board (just as the board *itself* had proposed in 1807 as part of its request for more state aid). Plumer called for a committee of delegates from each county to consider a proposed Act to Amend, Enlarge, and Improve the Corporation of Dartmouth College, which, among other changes, proposed a supplemental group.

Plumer's call to revise Dartmouth's charter received support from the founder's grandson, Eleazar Wheelock Ripley (a nephew of John Wheelock), who drafted a bill that recommended "material changes'" in the charter, including the adoption of a new institutional name, "Dartmouth University," along with a new board of overseers. The legislature's Republican majority passed a slightly revised act that adopted the name; increased the number of trustees from twelve to twenty-one (with all new appointments made by the governor); created a separate board of twenty-five public overseers with explicit visitatorial rights and the authority to veto the board of trustees; reorganized the university into departments; established a new "Institute" for applied science; and, finally, required the institution's president, faculty, trustees, and overseers to swear an oath to support the state and federal constitutions, in order to remove any vestige of monarchism.

When the college trustees heard about this so-called Act of 1816, they responded with an eight-page "remonstrance," which highlighted what they called the "illegal features of the bill," notably the fact that it transferred all college property into the renamed institution, required both the president and board of trustees to furnish annual reports to a public board of overseers, and, crucially, passed the legislature without the original board's consent. Such legislation, the board said, constituted a clear violation of its corporate rights. "The charter of Dartmouth College vests certain rights of property, for particular uses, in the trustees," they wrote on June 18, 1816. "The sovereign power, having once made this grant [of incorporation], cannot, as the trustees humbly conceive, devest them of it so long as they exercise their trust in conformity to the true intent and meaning of the charter."

The board went on to say that Dartmouth's charter was not subject to legislative alteration, because the college was not—and never had been—a public corporation. "Dartmouth College was not founded by the then-existing sovereign," it asserted in an interpretation that distinguished between the institution's *foundation* and its (subsequent) *charter*. "It was founded and endowed by liberal individuals, and the charter was given by the sovereign to perpetuate the application of the property conformably to the design of the donors." (Crucially, the board did not say which property, or which donors.) "If the property has been misapplied, if there has been any abuse of power upon the part of the trustees, they are fully sensible of their high responsibility, but they have always believed, and still believe, that a sound construction of the powers granted to the legislature gives [it], in this case, only the right to order, for good cause, a prosecution in the judicial courts." In short, the board said Dartmouth College was a private corporation subject only to judicial, not legislative, oversight.

Moreover, the board argued that a charter of incorporation was a contract protected by the US Constitution and therefore unalterable without the consent of the corporation itself. "By the charter of Dartmouth College, a contract was made by the then-supreme power of the state with the twelve persons therein named, by which, *when accepted by the persons therein named*, certain rights and privileges were vested in them and their successors for the guarantee of which the faith of government was pledged by necessary implication." The legislature had no authority to amend this contract, whose terms, said the board, had not changed in the revolutionary transition from a royal colony to a republic. On the contrary, it argued, if the legislature had the right to alter property contracts at will or adjust corporation's governance structures on political grounds, then "nearly all the titles to real estate held by our fellow citizens must be deemed invalid."

Yet, while the board declared its autonomous right to govern the college, it did not wish to be at odds with the public. It offered a compromise whereby New Hampshire's speaker of the house, with all senators and members of the governor's council, would form a public board of overseers for the college, with a right to "negatize" any vote of the board of trustees (like Harvard's structure). It was a major concession. Why did the board offer it? Because, in 1816, its chief goal was not to avoid public supervision but simply to get rid of John Wheelock as president. As historian John Shirley observes, "The truth is, the trustees were willing that almost any amendment should be made to the charter if so framed that they could exclude Wheelock and . . . retain possession [of the college's property] for themselves and their friends." But it was not to be. The legislature rejected the board's offer and moved forward with the Act of 1816 to amend the institution's charter. It was a fateful decision.

CHAPTER 7

Trustees of Dartmouth College v. Woodward

The so-called Act of 1816 appalled Dartmouth College's trustees. "I have no doubt in my own mind that the Act is altogether unconstitutional and must be so decided could the question come before a competent and dispassionate court," wrote trustee Charles Marsh from Vermont a week after the vote was taken. Marsh felt the board should fight the charter amendment from the first instant. "I think we shall be more likely to bring [the state legislators] to terms by resisting the act than by yielding to its provisions," he suggested as he proposed two possible strategies. The first was to refuse to attend the meetings of the new "university" board and thus deprive it of a quorum; the second was to refuse to collect rent on college property in Wheelock, Vermont, and thus deprive the new university of a crucial source of income.

The college trustees decided that obstruction would be their first tactic. When Governor Plumer called the "university" board to meet in Dartmouth's library on August 27, 1816, just one college trustee showed up (even though nine more were in town), and President Francis Brown said he could not give Plumer the key to unlock the library door. "I have no authority to cause the room occupied by the library to be opened," Brown wrote in a note carried by courier to Plumer and his fellow members of the university board. "As to rooms in other buildings, judge [William H.] Woodward, from his superior acquaintance with the place, will be able to give Your Excellency more satisfactory information than myself." Woodward, the college's secretary-treasurer, did not have a library key but allowed Plumer to host the university's board in his office.

Woodward—later the named defendant in *Trustees of Dartmouth College v. Woodward*—played an important role in the dispute between Wheelock and the college trustees. Not only was he Wheelock's nephew, but as secretary-treasurer, he was the keeper of the institution's official seal and records (for example, all its land titles and other financial documents), which he turned over to its new board. In response, the college trustees charged that Woodward had *stolen* items they considered their property by charter right. "I wish that we had seasonably removed the secretary so as to have possessed the records ourselves," Charles Marsh wrote as his fellow trustees proceeded to fire Woodward and replace him with a new secretary-treasurer, Mills Olcott, who promptly initiated a suit for the "safe return" of the documents. Woodward, however, refused to give up the seal or records, which he claimed to hold "only for the use of the rightful trustees."

Ultimately, the college trustees' effort to reclaim these items provided the pretext for the case that ended up in court, a legal process that began with a suit for "trover," or request to recover property unlawfully taken, entered on October 7, 1816, for a value of $50,000. Notice of this suit was duly served to Plumer and his fellow members of the university's board, then entered in the court of common pleas in Grafton County—in full knowledge of the fact that Woodward *himself* was the judge in that court and would have to recuse himself from the case. The suit then would be referred automatically to New Hampshire's Superior Court, where the college trustees hoped for a favorable outcome—not only to retrieve their "rightful" property (the seal, the records, and indeed the college itself) but also to reverse the Act of 1816.

Meanwhile, as they awaited trial, members of the *college* board continued to deprive the *university* board of a quorum. Plumer, unable to conduct any business on behalf of the university, expressed his frustration to New Hampshire lawmakers. He inquired "whether . . . a minority of the trustees of a literary institution formed for the education of your children shall be encouraged to inculcate the doctrine of resistance to law." Could the college trustees use their alleged corporate rights to evade laws duly passed by the state? Plumer drafted two bills to challenge the college trustees' resistance. One would lower the number of trustees needed for a quorum to nine (those appointed by the governor); the other would levy a fine of $500 on anyone in the college who defied the university board. Called the Penal Acts, these bills, when passed, concerned the Dartmouth College faculty, who faced a penalty for every day they refused to lecture in the new Dartmouth University.

In the meantime, Plumer checked with the New Hampshire Superior Court about the constitutionality of his latest bills. He asked two questions. First, "Has the legislature of this state authority to amend the charters or acts of incorporation of literary corporations by increasing the number of trustees, adding boards of overseers, and prescribing modes of visitation in cases where such corporations were established by the present government of this state, or by John Wentworth, formerly governor of the province of New Hampshire, exercising his authority in the name of the British king?" And second, in the absence of a quorum on a public corporation's board, "Have the governor and council of this state, in virtue of an act passed June 27, 1816, entitled 'An Act to Amend the Charter and Enlarge and Improve the Corporation of Dartmouth College,' authority to fill any vacancies in the board of trustees or overseers?"

Since the members of the superior court had been appointed by Plumer himself in 1814, he soon got a reply. As for his first question, whether the legislature could amend the charter, the court answered: "We have examined the constitution of this state and also the Constitution of the United States and have not been able even to conjecture any ground upon which such an authority in the legislature can be questioned, unless it be that such alterations, if made without the consent of the corporation, may possibly be construed to be a violation of private vested rights, which are protected by those constitutions." As for the second question, whether the legislature could alter the number of trustees required for a quorum, the court answered that such action would require special laws—which the legislature promptly supplied with its measures to reduce the size of the quorum and penalize trustees who did not comply.

The college trustees said these penalties were legally unenforceable. "I believe the Penal Act was intended as a scarecrow and ... cannot be carried into effect," trustee Asa McFarland wrote. Charles Marsh concurred: "Dr. Wheelock's men regard this last measure as a device with which to frighten us rather than as a law which they can ever execute." Marsh told his friends on the faculty not to be intimidated and, instead, to keep possession of at least one college structure (preferably the library) until Federalists could reclaim the legislature and reverse its recent acts. "We must maintain our possession and discharge our duties as though nothing has happened," he asserted. "It is an object to keep possession at least until after the next election. The Federalists, or a better sort of democrats, may become a dominant party."

Of course, if the faculty occupied the library or any other structure, the "university" board would not be happy. "They may indeed take forcible possession of the library," Marsh admitted, "but . . . I do not think they will dare attempt any such violent measures." But he was mistaken. On February 28, 1817, the university trustees dispatched a delegation to demand the library keys, and when Professor Shurtleff rebuffed their request (on grounds that his superiors on the college board "still claim a legal existence"), the university board sent "two assistants"—one a carpenter, the other a stonecutter—to enter through a window, remove the door lock, and "put on a [new] lock of their own." As historian John King Lord explains, they proceeded next to the chapel and forced the door open "with a bar of iron . . . and secured this also with a new lock." Next came the philosophy room, followed by the president's house and the "meeting house" in town.

Yet when the university delegates reached the meeting house, Professor Shurtleff along with sixty college students blocked the entry. "It began to be rumored that they intended to take possession of the building, and the students of the college, not to be out-generaled, at once garrisoned it in force," historian Frederick Chase recounts. After three days, President Brown proposed a way for the college and the university to use the meeting house at different times. "He offered on behalf of the college to begin at nine o'clock and end at one," Chase notes, "but, as the university people insisted on having precedence—which, since the college people were in possession of the meeting house, they were unable to enforce—no treaty was established." In the meantime, "college" students, barred from other academic buildings, held classes in a local hat store.

———

As these events unfolded, President Wheelock's health began to decline. Sixty-three years old, Wheelock had been "long afflicted with a disorder that the physicians called a 'dropsy of the chest,'" until finally, on April 4, 1817, he died. In his will, he passed his powers and privileges as Dartmouth's (now deposed) president to William Allen, his son-in-law. He also left Dartmouth University two houses in Hanover and several farms in Vermont, plus the forgiveness of all debts owed to him personally, a legacy valued at $40,000. Part of this sum was designated for professorships at the new university, though he stipulated that, if the Act of 1816 was "altered or repealed at any future time, except with the consent of the [university] board of trustees as then constituted," then all his contributions were to go to Princeton Theological Seminary instead.

The college, meanwhile, struggled financially. Support for Dartmouth College had come from lands first granted on behalf of the colony by governor John Wentworth in 1770 and, later, by private donors, with further public grants after the revolution from Vermont's legislature in 1785 (half to Dartmouth College and half to "The President of Moor's Indian Charity School") and from New Hampshire's legislature in 1789 (the "First College Grant," to replace the Landaff property) and 1807 (the "Second College Grant"). But these lands produced little revenue, and in fact the college was unable to collect *any* revenue on them as long as Woodward held the property titles on behalf of the "university" board.

Under these circumstances, the college board called on supporters in other colleges for aid. "While Harvard and Yale, Brown and Williams, Bowdoin and Middlebury are enriched by public or private benefactions, shall Dartmouth [suddenly] decay, merely for want of necessary funds?" the college trustees inquired. But the response was not what they expected. Even as they asked for money, other colleges saw a chance to benefit from their weakness. Middlebury invited Dartmouth professor Ebenezer Adams to join its faculty, and President Brown was asked to assume the presidency of five-year-old Hamilton College in New York. "The prospects of that institution are highly promising," he noted, "and the salary offered, $1,800, double the salary here." In the end, Brown stayed at Dartmouth but said he could not do much for the college unless its trustees found a way to shore up its balance sheet. "We must have substantial aid," he wrote, "or it will be impossible to go on."

In the summer of 1817, the dispute between the college and university was on full display when US President James Monroe—fresh off a landslide Republican victory in the elections of 1816—visited New Hampshire on a postinaugural national tour. The week before, Monroe had attended Harvard's commencement, full of paeans to nonpartisanship, but the president was not persuaded. "In all the towns through which I passed, there was a union between the parties, except in Boston," he informed Thomas Jefferson after his visit. And if Boston was split by partisan spirit, then Hanover was even more so. Monroe was asked to speak at separate graduation ceremonies for Dartmouth College and Dartmouth University, and since neither could stand to be upstaged, each awarded him an honorary LLD (though, given the litigation then underway, it was unclear which institution had the authority to grant such degrees).

Even before Monroe's visit, the college trustees had begun to gather legal documents to defend their presumed corporate rights. As early as May 16, 1817, Charles Marsh published his "Minutes of Authorities and Observations in Relation to the Affairs of Dartmouth College," which said that Dartmouth's "private" charter was unalterable without its trustees' consent. Specifically, he argued that postrevolutionary state legislatures did not have the same powers that Parliament had to amend charters at will. "The Parliament of Great Britain, consisting of the king, lords, and commons (the three estates of the kingdom), is said, in the vaunted language of legal and political writers, to be omnipotent," Marsh acknowledged, "having derived its powers from the king, as the source of power and authority, and not from the people." During the colonial era, he recognized, *all* charters of incorporation were effectively public and could be "dissolved by act of Parliament."

On the absolute power of Parliament to alter or amend charters, the university's board of trustees cited the case of Gresham College in London, where, in the late sixteenth century, the city had asked Parliament for permission to seize the college building to make way for a new tax office—a move upheld in court. Marsh, however, dismissed this reference. The property in that case was vested by Sir Thomas Gresham in the corporation of the City of London, and when the city took it, London's mayor asked permission to shift the college to a new structure ("built by Sir Thomas at his own expense") and to continue to pay its lecturers with Gresham's initial funds. Parliament granted the mayor's request with a stipulation that, in compensation for the loss of their original structure, the lecturers should receive fifty pounds more per year and release from a part of Gresham's will that required them to remain unmarried.

Had the permission of Parliament violated Gresham's original trust?

No, said Marsh, because the City of London, as trustee, consented to all the changes. "There is no attempt here to interfere with the property or powers of the corporation without its consent," he wrote. In the same way, any changes in the charter of Dartmouth College likewise required the consent of its original trustees. "It is said that, 'in this country, a number of states have passed laws which made material changes in the charters of their colleges,'" Marsh recalled of Plumer's inaugural speech as governor. Yet, "No instance can be found where this has been attempted without consent. The legislature of Massachusetts some few years since passed an act that ministers of such-and-such parishes should be, with others, overseers of Harvard College, but chief justice Parsons, who is said to have penned the act, inserted a proviso that it would be obligatory *when accepted by the corporation*, and not until then."

Marsh acknowledged that state legislatures could amend the charters of towns, villages, or municipalities, but he said towns were different from colleges. The former were civil, or public, corporations while the latter were charitable, or private, corporations. "Towns are corporations of a very different nature, and for different purposes, from those for which academies and colleges are incorporated," he argued. Yes, towns could hold property, but their charters of incorporation were mere acts of legislation that could be altered by further acts of legislation. "All these privileges are given . . . by statute," Marsh noted, "and thus are not to be regarded as [irrevocable] grants but as mere municipal regulations to be varied at the discretion of the legislature, not interfering with any constitutional principles." Private corporations, by contrast, were off-limits to legislative interference (unless a legislature reserved such power in the corporations' original charters).

The question of town corporations was front and center in New England when Marsh wrote these words. In 1816, the Supreme Court of Massachusetts had decided two cases on this issue—*Stetson v. Kempton* and *Inhabitants of the Fourth School District v. Wood*—both of which held that "municipal" corporations were public and thus subject to legislative intervention. Two years later, the Superior Court in New Hampshire heard *Eustis v. Parker* on the differences between public and private corporations. "Public corporations such as towns, counties, etc., are in their nature widely different from private corporations," the court observed. "They are created not for private emolument but for public purposes." A state had the power to change a town's "public" charter without its consent, Marsh admitted, but it had no such power when it came to "private" corporations such as colleges.

Yet when it came to institutions of higher education, distinctions between public and private corporations were subtle, at least in British law. William Blackstone had explained in his *Commentaries on the Laws of England* that both the University of Oxford and the University of Cambridge were public *universities* that had private *colleges* within them. He characterized both universities as "civil" (public) rather than "charitable" (private) corporations, because Oxford and Cambridge were incorporated by the Crown to grant degrees—a public act—while the independently endowed residential colleges within them (Magdalen College, Exeter College, etc.) were separately incorporated to oversee the use of funds given by founder-donors to provide rooms, meals, lectures, tutors, and other services to students—a private enterprise.

So was Dartmouth a public corporation like Oxford University (and thus subject to legislative oversight) or a private corporation like Exeter College (and thus more autonomous)? Marsh asserted that even if New Hampshire's legislature had a right to oversee civil (municipal) corporations, it had no such right with respect to charitable (eleemosynary) ones—a category that, in his mind, included Dartmouth College and its boards of trustees. Without the board's consent, he said, the legislature's Act of 1816 was void. "In all the authorities which are to be found on this subject," he argued, "there is not a solitary instance of any interference by the government which can at all compare with the present [Act], either in point of principle or extent, where a [legislature] has, without the consent of the corporation, endeavored to change the principles or take away the property or privileges of an institution of this kind." When it came to colleges, as private corporations, the legislature's role was "merely to foster and encourage, not to interfere with, their internal concerns, or to vary without their consent the structure of their policy or government."

———

Not long after Marsh penned these words, the college's lawsuit began in New Hampshire's Superior Court. The court heard preliminary arguments in Haverhill in May, then ended in Exeter four months later.

On both occasions, the "college" was represented by Jeremiah Mason and Jeremiah Smith (a former chief justice of the superior court), while the "university" was represented by Ichabod Bartlett and George Sullivan (the state's attorney general). The audience in court included trustees and professors from both the college and the university as well as numerous lawyers and clergymen. *The Exeter Watchman* reported after oral arguments: "We can say with proud assurance that it was, upon the whole, an exhibition of professional ability which has reflected an honor to our native state not easily to be sullied, nor soon to be forgotten."

When the arguments began, six-foot, seven-inch Jeremiah Mason opened for the college. He said the Act of 1816 represented a brazen assault on the autonomous governance of a duly chartered private corporation. Regardless of any presumed links between chartered rights and public interests, he asked, "Who would found an eleemosynary corporation—or give it property for the purpose of securing it for a special charitable use—knowing that he thereby subjected his property to any use that a legislature, under the influence of momentary passion or prejudice, might prefer?" It did not matter whether a corporation's property came originally from public or private sources, Mason argued. Once donated to an independent board of trustees, it was immune to all state control. "The circumstance that this state has made donations to [Dartmouth College]," he insisted, "does not alter its nature nor lessen or destroy [the corporation's private] rights."

According to Mason, the original charter of Dartmouth College had given the institution not only (material) property but also (immaterial) privileges, which represented another form of "property" that could not be revoked. One such privilege was its trustees' right to grant degrees, which, like its lands, the legislature could not rescind without its consent (though others said the power to grant degrees was a public, not private, act). "Consent" was a condition of any contract, Mason asserted. "The legislature of this state has granted certain lands to the corporation, under consideration, which they cannot take away, because the grant constitutes a contract and is therefore protected by the Constitution of the United States," he said. "Would it not be grossly absurd to hold that the legislature may, at pleasure, abolish the corporation and then take to themselves not only the lands they have granted but all the other property and privileges of the corporation?"

On the irrevocability of land grants as constitutionally protected contracts, Mason cited the US Supreme Court's recent decision in *Fletcher v. Peck* (1810), a case that had begun in 1795 when the state of Georgia granted four companies 35 million acres of Indian land in the state's Yazoo valley. While this original grant was based on bribes, and the state's title itself was suspect, all parties had accepted the land contract as valid, and the companies later sold their lands to Congress as well as several northern investors. When the bribes were discovered a year later, the citizens of Georgia called for these sales to be reversed. A new legislature revoked the original grants, but a New Hampshire investor, Robert Fletcher, who had bought a Yazoo plot from John Peck of the New England Mississippi Land Company, brought suit in Massachusetts's federal district court to challenge Georgia's reversal on grounds that it violated his ownership contract. (According to historian Peter McGrath, the lawsuit between Fletcher and Peck was collusively arranged between "friendly 'adversaries'" to validate the New England Mississippi Land Company's purchases.)

The question was: Did Georgia's original (corrupt) sale constitute a valid contract? Massachusetts's Supreme Court had ruled in 1799 that it did and concluded that Georgia's attempt to retake Peck's (then Fletcher's) land was a violation of the Contract Clause of the US Constitution—but others disagreed. Virginia congressman John Randolph asserted in 1804 (shortly after Fletcher had filed suit) that Georgia's original grant was tainted and that its legislative reversal was justified in order to protect the public interest. According to Randolph, it did not matter that Peck had promised Fletcher that Georgia's initial title was valid, because that statement was untrue. In 1810, however, the US Supreme Court took a different view. It sided with the Federalists on Massachusetts's court and ruled that, however corrupt its origins, Fletcher's land contract, once made, could not be unmade without all parties' consent.

Fletcher's lawyer in this suit was thirty-year-old Joseph Story, who months later joined the US Supreme Court as an associate justice. Story argued, first, that "a grant is a contract executed"; second, that Georgia's legislature "could not revoke a grant once executed"; and third, that all legislatures, state or federal, were forbidden by the US Constitution to pass laws that impaired "the obligations of contract." Chief Justice Marshall (who had befriended Story three years earlier when he was in

Washington to lobby for the New England Mississippi Land Company) summarized these arguments when he wrote that Georgia's legislature "was restrained, either by general principles which are common to our free institutions, or by the particular provisions of the Constitution of the United States, from passing a law whereby the estate of the plaintiff in the premises so purchased could be constitutionally and legally impaired and rendered null and void." It was a landmark decision—the first in which the high court nullified a state law—and it seemed to reinforce the view of Dartmouth's college trustees that legislatures could not alter contracts without all parties' consent.

———

Indeed, throughout his argument in the Dartmouth case, Jeremiah Mason stressed that New Hampshire's legislature had no power to seize college property (whether land, records, or campus structures) without consent. To reinforce the sanctity of corporate property, he cited another recent US Supreme Court decision, *Terrett v. Taylor* (1815), in which Justice Story had reversed the earlier decision of Virginia's courts in *Turpin v. Lockett* (1804) on the legislature's power to reassign Anglican glebe lands to state ownership. While some had said the Anglican church was a public corporation, because it was funded by public land grants and taxes, Story maintained that glebes, once granted, were vested in Anglican clerics as private individuals, and since Virginia, in 1784, had confirmed these land titles, they counted as private "contracts" under the US Constitution. "Title was indefeasibly vested in the churches, or rather in their legal agents," he concluded.

This ruling was important for Dartmouth's college trustees, because it rendered private corporate property off-limits to state takeover. As historian Johann Neem has explained, the postrevolutionary legislature in Virginia could legally disestablish the state church as a public entity and thereby render it a private entity, but it could not then *also* deprive individual churches, or clergymen, of their property. If the state wanted to control the church's property, then it had to keep the church a public institution. If the state did not want a public, or "established" church, then it had to leave the church's property to its duly incorporated private trustees (in this case, the ministers). Any other approach would allow public seizure of private assets. "We think ourselves standing on a principle of natural justice, the fundamental laws of every free government, the spirit and letter of the Constitution of the United States, and the decisions of the most respectable judicial tribunals, in resisting such a doctrine," Story wrote.

This reference to "natural justice" was important. Story's decision in *Terrett v. Taylor* drew on principles of natural law, because the US Constitution did not actually mention either "charters" or "corporations." He therefore avoided the Contract Clause in this case. "Without an expressed constitutional provision which seemed applicable, Story looked to natural law principles implicit in the Constitution to restrain legislative authority," observes historian J. W. Ely Jr. "The matter in dispute was not impairment of a contract but an attempted confiscation of church property by the state. It was analogous to a 'taking' of property without payment of just compensation. But the 'takings' clause of the Fifth Amendment governed only actions of the federal government." This point was not lost on Jeremiah Mason, who asserted that, constitutionally, Dartmouth College's trustees had the same corporate rights as Episcopal clerics, which meant the state could not seize their property without their consent.

Did the New Hampshire legislature have the authority to acquire Dartmouth's property or alter its charter of incorporation at will? Mason acknowledged that under British law, Parliament could abolish charters "because its power was boundless"—but American legislatures had less capacious powers. The US Constitution barred any legislation that "impair[ed] the obligation of contracts," yet the Act of 1816 had deprived the Dartmouth College trustees of their corporate property and privileges without their consent. According to Mason, if attempts to alter charters—or contracts—by legislative fiat were permitted, then "colleges and seminaries would never be free from subservience to state legislatures." (Indeed, he noted, even Wheelock himself sought to shield his *own* bequests to Dartmouth University from legislative appropriation, should that institution ever come to an end.)

Mason's arguments were supplemented by those of Jeremiah Smith, a former congressman and former governor of New Hampshire who had since returned to private law practice. Smith, a Federalist, argued that without legal safeguards for private corporations, legislative majorities would be able to seize the chartered property of their political opponents at will. This risk was particularly acute in colleges like Dartmouth, which claimed to be free of "party" influence. "I do not wish to see a time when the government of this or any other literary institution . . . shall be closely connected with the government of the state," he announced. "Changes in the latter, if not desirable, are . . . to be expected; permanence in the former is [in] every way important. There is, besides, something in political men, generally speaking, which unfits them for the management of academical institutions, or to be useful fellow workers in the instruction of youth."

Smith, like Mason, emphasized the legal distinction between civil (public) and charitable (private) corporations. He acknowledged that "in England, the general corporate bodies of the universities of Oxford and Cambridge fall under the head of civil corporations, because merely for government, not for dispensing alms but for governing the particular colleges which dispense them." Yet, he continued, Dartmouth College was more like an English college than university (or collection of colleges), because it was founded to dispense charitable property, which made it a private, or eleemosynary, corporation. "The very essence—*sine qua non*—of eleemosynary corporations is property dedicated to charitable uses," he observed. "A corporation without any funds can hardly be called an eleemosynary corporation, because there are no alms—no free bounty—to be distributed."

At the same time, Smith argued, what made Dartmouth College different from an English college was that its charter had incorporated trustees who also functioned as visitors, subject only to judicial (not legislative) oversight. He cited *Philips v. Bury* on the "final" authority of visitors to govern a college, and he compared Dartmouth College with Phillips Academy in Exeter, New Hampshire, whose charter dubbed its trustees its "sole visitors." Whether called "trustees" or "visitors," "The whole power of visitation is vested in them," he maintained. "They are visitors, governors, and overseers of the charity as well as legal owners of the funds, appointed by the founders and donors as their perpetual representatives to protect the interests of the charity." Perhaps unaware of *Eden v. Foster* (1744) on the impermissibility of trustees who doubled as visitors (a least under British law), Smith insisted there was no distinction between these groups' absolute power to govern the college.

Well aware that some wanted to call Dartmouth College a public corporation, subject to public control, Smith admitted that even charitable (eleemosynary) corporations "may, in a certain sense, be considered as public"—for example, in a situation where "the property may arise, and the endowment be made, by the king, in which case it is an institution of 'royal foundation.'" He added: "If the state founds a college and endows it out of state property, this would, in respect of the foundation, be 'a public institution.' And we freely admit that, where the state are the patrons of a college, they may justly claim the superintendence and government of it." But, he continued, "It will not be pretended that Dartmouth College, in this sense, is a public institution. Although the state have given lands, they were not the real founders. They were not the first benefactors, who, and who only, are considered as founders."

Who, exactly, did Smith consider to be the *first* benefactors of Dartmouth College? On this point, he fudged the facts. "Its original funds arose altogether from the donations of individuals, principally obtained through the agency of Dr. Eleaz[a]r Wheelock," he maintained as he framed the initial private contributions to Moor's Indian Charity School as contributions to Dartmouth College (whose first donations actually had come from the colonial governor, on behalf of the Crown). "In no sense, and in no way, can it be said [that Dartmouth College's initial properties] originated with the king or the public," he asserted, wrongly. "Not a cent of money, or acre of land, was given by the province of any public body until long after the college went into operation." For proof, he cited the charter, written before the Landaff grant was finalized a few weeks later.

Over and over, the college's lawyers insisted that Dartmouth College was founded with private donations. For example, Smith distinguished the college, founded with private resources, from its medical school, founded with public funds. "Is it pretended that the state has the same estate and interest in the college lands and funds as in the medical house?" No, he answered. In the case of the medical school, "The state had secured a title to themselves in the land before they erected the building, and then became proprietors of the land, building and all."

In the case of the college, by contrast, Smith said the initial land grant always had been assumed to be the property of the college, not the state. If the state now claimed the college's land for itself, then what could stop its claim to land given by others—for example, lands given by the state of Vermont?

Surely, argued Smith, the state of New Hampshire could not claim lands Vermont had given. "Did the state of Vermont understand that [New Hampshire] made any such claim when it made [its] liberal grant of lands?" No, he asserted. In the case of New Hampshire's grant of 1789 (the "Second College Grant," to replace the original Landaff grant), the grant was made "to the Trustees of Dartmouth College . . . for the benefit of said college," *not* for the benefit of the state of New Hampshire, just as the state's next grant of 1807, jointly superintended by the college and the state, was said to become the property of the college trustees, not the state. (He elided the possibility that public grants to colleges were grants to higher education as a public good.) "The truth is," he said, "the legal and equitable property is in the trustees, to be applied . . . in the manner usual in colleges, subject [only] to the control and superintendence of the judicial courts."

Smith asked the court to protect the rights of private corporations. "I know it has been objected that our doctrine places this institution beyond all control; that it takes away all security that the beneficial uses intended by the contributors and donors will be enjoyed; that it is at variance with the just claims of the state to cherish and protect the interests of literature." But this characterization was false, Smith argued. "We are so far from placing this institution above control that we claim for it the protection of the law against what we consider a deadly blow aimed at its existence by the persons exercising the supreme power of the state." Only the court had the power to guard private corporations from legislative interference. "On this subject, we have been explicit from the beginning," he concluded. "An institution like this, unprotected by the judiciary, could not exist." With that, the college rested its case.

CHAPTER 8

Founders and First Donors

With the college's arguments complete, New Hampshire attorney general George Sullivan rose to respond for the university. He built his case on the premise that Dartmouth College's "first donor" was, in fact, the public. "The court has been told this college was a private charity, that Dr. Wheelock was its founder and visitor, and that he transferred his rights of visitation to the trustees," Sullivan began. "Not one of these positions is well founded." Neither the charter nor any other document recorded *any* original transfer of property from Wheelock to the college or its trustees. "It has been asserted that Dr. Wheelock was the founder, but the assertion is supported by no evidence," Sullivan repeated, even as he recognized Wheelock's many "exertions" to lead the institution throughout its early years. "The charter, probably in consequence of these exertions, calls him the founder," he observed. "But this does not make him so."

Sullivan went on to note that all the funds Wheelock received from abroad were for his Indian Charity School, not for Dartmouth College (an institution the school's donors explicitly abjured): "The charter states that Dr. Wheelock, on or about the year 1754, at his own expense, and on his own estates and plantations in Lebanon, Connecticut, set on foot an Indian Charity School, and that, with the assistance of several well-disposed persons, he had for several years clothed, maintained, and educated a number of the children of the Indian natives. In no part of the charter is it mentioned that he made any donation to the college." In fact, Sullivan reiterated, "Dr. Wheelock made very liberal donations to Moor's [Indian] Charity School—an institution in the neighborhood of the college, though entirely distinct from it—but ... he made none to the college itself."

Sullivan went on to explain that if Wheelock was not the first donor, then under the law of corporations, he could not be the founder. And if he was not the founder, then he could not claim exclusive visitatorial rights for himself or his designees. Visitatorial rights belonged to the first donor, which, in the case of Dartmouth College, was the colonial governor (on behalf of the Crown) and the governor's postrevolutionary successor, the state legislature. Sullivan quoted William Blackstone on this point: "The first gift of the revenues is the foundation, and he who gives them is, in law, the founder." He added: "It does not appear . . . that [Wheelock] was the founder or that he had power to transfer the right of visitation to the trustees. If Dr. Wheelock was the founder and visitor of the college, he did not transfer to the trustees the right of visitation. There are no words in the charter making them visitors." That function rested with the legislature.

Sullivan emphasized that under the law of corporations, trustees could not also be visitors, lest they be accountable only to themselves. "Where the management and application of the funds given to a charity are vested in trustees, or governors, they are not visitors," he explained. "The reason is apparent. It would defeat the charity if the same men who have the right of applying its funds should possess also the exclusive right of deciding whether those funds were properly applied." Even if the college trustees were granted legal rights "in all the lands and property given for the use of the institution," still, visitatorial powers ultimately rested with the legislature. "Had we had a court of chancery [or court of equity] in this state, the trustees would have been subject to its inspection and control," Sullivan asserted with contemporary British law in mind, "but, as we had no such court, they were subject to the inspection and control of the legislature."

Sullivan had little patience for the argument that Dartmouth's trustees held a personal, or "individual," stake in the college's property that was somehow violated by legislative inspection. "The trustees complain that they have been deprived of their property," he noted. "If the property held by the trustees has been taken from them (which is denied), they had no beneficial interest in it. They did not hold it for their own use. They were entitled to no compensation for its loss. Have these acts made the trustees poorer than they were? This cannot be pretended without accusing them of a breach of trust—of appropriating for their own use property belonging to the public." According to Sullivan, the college trustees had no individual claim on—or contract for—college property and thus no individual concern when it was redirected by the state to a new university. "As respects the taking of property," he wrote, "they complain where no injury has been sustained."

Sullivan went on to emphasize the *public benefit* of the college. "This corporation . . . as its charter shows, was established not for the advantage of the corporators, not for the advantage of a small number of individuals, but for the benefit of the whole people of the province of New Hampshire," he argued. "It was vested with power to hold property in trust for the public, but it could hold none for the use of the corporators. It was clothed with various powers, capacities, and franchises, all of which were to be exercised for the benefit of the public, but not one of them for the advantage of its own members, nor of any individuals whatever. In short, it was created—it existed—only for public purposes." He added: "If a corporation of this description be not a public one, then, in my opinion, no public corporation ever did, or ever can, exist." Put simply, Dartmouth College was a public, not a private, corporation.

Even if the court said Dartmouth College was a private corporation, Sullivan insisted the legislature still would have a visitatorial right to oversee its operations in order to ensure that it met its charter obligation to serve the public interest. "On this principle, legislatures often take the property of individuals when the public good requires it; they often deprive individuals of some of their natural rights when the exercise of them would prove detrimental," he observed. "Why may they not, with equal right, take the property of corporations when the public welfare demands it? Why may they not, with equal propriety, deprive corporations of some of their rights and privileges when the exercise of them would produce mischief to the commonwealth? Does the law guard the property of corporations with more vigilance than that of individuals? Are the rights of the former more sacred than those of the latter?"

Sullivan cited the use of eminent domain—outlined in article XII of New Hampshire's bill of rights—as justification for the state's authority to seize property from private corporations. "Suppose the lands of a private corporation are wanted for a fortification or arsenal: may they not be taken? Suppose they are wanted for a highway or for any important public purpose: may they not be taken? Without a power in the government to take the property and the rights of private corporations, as well as those of individuals, its operations would often be obstructed, and the safety of society might be endangered." Sullivan pointed to *Brown v. Penobscot Bank* (1812), in which the court said it was a "duty incumbent on the legislature" to ensure that banks' charters served a public interest, since all corporate powers derived "from legislative grants" that could reserve a right of legislative oversight. Thus, even if Dartmouth College were a private corporation—which Sullivan denied—the legislature still held ultimate visitatorial authority to oversee its operations.

Sullivan's cocounsel Ichabod Bartlett picked up where he left off. He recited several occasions when the Dartmouth College trustees had described their role as servants of the public. For example, in a memorial in 1804, they said they had "no other interest than members of the legislature themselves." In another instance, they called themselves "mere stakeholders for the public," with no individual private claims on college property. Bartlett, like Sullivan, argued that Dartmouth College was like a British university—a public corporation with the civil power to grant degrees. Indeed, he added, the Dartmouth College trustees "have not only exercised the powers of a 'university' but have used and even preferred that *name* as the most appropriate until, by some strange coincidence, it became obnoxious at the moment it became the legitimate title by the act of the legislature."

Bartlett asked why the college trustees now rejected the name of a "university." Was it because they knew a university was a public corporation under British law? He quoted their own vote on "the duties of the president of this university" as recently as November 1814. "That the corporation with a new name remains the same in all its rights, duties, and privileges is most incontrovertibly settled in ... *King v. Pasmore* (1789)," he noted. This case involved the village of Helleston, incorporated by Elizabeth I and Charles I yet, because of deaths and dismissals over several decades, lapsed in regard to its corporate functions. A minority of the extant trustees had asked George III for a new charter under a new name, which the king granted—at which point the majority suddenly reconstituted itself to sue for the restoration of the original charter and name (much as Dartmouth College's trustees sued to uphold their original charter and name).

As historian Elizabeth Brand Monroe notes, the legal question in *King v. Pasmore* was "whether the crown could grant a new charter when a corporation no longer performed the functions for which it was created." Chief Justice Lord Kenyon said it could, because all corporations were "creatures of the crown." "Lord Kenyon found the failure of the majority of the old grantees to accept the new charter immaterial, as they [had essentially] dissolved as a body before the new charter was granted, and sufficient members of the expanded group of grantees had accepted the new charter." In this case, the Crown simply replaced a failed corporation with a functional one, and since the new charter technically included all the members of the old corporation, they could not appeal to private (individual) rights to stand in the way of a public (municipal) good.

This case bore a resemblance to several aspects of the Dartmouth College litigation. Bartlett, aware that Dartmouth College's trustees never considered themselves "dissolved," said they nonetheless were included on the new university board and were therefore uninjured by any change in governance structure. He quoted Lord Kenyon's observation in *King v. Pasmore* that "by the new charter, the king did not consider the old corporation dissolved to all purposes, but he granted its rights to a new set of men and super-added such other powers as he deemed necessary." He also cited Lord Ashurst's remark that, in fact, even if they had not given their consent, members of the old corporation had no cause for complaint, "for they are all included in the new charter. . . . And if any of them do not become members of the new corporation but refuse to accept, it is their own fault."

One did not have to look far to find cases where colleges were subject to involuntary legislative control. "In this country," Bartlett explained, "our provincial assemblies exercised the same power and often changed the whole organization of such institutions." In 1673, for example, "by an order of the General Court of . . . Massachusetts, an addition was made to the members of the corporation of Harvard College against the will of the corporation," just as the colonial assembly in Connecticut had passed a law in 1723 "without petition or consent of the corporation, 'for the more full and complete establishment of Yale College, and for enlarging its powers and privileges.' By this act, the number of trustees was enlarged, new offices created, and new regulations made with regard to the number which should constitute a quorum." New Hampshire's alteration of the governance of Dartmouth College was no different.

As proof that Dartmouth College was a public corporation, Bartlett drew attention to its first donor: the royal governor and, by extension, the Crown. "The plaintiffs have insisted that [Dartmouth College] 'is a private eleemosynary corporation,' and that statement is attempted to be supported, in the first place, by confounding this institution with 'Moor's Indian Charity School,' which Dr. Eleazar Wheelock claimed as his, and over which no other jurisdiction has been exercised but at his request." But "no fact on record is more clearly stated than that [Dartmouth College] and Moor's Indian Charity School were entirely . . . independent of each other in their origin and establishment [and] were ever governed separately, without the least connection, until the school solicited the interference of the legislature and college. Their funds and property are now distinct and separate."

Bartlett cited the letter the English trustees wrote to Wheelock on April 25, 1771, which forbade Wheelock from any use of their funds to support a college. He also cited the resolution passed by the college trustees on May 7, 1789, which distinguished the funds of the school from those of the college and conceded that, with respect to funds of the English trust for the Indian Charity School, the college trustees "have never had any control or direction of said monies, nor have they, to their knowledge, at any time received or applied any sum or sums thereof to the use and benefit of said college, etc.'" In short, Bartlett argued, the *school* was founded with private donations in which the college did not share; the *college* was created with no funds of its own but later got its first donation from the colonial governor (on behalf of the Crown) after the charter was granted.

Bartlett listed the many donations the college had received from the public. "Among the public grants for its establishment and support was that of the township of Landaff, containing [23,040] acres of land, January 19, 1770, long before the board of trustees [first met] under the charter; also a tract of 300 acres in Hanover, the same upon which the buildings are located," he noted. "In the same charter was made a grant of 200 acres adjoining to Dr. Wheelock's [land], in consideration of his services and expenses to aid the institution—services and expenses it would have seemed unnecessary for the government to remunerate if they were devoted, as the plaintiffs must pretend, to his private use and property." Public donations continued after the revolution. "The legislature in 1787 granted a lottery to raise $5,000 over five years in aid of its funds; in 1789, a tract of 42,000 acres of land; in 1805, $900; and in 1807, a [new] tract of 23,040 acres."

Based on its first donation, the Crown was founder of the college. "As a public institution we believe the *crown* has been shown to be the founder," Bartlett noted, and "the state, since the revolution, succeeds to the rights of the crown." The college therefore was a public corporation, subject to public visitation by the legislature: "As all the power which the king, as visitor, could exercise over these corporations resulted from their public nature—and the [public] interest which the people had in their general design and object and vested in him as the guardian and protector of the rights of the people," he observed. "It would be a doctrine unfit for this country to say that our legislators did not stand in as near a relation to the community, and that our constitution had not entrusted them with as ample authority in this particular as could be exercised by His Majesty." In the shift from royal to republican government, the rights of visitation had passed from Crown to state.

Bartlett pointed to Harvard as the best example of a college under "public" control. "The renowned university of Harvard, which has ever been subject to legislative control, exhibits an illustrious proof that the gloomy apprehensions of the plaintiffs in the present case are altogether imaginary." Whereas the college lawyers had warned that colleges "would be in danger from a design in the legislature to defeat their object or effect their destruction," in fact, Bartlett said, "its dangers are from a very different source," namely, the partisan interests of private trustees. "To avert those dangers," he asserted, "legislative acts have been passed" to protect the public. "Soon may the opposition to [these acts] be disarmed by judicial decision, and Dartmouth arise redeemed from the ruin which has been threatened by an effort to convert its public nature and design to private and personal interests." In the end, Bartlett concluded, "The government must control these institutions, or they shall control the government."

His cocounsel agreed. While the "college" lawyers had insisted that legislators could not be trusted with academic governance, Sullivan asked why private trustees should be considered more trustworthy. "The counsel on the other side have expressed an opinion that the legislature is a very improper body to superintend literary institutions," Sullivan noted. "But is there no danger that [a private] corporation will discourage donations by an abuse of its trust if it may claim to be independent of the legislature?" Sullivan cautioned against too much collegiate autonomy. "Suppose the trustees should appropriate the funds of the college to their own use," he suggested. "If they are visitors as to the application of the funds, as is contended, no court of law can make them accountable. . . . The very sight of such a monster—placed beyond all legislative, all judicial, control, like the terrific head of Medusa—would convert even charity herself into stone."

When it came to corporations, Sullivan trusted public over private control. "It is feared that the legislature, under pretense of aiding these institutions, will deprive them of their property, or their most valuable rights and privileges," he recognized. "But no such danger is to be apprehended. If the property of a literary institution should be seized by a legislature and appropriated to a use different from that for which it was designed, or if any oppressive laws should be passed, injuring and retarding its growth, there would be a universal burst of indignation throughout the state. Any legislators who should act in this manner would be considered unworthy of confidence and would lose their offices." The public held legislators—who, in turn, held college trustees—accountable. Or as Sullivan put it, "Our frequent elections make them feel their dependence on the people."

Of course, the college lawyers saw things differently. Jeremiah Smith asserted that institutions of higher education should *never* be run by legislators. "It has been intimated that much good would result to this seminary and to the public from governmental checks on its officers," he concluded. "I am not a convert to these opinions. As there is no royal road to science, so there is no republican road. The best road is that which has been marked out and trodden by learned men, those who are themselves proficients in science." In other words, the best supervisors of a college were scholars themselves and the donor-trustees who managed property on their behalf. "The best reliance for funds is on munificent individuals—men who have wealth to bestow and hearts to bestow it—to found colleges and... to improve the literary seminaries we have," Smith concluded. "It is the duty of the legislature... to respect the rights, privileges, and immunities of the seminaries they endow." And with that, he left the matter for the court to decide.

New Hampshire's three superior court judges comprised a notable group. Levi Woodbury, just twenty-eight, was considered a legal prodigy. A graduate of Dartmouth who later joined the US Supreme Court, he was a man of Republican sentiments whose partisan ties led him to accept a seat on the "Dartmouth University" board of trustees, a post that obliged him to recuse himself from the case. Samuel Bell, likewise a Dartmouth graduate, had served on the college's board until 1811, when his own Republican sympathies led him to resign from that increasingly Federalist body. (He was by then embroiled in *Bullard v. Bell*, which concerned whether he was personally liable for a series of financial losses suffered by the Hillsborough Bank, of which he was president. This case eventually was heard by the US Supreme Court during the same term as the *Dartmouth* case.)

Sitting alongside Woodbury and Bell was Chief Justice William Richardson, a Harvard graduate who had studied law with Judge Samuel Dana in Massachusetts before he was elected to Congress in 1812 and 1814. Despite his reelection, he opted instead to serve as US Attorney in Portsmouth, New Hampshire, then in 1816 was chosen by Governor Plumer for a seat on the state's highest court. (Ironically, the governor's first choice for chief justice had been Jeremiah Mason, selected to replace Jeremiah Smith after Smith's brief tenure as chief on the Federalists' illegitimate court, but Mason had declined.) Richardson was a respected jurist. "He was a great and honest judge," historian John Major Shirley writes. "His reasoning and his heart alike were as open and ingenuous as the light of day."

When the superior court reached a decision on November 6, 1817, two months after oral arguments had ended, Richardson delivered the verdict: the court had decided for the university and, hence, the state's authority to amend Dartmouth's charter. "This cause has been argued on both sides with uncommon learning," he began. "If the counsel of the plaintiffs have failed to convince us ... it has not been owing to any want of diligence in research or ingenuity in reasoning but to a want of solid and substantial grounds on which to rest their arguments." The court found that Dartmouth was a public corporation, that its founder and first donor was the Crown, that its charter was not a private "contract" within the meaning of the US Constitution, and that New Hampshire's laws to add new members to a public corporation without the consent of the old corporation were "not repugnant to the constitution of the state."

Richardson accepted virtually every part of the university's argument. He concluded that Dartmouth was founded with public grants of property and privileges. "A gift to a corporation created for public purposes is, in reality, a gift to the public," he ruled. The trustees, as individuals, had no claim in the charter to personal contracts for property or privileges. They had no "private interest in the property of this institution, nothing that can be sold or transferred, ... descend to heirs, or be assets in the hands of their administrators." The college's property, in short, was public. "If all the property of the institution were destroyed, the loss would be exclusively public, and no private loss to [any trustee]," Richardson held. "Nor is it any private concern of theirs whether their powers, as corporators, shall be extended or lessened.... If such a corporation is not to be considered a public corporation, it would be difficult to find one that should be so considered."

Even if the college were a private corporation, Richardson insisted that *King v. Pasmore* gave the state—whether the Crown or the legislature—the power to amend its charter to serve the public interest. "It is said that these acts in fact attempt to dissolve the old corporation, to create a new one, and to transfer the property of the old corporation to the new," he noted. "But admitting this to be the attempt, we might with great propriety remark, in the language of justice Ashurst in ... *King v. Pasmore*, that 'members of the old body have no injury or injustice to complain of, for they are included in the new charter of incorporation, and if any of them do not become members of the new incorporation but refuse to accept, it is their own fault.'" He added that (presumably by the ancient principle of cy pres), a legislature could add new members to a public corporation—even without the other trustees' consent—with no alteration of the corporation's legal identity.

This point was important. A corporation was, according to William

Blackstone, a great "artificial, invisible body, existing only in contemplation of law." Its property and privileges did not change with its number of trustees. "The addition of new members by a legislative act, even to a private corporation, does not necessarily devest the old corporators of any private beneficial interest, which they may individually have in the corporate property," Richardson wrote. And the case was even clearer with public corporations, which had no private beneficial interests to bestow. "We are therefore of opinion," he added, "that these acts, if valid, do not dissolve the old corporation nor create a new one, nor do they operate in such manner as to change or transfer any legal title, or beneficial interest, in the corporate property." On the contrary, "The legal title remains in the corporation, and the beneficial interest in the public, unaffected."

On this point, Richardson cited the US Supreme Court decision in *Bank of the United States v. Deveaux* (1809), which acknowledged that corporations were not mentioned in the US Constitution but held that such associations were composed of "natural persons" with legal rights to property and privileges. The court, wrote John Marshall, needed to "look beyond that intangible creature of the law, the corporation, which in *form* possesses [rights], to the individuals... to whom, in reality, [all rights] belong, and who alone can be injured by a violation of them." *Devauux* found that "all beneficial interest, both in the franchises and the property of corporations, must be considered as vested in natural persons—either in the people at large or in individuals—and that, with respect to this interest, corporations may be divided into *public* and *private*." Richardson used this decision to say that Dartmouth College's property was vested not in the individual trustees but "in the people at large," which made it a public corporation.

What then of the claim that Dartmouth's charter was a "contract" between the Crown and the college's individual trustees? Richardson addressed this claim head-on. "It is said the charter of 1769 is a contract, the validity of which is impaired by these acts in violation of that clause in the tenth section of the first article of the Constitution of the United States, which declares that 'no state shall pass any law impairing the obligation of contracts.'" This clause, he acknowledged, "embraces all contracts relating to private property, whether executed or executory, and whether between individuals, between states, or between states and individuals." But it "was not intended to limit the power of the states in relation to their own public officers and servants, or their own civil institutions." Dartmouth College was a public corporation, Richardson held, so the Contracts Clause ("obviously intended to protect private rights of property") did not apply.

According to Richardson, the Contract Clause "must not be construed to embrace contracts which are, in their nature, mere matters of civil institution, nor grants of power and authority by a state to individuals to be exercised for purposes merely public." This point was "obvious," he repeated. A charter for a public corporation was not a private contract: "If the charter of a public institution, like that of Dartmouth College, is to be construed as a contract within the intent of the Constitution of the United States, [then] it will, in our opinion, be difficult to say what powers in relation to their public institutions, if any, are left to the states." Such a view, he added, represented "a construction ... repugnant to the very principles of all [republican] government, because it places all the public institutions of all the states beyond legislative control." Ultimately, argued Richardson, the Act of 1816 was constitutional, because Dartmouth College was a public corporation.

Richardson hoped the court's decision would stand. "The education of the rising generation is a matter of the highest public concern and is worthy of the best attention of every legislature," he concluded. "The immediate care of these institutions must be committed to individuals, and the trust will be faithfully executed as long as it is recollected to be a mere public trust, and that there is a superintending power that can and will correct every abuse of it." But if the trustees were considered independent, he warned, "They will ultimately forget that their office is a public trust—will at length consider these institutions as their own—will overlook the great purposes for which their powers were originally given—and will exercise them only to gratify their own private views and wishes or promote the narrow purposes of a sect or a party." New Hampshire could not let Dartmouth College fall prey to narrow private aims. It had to ensure that its public institutions served public interests.

CHAPTER 9

Advice from a "High Authority"

Dartmouth University president William Allen relished the state's victory. Shortly after the court released its decision, he invited all students who remained in the college to join the university as New Hampshire's only legitimate institution of higher education. He then sent a letter to "parents and friends of the students, late of Dartmouth College," in which he cast the college's professors as scoundrels who harbored partisan bias "in a manner prejudicial to the literary and moral improvement of their pupils." He went on to cast the students who stuck by the college as "gullible children, ensnared by the passions of their professors" and urged their "reunion with the legal seminary at Hanover." Few took him up on his invitation, however, so Allen took a more drastic step: he seized college property and claimed it for the university.

He started with its books, held in two literary societies: the Social Friends and the United Fraternity. On November 11, 1817, just five days after the superior court's decision, he directed groundskeeper Henry Hutchinson to "take possession of the library room of the societies," whereupon Hutchinson, with help from university professors James Dean and Nathaniel Carter (both members of the Social Friends), entered the library to collect the books. "They had not the key, nor had they applied for it, but attempted to force the door by stepping back across the hall and running against it," historian Frederick Chase notes, and when this approach failed, Dean had the door cut down with axes. "It was a firm double door, and many blows by a strong laboring man were necessary to open a place large enough for them to crawl in."

So loud was the racket from this incursion that members of both the Social Friends and the United Fraternity ("then in session in the hall below") rushed to protect their books. "Finding their opponents armed, they supplied themselves with clubs from a pile of firewood that lay in the hall," Chase notes. "One of their number, H. K. Oliver, blessed with a powerful voice, shouted: 'Turn out, Social Friends, your library is broken open.'" Another student recalled the mêlée that followed: "I was soon at the scene of action. . . . Professors Dean and Carter were also present, with . . . three shoemakers and others unknown to fame. The first sensible speech I heard was from one of the shoemakers who addressed his associates, saying, 'it appears to me we are in a cursed poor scrape. I had rather be in a nest of hornets than among these college boys when they get mad.'"

College president Francis Brown described this skirmish in a letter to his trustees. "An event occurred on Tuesday evening last, which, I believe, may well put to rest all the hopes of the university of an increase of their number by the diminution of ours," he wrote. "This was an attempt to seize the libraries of the private societies in the college. Professors Dean and Carter, Mr. Hutchinson, Messrs. Cook and Bissel, and fifteen or twenty more of the same commenced the assault between 7 and 8 o'clock," after which the whole student body converged on the scene. "A parley ensued. The professors and their company surrendered themselves as prisoners and were conducted into an adjoining room until the societies had removed all their books to a place of safety." The attack, said Brown, had discredited the university in that it suggested a plot to seize distinctly *private* assets (the societies' books).

After the library incident, students in the college recounted their defense of their books in a series of letters to newspapers across the state. They maintained that college property—whether books or buildings—was privately owned and thus could not be seized by the university (or the state). The fact that Professors Dean and Carter had no keys for the societies' rooms showed that library access was private; indeed, the "shivered fragments" of the library door were "sufficient to show in what manner they expected, from the first, to execute their commission." If anything, their attempt to seize private libraries by force had the appearance of mob rule. College historians Frederick Chase and John King Lord agree: the affair gave the university's republican (or Republican) principle of "public oversight" a bad name.

The university saw the situation differently. It said the college students defended their libraries from a sense of institutional desperation. David Ames—among the dozen students who sided with the university—said the college was "reduced to the miserable necessity" of holding

{ *Advice from a "High Authority"* }

classes in a small room in town. With "no library" and "no philosophical apparatus," its faculty taught merely "as private instructors," stripped of any official power to grant degrees. William Allen reinforced this argument in a published "Address to the Public," which claimed that Dean and Carter acted only "to secure the books to the [public] object for which they were given: that every member of the society, whether connected with the university or not, might have access to them." In other words, it was the college's students, not the university's professors, who had seized (or stolen) property *from the public.*

It was a clever argument, but it appeared the college had the upper hand, for the simple reason that it had more students: a hundred in the college versus twelve in the university. In the pamphlet war that followed, Brown assured parents that every student in the college remained "well-supplied with books from the libraries of the two literary societies," whereas students in the university had almost no books at all. He thanked parents who kept their sons in the college. "It would be unjust in the trustees not to acknowledge their obligations to those parents who have afforded countenance and encouragement to the college, under its numerous embarrassments, by committing their sons to its instruction," he wrote. "The internal state of the college, including the moral and literary habits of its members and their proficiency in all the branches of literature and science, has at no time been better."

For the next fourteen months, two Dartmouths existed side by side. The university continued to say it was the state's only legitimate institution of higher education, but most students remained with the college (they occupied campus dormitories and "refused to pay their rent until the university's legal status was established"). In effect, observes historian Jane Fiegen Green, the college's students exercised their power of the purse and refused to pay any bills that might support the university. "One newspaper editorial warned that, if the university asserted its legal authority over the students, they 'would defend themselves with arms, or else leave the naked college walls to a new government . . . and that, not a government over men, but an empty edifice." The image of a vacant university raised a key question: How "public" could an educational institution be without students?

The answer seemed to hinge on the university's success in court, which, as far as Governor Plumer was concerned, was secure ... even as the college began to prepare its appeal. "The decision of the Superior Court in the suit against the university is an important and correct decision," Plumer wrote. "My confidence [is] founded on a knowledge of the law and the talents and integrity of the judges. It is said [that] Brown and Co. intend on carrying the suit by writ of error to the Supreme Court of the United States.... I think they can have no rational grounds to hope for success in the national court, and the friends of the university have nothing to fear from the result but the expense, and the evil which proceeds from a state of suspense." Plumer was sure the Act of 1816 would be upheld.

Daniel Webster, friend of the college trustees, feared Plumer might be right. As he drafted the college's appeal, he corresponded with US Supreme Court justice Joseph Story on the prospects for reversal. "The truth is, the New Hampshire opinion is able, ingenious, and plausible," he wrote as he worried that his appeal (or "writ of error") might be a "forlorn hope." Still, he agreed to do what he could for his alma mater. He circulated the arguments that college lawyers Mason and Smith had made in the superior court and offered to reargue the case in Washington for a flat fee of $1,000—all-inclusive—with part of this sum to pay for cocounsel. He suggested Joseph Hopkinson of Philadelphia for that role. "He is well known," Webster said of Hopkinson, who had argued several cases before the court. "I think him capable of arguing this cause as well as any man in the United States."

For his part, forty-five-year-old Webster was already well known for his many successes before the bar. Born on a farm in rural New Hampshire, he matriculated at Phillips Academy in Exeter for a year before he entered Dartmouth College at the age of fifteen. He graduated in 1801, first in his class, then apprenticed in law and taught school to help pay his younger brother's Dartmouth tuition. In 1804, he made his way to Boston and took a position in the firm of Christopher Gore, a prominent Federalist attorney. "Gore was one of the city's most distinguished commercial lawyers and moved easily in the rarefied atmosphere of Massachusetts high politics," historian R. Kent Newmyer notes. "With a fine legal library at his disposal, [and] with friendly, informed direction from his mentor ... Webster sharpened his legal tools and demonstrated his Federalist orthodoxy."

In 1812, Webster returned to New Hampshire to run for Congress and won a Federalist seat in the House of Representatives, where he served three consecutive terms. A year after his first race, he delivered a famous speech in which he opposed the Madison administration's decision to go to war and hinted at the possibility of New England secession, a message that garnered considerable praise during the conflict but contributed to Webster's reputation for partisan views. (His zealous support for the Federalists' positions on tariffs and the national bank exacerbated this reputation.) In 1816, when the Republicans put William Plumer back in the governor's office, Webster declined to run for a fourth term in Congress and instead returned to Boston to open a private law practice. A year later, he accepted Dartmouth College's appeal.

Webster had argued his first case before the US Supreme Court in 1814 (he eventually argued over two hundred and won more than half). So extraordinary was his success before that body that Federalists across the country began to rely on him for legal strategy—and paid handsomely for his guidance. According to one recollection, "Webster earned as much as $17,000-$20,000 a year" in an era when the court's own justices earned less than one-fifth that amount. The case of Dartmouth College was his ninth before the high court, and while he believed the college had a valuable educational mission, it seems his principal motives were economic: to protect the "rights" of private—and propertied—corporations, including colleges, from the encroachments of public legislative oversight.

Indeed, other colleges were fully aware of the implications of Dartmouth's case. In the fall of 1817, trustees from Harvard, Yale, Bowdoin, and Middlebury gathered in New Haven to discuss it. Later that year, Dartmouth supporter Benjamin Gilbert "made an attempt to see president [Jeremiah] Day of Yale at New Haven, but without success, and left papers for him and a letter from President Brown soliciting the assistance of Yale in the prosecution of the suit." This intercollegiate (Federalist-Congregationalist) alliance did not go unnoticed. Republican editor Isaac Hill at the *New Hampshire Patriot* noted that "nearly every college north of the Delaware [river], as soon as they ascertained this question was to be tried before the U.S. [Supreme] Court, entered [a] combination and exerted their influence to procure a decision which should forever place them beyond the control of the people."

Even as the college rallied its allies, however, the Supreme Court's disposition toward Dartmouth's case was unknown, and this uncertainty put many on edge. Harvard president John Thornton Kirkland, for example, warned President Brown that Dartmouth's appeal might backfire. "Some of my friends here, who sincerely wish success in the cause of your college, have yet a strong wish that it should *not* be carried to Washington," wrote Kirkland, "from an apprehension that, even should the U.S. Supreme Court take up the cause and consider it in all points, [the justices might] confirm the present decision and thereby increase a hundredfold the weight of its authority." Kirkland dreaded that prospect. "The result of a hearing at Washington could be worse than leaving the cause where it is," he told Brown, "so far, at least, as respects *our* institutions."

Others feared the problem was even more serious, for it was rumored that Supreme Court justice Joseph Story had advised the New Hampshire legislature on its Act of 1816 and now was to sit in judgment of the constitutionality of that very act. David White, a judge in Story's hometown of Salem, Massachusetts, told President Brown that he took it on "high authority" that Story had drafted the legislation under review. Though he did not say who this "high authority" was, many suspected it was Story himself. T. J. Murdock, a Dartmouth graduate then at the Andover Theological Seminary, told Brown on December 27, 1817, that "folks in this region are frightened . . . because it is ascertained that judge Story . . . is the original framer of the law you are opposing. They suppose that, on this account, the cause is hopeless before the Supreme Court."

When these concerns reached Webster's cocounsel Joseph Hopkinson in Philadelphia, he immediately contacted trustee Charles Marsh to ask whether they were true. "The situation in which, if you are not misinformed, judge Story has placed himself is . . . alarming to us, and so disreputable to him, should he sit in the case, that I confess I am inclined to believe that your information in this respect must be mistaken," Hopkinson wrote on December 31, 1817. "Should it, however, be otherwise, and he is about to sit as a judge in a cause in which he has been a feed counsellor, I should have no hesitation in resorting to any legal and proper means to prevent such an abuse of power and office. The influence of the judge with the court in general cases is, I think, considerable and will probably be very great in one like the present."

Rumors were rife about Story's role in the original legislation. "Story was known as an old friend and confidant of governor Plumer," historian Frederick Chase observes. "He even had been appointed an overseer of [Dartmouth] University (though he did not accept)." It was not inconceivable that he advised New Hampshire lawmakers on the Act of 1816, and some intimated that "even if he had not drafted the act, he had, at all events, advised on it and—with his usual industry and indiscretion—examined it at an early stage and vouched for its legality." Indeed, notes historian John Major Shirley, Governor Plumer had visited Story in Salem on September 16, 1815, three weeks after the college trustees dismissed John Wheelock as president. Had they discussed the possibility of legislative retaliation?

Had Justice Story been tainted in this case? According to Shirley, yes. "The tradition is that judge Story, at an early day, carefully examined the question with his characteristic zeal and indefatigable research and arrived at the same result [later] reached by his friend chief justice Richardson," and, moreover, that "he communicated this fact semi-confidentially to his friend Ichabod Bartlett, one of the counsel for the state." Despite these allegations, the college lawyers did not seek to have Story recused from the case. Why not? Apparently because they felt Story would give them a fair trial. "As we hear no more of impeachment," Shirley notes, "it is evident that means were found to convey to ... Story, in a friendly way (apparently through Mr. Mason, whom the judge held in high esteem), the sentiments of Mr. Hopkinson's letter and to obtain assurances of impartiality."

The college's trust in Story probably stemmed from his Federalist sympathies. During his youth, Story had been a fervent Republican but, over time, had migrated into the Federalist camp. His transition began in 1806 when he won a seat in Massachusetts's legislature. Two years later, when he chaired a subcommittee to establish a state court of equity to oversee a range of property concerns (from contracts to wills, trusts, and estates), he took on a more conservative outlook. "Story condemned the exercise of equity powers by the legislatures, which often, under political influence ... tended to 'dispense with strict compliance' of the terms of contracts," historian Peter Dobkin Hall remarks. As chair of the subcommittee on the court of equity, his aim was to protect contracts from politics, that is, to defend private assets from public interference.

He worked hard on this project. "On the one hand, equity, by protecting contracts from meddling legislatures and vexatious suits over estates and land titles, would ensure legal transformations that could have far-reaching impacts on commerce, real estate, charities, and testation," Hall notes. "On the other hand, it promised to ensure the free circulation of property essential to a growing entrepreneurial economy." Yet, despite his efforts, Story's committee failed. In 1810, when Republicans took control of Massachusetts's legislature, they defeated its Act Providing for Relief and Equity and dismantled plans to protect contracts and charters of incorporation from legislative oversight (Harvard's charter included). Story felt that Republicans had disrespected the laws of equity and property, and the next year, 1811, he brought this concern with him to his new seat on the US Supreme Court.

The prominence and peculiarities of Story's role in the case of Dartmouth College have long attracted historical speculation. As early as December 1817, when Judge David White of Salem visited President Kirkland at Harvard, he also visited Story, then in Boston, to discuss the case. Their conversation was private, but afterward White discreetly told President Brown at Dartmouth that it would be risky for the college to bring its suit to Washington on the "single point" of the amendment of the charter, or impairment of contract. "Should this course be taken," he noted, "it is supposed the merits of the cause will not be brought into view." A few days later, Daniel Webster and Jeremiah Smith looked for ways to broaden their appellate strategy. As they did so, they said they followed advice that White had received from a "high authority."

Webster got creative as they searched for a broader strategy. He told Smith: "It is our misfortune that our cause goes to Washington on a single point.... I have thought of this more from hearing of sundry sayings of a great personage." Although he declined to name this "great personage," he repeated in a message to Jeremiah Mason the same day: "I am sorry our college cause goes to Washington on one point only. What do you think of an action in some court of the United States that shall raise all the objections to the act in question?" Was there a way to bring a parallel suit at the circuit level and, specifically, the circuit overseen by Story himself—a suit that Story might decide in the college's favor? "Such a suit," were it to involve litigants from different states (and thus be subject to federal jurisdiction), "could easily be given to the court of the United States by bringing in a Vermont party."

Webster had long been concerned about the narrow scope of the college suit: a mere claim of trover for recovery of college records on the basis of chartered rights to corporate property. He wanted the case set on a broader foundation, one that could establish the college trustees' right to control the institution's property—including its library and lands—as a matter of legal *contract*. It was the college's ownership of *land* that he particularly wanted to establish. "Suppose the corporation of Dartmouth College should lease to some man of Vermont (e.g., trustee C[harles] Marsh) one of their New Hampshire farms [now claimed by the university], and the lessee should bring ejectment for it," Webster suggested to Jeremiah Smith a few days after White's letter. In that case, "The whole question [of who owned these lands by charter, or contract] might get before the court at Washington."

Webster knew the success of the college's appeal hinged on whether its "first donor" of property was Eleazar Wheelock or the Crown. "In relation to the special verdict [in other words, the superior court decision], my impression has been that we should insert everything to show, as far as we can, that the state did not found and endow the college," he wrote to Smith. "I should wish it rather to appear what they had *not* done than what they had. . . . For like reason, I should think it well to find the original grants, gifts, or endowments upon which the college set out." The aim was to show that Dartmouth College's original grants had come entirely from "private" individuals—and to do so in Story's court. Should the college fail to make this case, Webster feared, "I think the jury had better find . . . they are all the grants and acts made by the state" (as, in fact, they were).

Webster's plan was clever. Some called it devious. It began when trustee Charles Marsh contacted friends in Vermont and convinced them to file suits against the college over its ownership of land across the border. These suits would trigger interstate legal questions that only Story's federal circuit, and ultimately the US Supreme Court, could answer.

(Recall that in *Fletcher v. Peck* (1810), Story, the plaintiff's lawyer, concocted a similar case to convince the high court that Georgia could not undo a contract with a Massachusetts buyer, even if Georgia's original contract was based on bribes.) Webster filed three such lawsuits. The first, *Hatch v. Lang*, began with Richard Lang of New Hampshire, who had leased two plots from Dartmouth College in 1807 for thirteen dollars in yearly rent. After the Act of 1816, Lang paid his rent to Dartmouth University, which he thought was the rightful owner. The college trustees, however, said Lang was delinquent on his rent and promptly sold both plots to Horace Hatch of Vermont, who then filed a suit that claimed Lang was a squatter. Hatch's "plea of ejectment" against Lang went to Story's circuit for a decision.

The second lawsuit, *Marsh v. Allen*, was even more convoluted. In this case, the college's trustees leased all of the campus land to Charles Marsh, who then accused Dartmouth University's president William Allen (and two others) of an illegal occupation of his leased property. He, too, filed a "plea of ejectment" in Story's circuit to remove Allen from the premises. Of course, the plea was simply a ruse to call into question the legitimacy of Dartmouth University's claim to own campus property and a way to take a case with disputants from different states (Marsh was a Vermonter) away from New Hampshire's state courts and into federal court. "In this and the other cases," historian Francis Stites observes, "Dartmouth College was the true party in interest. The question was the effect of the Act of 1816 on the college's title to its lands—and, the validity of the legislation [that challenged its trustees' claim to be its sole owners]."

The final suit, *Pierce ex dem. Lyman v. Gilbert*, was similarly formulated to undermine the university's property claims. Here, the college leased Commons Hall to Job Lyman, a Vermont resident, who subleased the hall to David Pierce, also of Vermont, who then said that Benjamin Gilbert (who occupied the structure) refused to let him enter and thus "dispossessed" him of his property. In fact, Stites notes, Gilbert "did not actually dispossess Pierce" but only staged a refusal of entry so that Pierce could lend his name to a legal process against the university in Story's circuit. As required by law in actions of this sort, Gilbert informed the university that its board members would have to "appear in court and have themselves made defendants in his stead, since only they had title to the property." If they did not appear, the university would lose its title.

At first, Webster had suggested a suit for the "Wheelock" township in Vermont, but since that land had been granted in 1785 to both Dartmouth College and "The President of Moor's Indian Charity School," the college was unable to sell or lease it without the school's consent. Webster also suggested a suit for "portions of the New Hampshire lands," but those lands were cogoverned by the college and the legislature and thus were similarly off-limits to sale or lease. A third idea was to sell the college's "last-granted township of wild land in the north part of this state," but in that case the donor was the state, which undermined the argument that Dartmouth's first donors were private citizens. Webster thus opted to sell various smaller parcels for which the college trustees held clearer titles. While these parcels were not the college's *first* donations, they were construed as its property, allegedly "vested" in the college's individual trustees under the charter.

Webster asked Charles Marsh to lead these suits, but Marsh had reservations about the strategy of ejectments, or writs of entry, to validate ownership titles—an English legal maneuver that to his knowledge had not been tried in American courts. "There has never been anything in practice in Vermont analogous to the 'writ of entry' in England," he wrote to fellow trustees in February 1818 as he worried especially about the college's plan to repossess land that had never been possessed by its trustees in the first place. "It is proposed to bring a 'writ of entry' directly against trustees of the university for the last-granted township of wild lands in the northern part of New Hampshire," he noted. "I do not find that a writ of entry will do to try the title to land of which no one has ever been in possession." At the very least, he added, since a writ of ejectment had to be served in person, it would have to wait until spring, after the snow melted.

Webster, however, was determined to proceed quickly in order to cast the legislature as the usurper of property rightfully controlled by the college trustees. If accusations of usurpation came from residents of a different state, then he could suggest in Story's circuit that his clients had a "vested" (private) right to control the college's property—*regardless* of its first donor. After his chats with a "high authority" and "great personage," he was certain his strategy would succeed. He said the college had "reason to expect that a case would be presented at the circuit court raising the question in its amplest form." He added furtively: "I am very confident the court at Washington would be with us.... If we can get up one of these cases in due form, we shall defeat our adversaries."

CHAPTER 10

"It Is, Sir, a Small College, and Yet There Are Those Who Love It"

Webster presented his arguments in Washington on March 10, 1818, four days before the end of the Supreme Court's spring term. The gallery was full in the cramped basement quarters the court occupied in the Capitol building (after its usual rooms had been torched by the British army four years earlier). In this era, the justices usually heard arguments "from 11 a.m. to 4 p.m.," explains historian G. Edward White, and the attorneys who appeared before them had no time limits, so oral arguments "sometimes lasted as long as six days." Ordinarily, the prospect of a long trial in a subterranean courtroom might have deterred visitors, but *Dartmouth v. Woodward* attracted considerable attention. "The case was widely known, and of great importance," notes historian Frederick Chase, so much so that Chauncey Goodrich, a professor of oratory at Yale, "went from New Haven to listen." He was not alone.

Webster opened with the central issue: whether New Hampshire's legislature could alter the charter of Dartmouth College without the consent of its trustees. The Act of 1816, he argued, had replaced the old corporation with a new one and had transferred its property and privileges to a new body. "The two corporations are not the same in anything which essentially belongs to the existence of a corporation," he asserted. "They have different names and different powers, rights, and duties. Their organization is wholly different." Dartmouth College had been turned into a "university," complete with specialized departments and topped with an "Institute" for scientific research. "To these new colleges, and this *Institute*, the funds contributed by the founder, Dr. Wheelock, and by the original donors, the Earl of Dartmouth and others, are to be

{ 132 }

applied, in plain and manifest disregard of the uses to which they were given."

While he presented no evidence to show that Wheelock (let alone the Earl of Dartmouth) had contributed any property to found Dartmouth College, Webster nonetheless said Wheelock enjoyed all the rights of a first donor. "Eleemosynary corporations are for the management of private property according to the will of the donors," he argued (as if Wheelock had been the donor). "A college is as much a private corporation as a hospital, especially a college founded, as this was, by private bounty"—an untruth. He went on: "The government, in these cases, lends its aid to perpetuate the beneficent intention of the donor by granting a charter under which his private charity shall continue to be dispensed after his death. This is done either by incorporating the objects of the charity—as, for instance, the scholars in a college, or the poor in a hospital—or by incorporating those who are to be governors, or trustees, of the charity."

Webster cast the idea that Dartmouth College was a public corporation as inconceivable. "Who ever heard before that a gift to a college or hospital or asylum was, in reality, nothing but a gift to the state?" he inquired as he cited the court's recent decision in *Town of Pawlet v. Clarke* (1815), where a colonial grant to fund churches in New Hampshire border towns was redirected after the revolution by the new jurisdiction of Vermont to fund charity schools. Webster, lawyer for the churches, had argued that colonial grants, once made, could not be redirected by new states' legislatures. And if Vermont could not redirect grants from churches to schools (as John Wheelock *himself* had asked Vermont to do in 1780 with a transfer of the "Kingsland" grant in New York from the Anglican Church to Dartmouth College), then how could New Hampshire redirect a grant allegedly given to a "college" to a new "university"?

Having designated Wheelock as the college's first donor, Webster assigned to him all the rights of governance that such a donor would have to oversee the dispensation of "his" property. He schooled the justices on the English law of eleemosynary corporations. "In early times, it became a maxim that he who gave the property might regulate it in future," he noted. "This right of visitation descended from the founder to his heir as a right of property," with heirs entitled to a right of perpetual succession. "The founder may, if he pleases, part with it at the time when he establishes the charity, and may vest it in others," Webster explained. "Therefore, if he chooses that governors, trustees, or overseers should be appointed in the charter, he may cause it to be done, and his power of visitation will be transferred to them, instead of descending to his heirs."

Webster never acknowledged that in English law, whenever trustees were also visitors, they were subject to royal courts of chancery in the interest of public review; rather, he insisted that Wheelock, as "first donor," could transfer all visitatorial power to his chosen trustees, with no other review whatsoever. He elided the fact that Wheelock's son was both heir and trustee (and given explicit governance rights in the charter); instead, he emphasized the absolute power of the college trustees after the elder Wheelock's death. "A right of visitation accrues to them as a matter of property, by the gift, transfer, or appointment of the founder," he said. "As visitors, they may make rules, ordinances, and statutes, and alter and repeal them, as far as permitted so to do by the charter." The charter, in turn, represented a contract between Wheelock and his trustees for control of the property that Wheelock himself (purportedly) had given.

In the lower court, lawyers for the university had pointed to Oxford and Cambridge to say that Parliament had the authority to make rules for universities as public corporations. Webster countered that Dartmouth was not a university like Oxford and Cambridge but, rather, a college like the separately endowed residential units that comprised those broader institutions. Colleges "were originally charitable organizations that housed poor students at Oxford and Cambridge; later, the colleges took over teaching functions and prepared students for 'university' examinations and degrees." Despite his own claim that Dartmouth was "not inferior to any university on the continent," Webster placed the establishment "in the category of an English college" whose private (charitable) property was governed solely by its private trustees—and was thus off-limits to public oversight.

Webster's interpretation of English precedent has attracted scrutiny. As historian Bruce Campbell notes, "Webster contended that *Dartmouth College*—properly considered in light of applicable English law—was a property case; that Dartmouth College itself was, under English law, a private charitable corporation; that the trustees were the only visitors; and that these propositions, taken together, compelled the conclusion that the New Hampshire legislature could not constitutionally amend the college charter." Were all these contentions true? Campbell says no. "Although Webster's argument was ingenious, a close examination of English precedents... in light of the facts and ultimate issues in the Dartmouth College case reveals many serious flaws." In particular, Webster's presumption that Dartmouth was inherently a "private charitable corporation" of the English type was "questionable."

Indeed, notes Campbell, the argument that Webster presented was full of holes and half-truths. "Webster persistently distorted the concept of 'visitatorial power' to make it include not only judicial functions but *all* the governmental and administrative power within the charitable corporation. Apparently, this was [his] effort to inflate the significance of the English cases by making it appear that they meant to find a total corporate independence." In fact, it was not clear even to Webster that Dartmouth's trustees were also its visitors, since no such language was in the charter. "Although Webster contended before the Supreme Court that Dartmouth's trustees were legally the visitors, privately he had doubts on this point," Campbell notes, particularly since, as Webster acknowledged, even "in the case of Harvard College... some power of inspection [was] given to the [institution's public] overseers."

Halfway through his argument, Webster turned his attention to a crucial point, namely, whether a charter of incorporation for a college fit the constitution's definition of a contract. He said it did. "There is something to be contracted about, there are parties, and there are plain terms in which the agreement of the parties on the subject of the contract is expressed," he argued. "The charter recites that the founder, on his part, has agreed to establish his seminary in New Hampshire and to enlarge it beyond its original design—among other things, for the benefit of that province—and thereupon a charter is given to him and his associates, designated by himself, promising and assuring to them under the plighted faith of the state the right of governing the college and [thus] administering its concerns in the manner provided in the charter."

Traditionally, a contract was defined in terms of a "bargain," or agreement, sanctioned by the state between at least two parties, each of whom derived a benefit from the deal. Such a bargain occurred in the form of an exchange of "interests" or "considerations"—either material property or immaterial privileges—on both sides. So in a business contract, for example, the state might sanction a bargain or agreement between a buyer and seller, each of whom derived a financial benefit from the exchange. The question for Dartmouth College was: If the original charter was a contract, then who constituted the parties, and what constituted the interests, considerations, or benefits exchanged? Was the charter a private contract between Wheelock and his trustees for the right to oversee the use of his individual donations of property? Or was it a public contract between Wheelock and the Crown for the right to oversee the use of royal donations of land?

Webster, aware of the ambiguities that surrounded the college's property, answered this question in an unexpected way. Despite his earlier statement about the trustees' right to oversee donations of property, he now said the charter was a contract between Wheelock and the Crown, *not* in exchange for a grant of property (in which case the college's first donor would have been the royal governor, who gave its first land grant) but rather in exchange for the "franchises," or "privileges," of corporate governance itself, and particularly the privilege to govern property. "Is there any difference in legal contemplation between a grant of corporate franchises and a grant of tangible property?" he inquired. "No such difference is recognized in any decided case, nor does it exist in the common apprehension of mankind. It is therefore contended that ... the charter of 1769 is a contract—a stipulation or agreement, mutual in its considerations, express and formal in its terms, and of a most binding and solemn nature."

On the idea that charters were contracts that bestowed privileges in the form of governance rights, Webster cited *King v. Vice Chancellor of Cambridge* (1765), where the university's charter was considered to be "a compact between the crown and a certain number of the subjects, the latter of whom undertake, in consideration of the privileges which are bestowed, to exert themselves for the good government of the place." Webster applied this language to Dartmouth College: "It was in consequence of the 'privileges bestowed' [in the charter] that Dr. Wheelock and his associates undertook to exert themselves for the instruction ... of youth in this college, and it was on the same consideration that the founder endowed it with his property. And because charters of incorporation are of the nature of contracts, they cannot be altered, or varied, but by consent of the original parties." Webster disregarded the fact that Cambridge University's royal charter did not disturb Parliament's visitatorial right to oversee the institution on behalf of the public. He also disregarded the fact that Wheelock did *not* "endow [the college] with his property."

Webster said that Dartmouth's charter granted privileges of governance to each trustee as a private individual. "The plaintiffs have such an interest in this corporation, individually, as they could assert and maintain in a court of law, not as agents of the public, but in their own right," he argued in the language of *Bank of the United States v. Deveaux*. "Each trustee has a *franchise*, and if he be disturbed in the enjoyment of it, he would have redress, on appealing to the law, as promptly as for any other injury. If the other trustees should conspire against any one of them to prevent his equal right and voice in the appointment of a president or professor, or in the passing of any statute or ordinance of the college, he would be entitled to his action for depriving him of his franchise." He added: "It makes no difference that this property is to be held and administered, and these franchises exercised, for the purpose of diffusing learning."

According to Webster, the charter of Dartmouth College granted each trustee individual control over *privileges* just as other private contracts granted each party individual control over *property*. Once granted, neither property nor privileges could be revoked without each trustee's individual consent, and they alone could decide how to use their individual powers of governance. "The use being public in no way diminished their legal estate in the property or their title to the franchise," Webster argued. On the contrary, the Act of 1816 marked an illegal seizure of governance powers, or privileges, *as* property. "The acts in question violate property," he asserted. "They take away privileges, immunities, and franchises; they deny the trustees the protections of the law; and they are retrospective in their operation—in all which respects they are against the constitution of New Hampshire"—and presumably also the Contract Clause of the US Constitution.

In his closing statement, Webster anticipated the consequences of the court's decision for "all the literary institutions of the country," north, south, east, and west. "They all have a common principle of existence: the inviolability of their charters," he explained. "If their franchise may be at any time taken away, or impaired, their property also may be taken away, or its use perverted. Benefactors will have no certainty of effecting the objects of their bounty, and learned men will be deterred from devoting themselves to the service of such institutions from the precarious title of their offices." In that case, he warned, "Colleges and halls will be deserted by all better spirits and become a theater for the contentions of politics. Party and faction will be cherished in the places consecrated to piety and learning." These consequences, he added, were hardly "remote." On the contrary, they were "certain and immediate."

Webster then looked Chief Justice Marshall straight in the eye and unleashed the peroration of a lifetime: "*This, sir, is my case.* It is the case not merely of that humble institution. It is the case of every college in our land. It is more. It is the case of every eleemosynary institution throughout our country—of all those great charities founded by the piety of our ancestors to alleviate human misery and scatter blessings along the pathway of human life. It is more. It is, in some sense, the case of every man who has property of which he may be stripped." The essential question, he said, was this: "Shall our state legislatures be allowed to take that which is not their own, to turn it from its original use and apply it to such ends or purposes as they, in their discretion, shall see fit?" Could the law permit the private rights of property to be so brazenly subverted?

He continued: "Sir, you may destroy this little institution. It is weak. It is in your hands! I know it is one of the lesser lights on the literary horizon of our country. You may put it out. But if you do, you must carry through your work! You must extinguish, one after the other, all those great lights of science, which, for more than a century, have thrown their radiance over the land! It is, sir, as I have said, a small college, and yet *there are those who love it.*" Here, observed historian Frederick Chase, "The feelings which he thus far had succeeded in keeping down, broke forth. His lips quivered; his firm cheeks trembled with emotion; his eyes were filled with tears; his voice choked; he seemed to struggle to the utmost simply to gain the mastery over himself which might save him from an unmanly burst of feeling.... Everyone saw that it was wholly unpremeditated—a pressure on his heart which sought relief in words and tears."

Most agreed that Webster had delivered a commanding performance—a "consequentialist" narrative that seemed to reduce constitutional questions to mere quibbles. He spoke not only for his alma mater but for every college in the country. As he brought his comments to a close, he again looked at Marshall and said, "Sir, I know not how others may feel, but for myself, when I see my *alma mater* surrounded—like Caesar in the Senate—by those reiterating, stab upon stab, I would not, for this right hand, have her turn to me and say, *Et tu quoque mi filii!* [And you too my son]." It was a masterstroke. The entire courtroom broke down. "The depth of personal feeling in this remark reportedly moved Marshall to tears," historian Francis Stites notes. "This was the consensus, and none withheld encomiums." One audience member later reported to William Plumer that Webster's "character, his manners, and his artful statement of the case . . . had great weight with some of the judges."

Clearly, the university's counsel had its work cut out. To present its case, the university had chosen Massachusetts congressman John Holmes from the district of Maine (then a frontier region). "Holmes was a famous[ly] kaleidoscopic politician," historian John Major Shirley notes. First a Federalist, Holmes suddenly became a Republican in 1811 when his constituents swung that way. "Federalists had a strong majority in Massachusetts proper," Shirley notes, but after Maine went Republican, its congressional delegation followed. Holmes thereafter "was elected to the House and Senate by his new friends" and served during the War of 1812, after which President James Monroe, grateful for his contributions, named him US commissioner to enforce article IV of the Treaty of Ghent, which specified the US-Canadian border and thus Maine's eastern boundary line.

"Holmes was not without talent," Shirley comments. But was he the right person to argue the *Dartmouth* case? University trustee William Hale, a New Hampshire congressman, was doubtful. As he wrote to secretary-treasurer William Woodward: "Were you sensible of the low ebb of Mr. Holmes's reputation here, you would, I think, be unwilling to trust the cause with him. It might in the end be decided right, but a lawyer of higher standing would be much more likely to persuade the court." Woodward, however, liked Holmes's chances. "I have thought him extremely ready—of sound mind and [a] good lawyer, inferior only to Daniel Webster in point of oratory," he replied a few weeks before oral arguments. But when Hale suggested that US attorney general William Wirt might be a better choice, Woodward agreed that Wirt should join Holmes as cocounsel, which he did.

When they appeared before the court, Holmes and Wirt offered the best arguments they could muster. Holmes went first. He said that when it came to deciding whether a corporation was public or private, its *function* was as important as its *funds*, and nowhere was the public function of a corporation more clear than it was in the case of a college. "The education of youth, and the encouragement of the arts and sciences, is one of the most important objects of civil government," he argued. "By our constitutions, it is left exclusively to states (with the exception of copyrights and patents).... The constitution [of New Hampshire] admonishes the legislature of the duty of encouraging science and literature and thus seems to suppose its power of control over the scientific and literary institutions of the state." In fact, "It was in the exercise of this [public] duty of [educational] government that a charter was originally granted to Dartmouth College."

If education was a public function subject to legislative control before the revolution, then it remained so after the revolution. "The revolution, which separated the colony from the parent country, dissolved all connection between this corporation and the crown of Great Britain," noted Holmes, "but it did not destroy that supreme authority, which every political society has over its public institutions. That still remained, and was transferred unto the people of New Hampshire." A charter originally granted by the Crown subsequently fell under the authority of the state, which inherited the Crown's rights of alteration or amendment. "Its amendment, or even repeal, can no more be considered as the breach of a contract than the amendment or repeal of any other law," Holmes argued. "Such repeal or amendment is an ordinary act of public legislation, not an act impairing the obligation of a contract between the government and private citizens."

Holmes went on to say that even if the charter of Dartmouth College were a "contract," the Act of 1816 had not impaired that contract, because the charter was a civil (public) contract between the Crown and the people of New Hampshire, with the college trustees as caretakers of that (public) trust. "If, by a technical fiction, the grant of the charter can be considered a contract between the king (or the state) and the corporators, the obligation of that contract is not impaired but is, rather, *enforced* by these acts, which continue the same corporation, for the same objects, under a new name," he concluded. "It is well settled that a mere change of the name of a corporation will not affect its identity," he noted, citing *King v. Pasmore*. "An increase in the number of trustees does not impair the franchises of the corporate body, nor is the franchise of any individual corporator impaired." And with that brief summation, Holmes rested his case.

As he listened, Webster felt his own chances improve. He wrote to Jeremiah Smith that Holmes "spoke three or four hours" but "did not make a figure." (The published version of his argument filled barely four pages.) "I had a malicious joy in seeing [New Hampshire Superior Court judge Samuel] Bell sit by to [listen to] him while everybody was grinning at the folly he uttered," Webster noted. "Bell could not stand it. He seized his hat and went off." Others were equally nonplussed. David Daggett, a senator from Connecticut who later served as chief justice of that state's high court, wrote to Jeremiah Mason with a quotation from Thomas Paine that he said applied to Holmes's performance: "He went up like a rocket and came down like a stick. . . . In the Dartmouth College cause, he sunk lower at the bar than he had in the legislature."

But if Holmes fared poorly, his cocounsel fared only marginally better. William Wirt had appeared before the US Supreme Court twice: first in 1807, in Aaron Burr's trial for treason, and then in 1817, when he defeated Webster's cocounsel Joseph Hopkinson in a commercial-law case. But as historian Joseph Burke notes, his duties as President Monroe's attorney general had left him little time for preparation. The case of Dartmouth College joined ten other cases on his desk, and with no chance for research, he relied on a set of documents shipped from Hanover at the last minute. "All he received was a bare list of [references]," Burke recounts, "and when it arrived, late in February 1818, he was sick in bed." His prospects for a successful argument were not strong.

Wirt knew his task was to show that Dartmouth was a public

corporation, founded with public funds to serve public ends. He therefore began with George Sullivan and Ichabod Bartlett's assertion that even if Eleazar Wheelock had given property to his Indian Charity School, he never gave anything to the college and thus could not claim a "contract" to control property that had, in fact, come from the Crown. "The fact that Dr. Wheelock was a contributor is not found," Wirt emphasized. "Are the other contributors alluded to in the charter ... contracting parties? They are not before the court, and even if they were, with whom did they contract? With the king of Great Britain? He, too, is not before the court and has declared, by his chancellor, in *Attorney General ex rel. Bishop of London v. College of William and Mary* [on the redirection of Robert Boyle's scholarships for Indian students] that he no longer has any connection with corporations in America."

Webster had argued that Dartmouth's charter was a contract between Wheelock and the Crown, principally for his trustees' privileges, or franchises, of corporate governance, but Wirt disagreed. The charter was not a contract, he said, because it bestowed no beneficial interest on any individual college trustee. "To make this charter a contract," he argued, "there must be a private beneficial interest vested in the party ... the right of appointing the president and professors of the college, of establishing ordinances for its government, etc.—but to make these rights an interest that will constitute the end and object of a contract, the exercise of these rights must be for the private individual advantage of the trustees. Here, however, so far from that being the fact, it is solely for the advantage of the public, for the interest of piety and learning." The contract, if one existed, was between the Crown, which donated the property, and the public, which received the benefit.

According to Wirt, the people of New Hampshire, not the individual trustees, had received Dartmouth College's property and privileges from its original donor, the king, with the college board of trustees as caretakers and subject to legislative oversight. "By the revolution, which separated this country from the British empire, all the powers of the British government devolved on the states," he reminded the court. In the case of Dartmouth College, "The legal estate was indeed vested in the [college's] trustees before the revolution by virtue of the royal charter of 1769, but that charter was destroyed by the revolution, and the legal estate of course fell on those who held the equitable estate: upon the people." The college trustees merely directed the use of the property on behalf of the public. "If those who were trustees carried on the duties of the trust after the revolution," Wirt reasoned, "it must have been subject to the power of the people," represented by the legislature.

Webster described Wirt's performance in court in a letter to Jeremiah Mason back at the college. "He is a good deal of a lawyer and has very quick perceptions and handsome powers of argument, but he seemed to treat this case as if his side could furnish nothing but declamation," Webster noted. "He undertook to make out one legal point on which he rested his argument, namely, that Dr. Wheelock was not [the] founder. In this, he was, I thought, completely unsuccessful." In fact, during Wirt's argument, Webster had interrupted him to cite the clause in the charter that explicitly identified Wheelock as "founder." Wirt confessed that he was unaware of that clause and, untutored on the complex historical relationship between Moor's Indian Charity School and Dartmouth College, "abandoned the point" to request a recess. "He made an apology for himself," Webster noted, and disclosed that he "had not had time to study the case."

It was a disaster for the university's side. "No man could make a good legal argument in such a cause who had 'hardly thought of it,'" Shirley remarks. "Whether in consequence of Webster's disabling him in the tilt about the 'founder,' etc., or from his vehemence, or what is more probable, from both, does not distinctly appear, but contemporary accounts show that he [Wirt] utterly broke down." Webster chuckled. In a letter to Jeremiah Smith he noted that "Wirt said more nonsensical things than became him." Still, the friends of the university held out hope. William Hale did his best to bring Wirt up to speed—literally overnight. "It cost me almost the night's labor to furnish Mr. Wirt with facts and authority," he wrote. But the next day was no better. Wirt could not recover from missteps already made.

With the university's case apparently dead on arrival, Webster's co-counsel put the last nail in the coffin. In his rebuttal, Joseph Hopkinson repeated that Wheelock was the founder and first donor. "It is clear that Dr. Wheelock's original school was founded by him at great labor and expense [and] that Dartmouth [College] was but an enlargement of that seminary, made by his own consent," he claimed (with no acknowledgment of the English trustees' lack of consent to enlarge their original institution). "How otherwise could he [be] considered the founder? It is therefore not correct, neither in point of fact nor material in point of law, to say he contributed nothing to Dartmouth College if this college is but a graft on his original stock, because the law is clear that if the original foundation of a charity is ever [so very] small, and subsequent donations or additions ever so large, they are considered but additions to the first establishment, submitting to its power and coming under its government."

Critics have questioned Hopkinson's theory of "grafted" foundations, whereby the college trustees simply presumed a right to control the school's original property (whether that of Wheelock or the English trustees). Moor's Indian Charity School may have been a private corporation under the control of its original English donors, but Dartmouth College, with its original Landaff grant from the colony, appeared to be a public corporation. "The king first gave Landaff to Dartmouth and was, in consequence, its founder," Shirley notes. "It is true that the grant of Landaff was overturned, as were many other grants by the same authority, after the revolution, but that would seem to be immaterial. If the least private interest transforms what otherwise would be a public into a private corporation, [then] it would be a work of great difficulty to discover a public corporation in [any] of the states."

Hopkinson asked when the "corporation's property" had become "public," but the more salient question was at what point—if any—had the Crown's initial grant of land become "private"? At what point were public grants to Dartmouth College converted into private grants to its trustees? "The property of this college was private property before the charter, and the charter has wrought no change in the nature or title of this property," Hopkinson misleadingly averred. "Dr. Wheelock had a legal interest in the funds with which the institution was founded; he made a contract with the then-existing government of the state [the Crown] in relation to that interest, by which he devoted (to uses beneficial to the public) the funds he collected in consideration of the covenants on the part of the government contained in the charter; and these [covenants] are violated, and the contract impaired, by the acts of the legislature of New Hampshire."

It was a convoluted narrative, but Webster applauded. "Mr. Hopkinson understood every part of the cause, and in his argument did it great justice," he wrote to President Brown in Hanover, sure the college would prevail. "I am informed that the bar here are decidedly with us in opinion." William Hale, by contrast, felt the university still had a chance. "Mr. Wirt grasped the cause with the mind of a giant and made Webster lower his crest and sit uneasy," he avowed. But most agreed that Holmes and Wirt had been outmatched. As Judge Daggett of Connecticut put it: "The opinion was entirely universal that Webster rose superior even to Wirt (though it is said he appeared very well) and infinitely so to Holmes," whose performance was panned by everyone except himself (in fact, Holmes asked for an extra fee to recognize his achievement). But whose arguments would the court accept? It would take more than a year to find out.

PART III
The Consequences

CHAPTER II

How to Win Friends and Influence Justices

Holmes and Wirt's lack of preparation, together with the fact that arguments in the case occurred at the very end of the court's term, led the justices to postpone their decision. The court notified counsel on March 13 (the day after oral arguments concluded) that it would continue the case at its next term, scheduled to begin on February 1, 1819. On the one hand, this postponement gave the university a chance to regroup; it promptly replaced Holmes with a new lawyer, William Pinkney, who had won several cases before the high court. On the other hand, it gave the college a chance to strengthen its appeal even further. Neither side wasted any time. As the justices "rode circuit" in their respective geographic regions to hear cases in the lower appellate courts, both the university and the college looked for new strategies—judicial and political.

The college's first strategy was to publish Webster's arguments in an effort to influence public opinion. He sent his *Argument in the Case of the Trustees of Dartmouth College v. William H. Woodward in the United States Supreme Court* (1818) to a "few friends," including Jacob McGaw in Maine, whom he knew from his legal apprenticeship in New Hampshire, with a request to show it to Judge Samuel Wilde of Massachusetts's Supreme Court or "any professional friend, in your discretion" (though McGraw noted that "general decorum" would seem "to prohibit the publishing of an argument while the cause is pending"). Among others who received Webster's pamphlet was Massachusetts's chief justice Isaac Parker, who forwarded a copy to Justice Joseph Story, though Webster already had sent that justice five copies with a request to share them with his colleagues on the court.

Parker, recently named the first professor at Harvard Law School (established the previous year), had encouraged the publication of Webster's argument in hopes that it would influence the justices. "Public sentiment has a great deal to do in affairs of this sort," Parker confided. "If there be any members who wish to do right but are a little afraid, it will be a great help to know that all the world expects they will do right." In any democracy, he added, "There is a natural leaning in favor of legislative power, for it is the power of the people when constitutionally exercised. But the people ought to be made to know that, in certain cases, their rights are above the reach of the legislature, and thus popularity may be given to a denial of legislative power." In short, Parker said, the best security against public majoritarian rule was private corporate rights, as protected by constitutions and courts.

Delighted with Parker's letter, President Brown sought the widest possible distribution for Webster's argument in hopes that every college in the country would see the case from Dartmouth's perspective. Brown thanked President John Thornton Kirkland at Harvard for his offer to share the argument with other college leaders. "It has already been, or shortly will be, read by all the commanding men of New England and New York," he wrote, "and, so far as it has gone, it has united them all, without a single exception within my knowledge, in one broad and impenetrable phalanx for our defense." It was true. On May 26, 1818, two months after oral arguments, a "Congress of Colleges" met in Boston to present a united front against state interference. Aside from Dartmouth, the participants included Harvard, Yale, Middlebury, Bowdoin, Williams, and the Andover Theological Seminary . . . all Federalist strongholds.

Not to be outdone, representatives of the university initiated a public relations campaign of their own. They first contacted legal expert James Kent of New York, his state's "chancellor," or highest judicial officer, to build support for their side in the contest. As historian Francis Stites notes, Kent had vacationed in the Connecticut Valley that summer. While in Windsor, Vermont, he visited university supporter Josiah Dunham, who brought him to Hanover and "introduced him to president Allen and the officers of the university." Kent, eager "to learn something of the college quarrel," bought a copy of Richardson's superior court opinion and, on his ride back to Windsor, concluded that Dartmouth was "a public establishment" and that New Hampshire's legislature was "competent to pass the laws in question."

The college party was alarmed. Kent, a Federalist, was a close friend of two US Supreme Court justices, Henry Livingston and William Johnson, and was likely to influence their interpretations of the case. In fact, notes historian Frederick Chase, Kent was likely to be asked "to write Mr. Justice Johnson's opinion" for the court. To sway his views, the college therefore sent him a copy of Webster's argument, together with a copy of Dartmouth's charter, and dispatched President Brown to meet him in person. "Brown, in the course of a vacation trip undertaken for the help of the college, stopped at Albany, where he dined with Kent and conferred upon college matters," Chase writes. It must have been a persuasive conference, because "Kent at once expressed regret for the hasty [support he expressed for the university when he was in] Windsor and said that Mr. Webster's argument had thrown a different light upon the case."

Brown jotted a note to Webster after this dinner. "I have been with the chancellor," he reported. "I asked him if the corporation of Dartmouth College did not appear to be a private eleemosynary corporation. He smiled and said he believed he must express no more opinions until the cause should be decided." Brown, however, did not leave anything to chance. He met Kent again the next day and evidently was happy with their discussion. "There is no doubt that, by the argument and the charter, he is brought completely over to our side," he wrote to Webster on his way home. "I believe he will take every proper and prudent measure to impart correct views to others. While I remained in Albany, another copy of your argument fell into his hands, which, he said, agreeably to the strong wish of [Justice] Johnson, he should transmit to him." Brown felt confident that Johnson would support the college side.

Aside from his meetings with Kent, President Brown also met with New York's former governor DeWitt Clinton, a close friend of Justice Livingston, to whom he gave another copy of Webster's argument. "I hope he will incline to favor us rather than our competitors," Brown told Webster, aware that Clinton, a Columbia graduate (the first after its conversion from the original king's), had studied the law of charters as it applied to colleges when he served with Kent on New York's Council of Revision. This "Court of Errors" had advised the legislature on similar collegiate matters. "The Court of Errors . . . is unquestionably in our favor," Brown wrote from Albany, where he saw the court in session. "Clinton said he understood the Supreme Court would ... probably decide for the college." With both Kent and Clinton in the college's pocket, Brown felt his visit to Albany had gone very well, indeed.

Why did Kent in particular seem to support the college argument? "The nominal basis, if we are to credit Kent," writes historian John Major Shirley, was their familiarity with a series of cases from the Council of Revision on the protection of royal grants and charters under New York's postrevolutionary constitution. The constitution explicitly held that none of its provisions "shall be construed to affect any grant of land within this state made by the authority of [the] king or his predecessors, or to annul any charters to bodies-politic, by him or them ... and that none of the said charters shall be adjudged to be void by reason of any non-user or mis-user of any of their respective rights and privileges between [1775] and the publication of this constitution." In other words, New York's legislature could not alter colonial-era grants or charters without all parties' consent.

Over the years, the Council of Revision had ruled on this issue several times. In 1801, for instance, the legislature had asked Kent to review a proposed Act Relative to the Election of Charter Officers in the City of New York, which sought to change the way public officials were selected under the city's original public charter. Kent replied: "It has been ... a settled and salutary principle in our government that charters of incorporation were not to be essentially affected without due process of law, or without the consent of the parties concerned. Nothing but a strong public necessity would justify such an interference." He added, however, that public and private corporations differed, and he was not sure that his views on consent and the inviolability of charters "applied to corporations for the purpose of government, etc." Given this caveat, his fellow judges permitted the state legislature to alter the city's rules of election.

A similar question surfaced three years later when, in 1804, the Council of Revision considered a *revised* act: Relative to the Election of Charter Officers in the City of New York. In this case, Kent strengthened his opinion that both private *and* public corporations were immune to legislative intervention unless they gave their consent, or unless state action was "necessary" to protect the public interest. "Charters of incorporation containing grants of personal and municipal privileges were not to be essentially affected without the consent of the parties concerned," Kent ruled. "Although it be granted that such an interference would be justified by some strong public necessity, it is not to be presumed . . . that any such necessity exists in the present case." Here, the council stressed that corporations in general were to be shielded from legislative action. But since the council's decisions were merely advisory, the legislature passed its revised bill anyway.

Why had these disputes over charters and city elections arisen in the first place? Because, after 1800, state legislators in Albany had become increasingly frustrated with the management of the state's largest city. The City of New York had been founded with a royal charter that made it a "corporation" and gave its officials—the Common Council—a vast tract of land, which council members were permitted to sell in pieces to private buyers (often themselves), ostensibly to benefit the city. By the early nineteenth century, state legislators (mostly rural and Republican) felt the Common Council (mostly urban and Federalist) had abused its corporate privileges to enrich itself. As historian Elizabeth Mensch explains, "'Corporations' in general, and New York in particular, were viewed as illegitimate vestiges of crown rule," a reputation exacerbated in New York by a series of contemporary bribery scandals linked to state-issued bank charters.

To improve their image, New York's corporations began in the early nineteenth century to pitch themselves as "public" more than "private" entities. This shift was evident in 1806, when a Republican legislature chartered a new Medical Society of New York and inserted a clause in the act of incorporation that gave the state a right to amend the charter "at any time it saw fit." Then a year later, in 1807, the legislature took steps to amend the charter of Columbia College to make it more accountable to public interests. Notably, the legislature sought to give the public regents of the State University of New York the power to fill vacancies on Columbia's board of trustees. However, this effort failed because, as historian Bruce Campbell notes, "The attempt to terminate the independence of Columbia was primarily the result of factional divisions which agitated New York politics"—not least, divisions *within* the Republican Party itself.

Republicans in New York were divided between the more conservative "Livingstonians," associated with the powerful Livingston family, and the more liberal "Clintonians," aligned with DeWitt Clinton as governor. In 1807, when the Livingstonians united with the Federalists to fill government posts, the Clintonians retaliated with their attempt to seize control of Columbia—a Livingstonian stronghold. The defense of Columbia and its charter fell to college treasurer (and US Supreme Court justice) Henry Brockholst Livingston, who had been named to Columbia's board of trustees after its charter revision of 1787 restored its original "city"-dominated governance structure. Although his father William Livingston had sought greater public control of the college at its origin, Henry Livingston wanted to keep the college firmly under the private control of its (city) trustees.

Chancellor Kent, a Livingstonian, agreed that Columbia should be governed by its private trustees. Kent had served as Columbia's professor of law during the 1790s, and when he became New York's chancellor he made the state's Council of Revision a bastion of Livingstonian support for collegiate "independence." In 1807, he ruled that Columbia's original charter had granted its trustees a right to fill all their own vacancies "forever." He added that Columbia was "entitled to all the security which any grant of chartered rights could receive under the state constitution." Indeed, he noted, "Charters of incorporation—whether granted for private, or local, or charitable, or literary, or religious purposes—were not to be affected without due process of law, or without the consent of the parties concerned."

Of course, the Council of Revision was merely advisory to the legislature, which split on the question of Columbia's autonomy. In 1807, when Kent said the legislature could not amend Columbia's original charter without its trustees' consent, the Clintonians in the Senate voted to override his opinion, only for Livingstonians in the House to block that effort, which meant the bill for legislative control failed and Columbia's trustees retained their chartered authority. The conflict did not end there, however. Three years later, in 1810, at Columbia's own request, a Livingstonian majority in the legislature granted a revised charter that placed all college property donated before the revolution under the control of its trustees (but, in exchange, capped the value of its real estate in the city at $20,000 and stated that all land titles granted by the former Anglican church would expire in sixty-three years).

This revised charter temporarily quieted tensions between the legislature and the college, and over the next few years Columbia received significant aid from the state. Moreover, in 1813, when the nation was at war, the college joined its medical school with the New York College of Physicians and Surgeons (a public corporation) and, in 1814, received public land for a new campus. Meanwhile, however, Clintonian governor Daniel Tompkins sought to merge Columbia with a new public college established with a seven-hundred-acre state grant on Staten Island. Columbia's trustees rebuffed this (hostile) takeover bid in 1817 on grounds that a merger would be inconsistent with "the duty of faithful trustees." Justice Livingston, as chair of Columbia's board, "personally informed Tompkins of the trustees' decision" to remain independent of state interference.

All these events undoubtedly shaped Justice Livingston's views of the Dartmouth College litigation, which raised similar questions about corporate autonomy, or charters as contracts. So did another case that played out in New York in this period. In 1817, in *Adams v. Storey*, the justice ruled at the circuit level that a particular variety of private contracts—namely, financial contracts—*could* in fact be altered by legislation if a state had laws that allowed debtors to declare insolvency. New York had passed a series of insolvency acts, first in 1778, then in 1801, 1811, and 1813, each with the endorsement of Kent and his colleagues on the Council of Revision, who concurred with Livingston that since Congress had not (yet) passed a federal bankruptcy act, the states could pass their own laws to deal with debtors' inability to pay. But if states could alter financial contracts with insolvency acts, could they not alter other kinds of "contracts," too?

Three years earlier, a divergent opinion had been handed down in a different circuit in the case of *Golden v. Prince* (1814), which held that states could not pass insolvency laws. This case had begun with a bill of exchange written in 1810 on the island of St. Bart's in the Caribbean but never repaid. The defendant later declared insolvency in Pennsylvania (under that state's insolvency law of 1812) and defaulted on his debt. Pennsylvania's law said a certificate of insolvency could discharge a debtor from "all debts ... for which he was liable at the date of such certificate, and from all contracts originating before that date (though payable afterwards)," but the court struck down this law. It said a certificate of insolvency could not discharge past debts retroactively and that, in fact, Congress alone had the power to pass such laws under the Constitution's bankruptcy clause—even though it had not yet done so.

Livingston was aware of *Golden v. Prince* when he decided in *Adams v. Storey* that states could alter financial contracts. He felt strongly that, in the absence of any federal bankruptcy law, states could act on their own. "This court is of the opinion that the act of April 3, 1811, is an insolvent, not a bankrupt law," he asserted; "that, [even] if it be of the latter description, the several states have a right to pass bankrupt laws for themselves until Congress shall establish a uniform system on the subject; [and] that an insolvency act extending to past as well as future debts is not a law 'impairing the obligation of contracts' within the meaning of the Constitution." Livingston's thirty-page decision from 1817 worried the lawyers for Dartmouth College, who feared that he might uphold legislative actions that "impaired" other kinds of "contracts" as well.

Daniel Webster studied Livingston's decisions in these cases with interest. As he learned more about their legal implications, he looked for ways to shift the focus of *Dartmouth* away from "public" and "private" contracts toward a simpler focus on property ownership. If he could establish the college's original property claims—and do so in justice Story's circuit—then he felt he could establish the "vested rights" of the college trustees in all matters related to corporate property and privileges. "I saw judge Story as I came along," he told Jeremiah Mason after his preliminary arguments. "He is evidently expecting a case which shall present all the questions," not least whether states had the authority to alter contracts, or charters, and their attendant property rights. "The question we must raise ... is 'whether ... state legislatures be not restrained from devesting vested rights,'" he wrote. "On this question, I have great confidence in a decision on the right side."

To foreground the questions of vested rights and property ownership, Webster relied on the interstate property suits he filed in Story's circuit. Story had scheduled an initial hearing on these suits for May 1, 1818, and had said he wanted all the evidence presented in time for a possible referral to the full Supreme Court later in the year. Webster felt he stood on solid ground. "The circuit judge expressed particularly his approbation of the action of ejectment brought in the English form," he told President Brown after the May 1 session. "It was evident [the university] counsel did not feel much confidence in their defense." Indeed, the university was dismayed by Story's willingness to entertain an entirely new angle on the case. Still, it hoped to use any "new facts" it could find to bolster its claim that Dartmouth's initial property had come from the Crown, whose visitatorial rights after the revolution had passed to state legislators.

For the university, everything seemed to hinge on its new facts. William Plumer, who received periodic reports on the university's research into Eleazar Wheelock's archived papers, hoped that four justices—Henry Livingston, William Johnson, Gabriel Duval, and Thomas Todd—would favor the view that Dartmouth was a public corporation whose governance rested with its first donor, the Crown, and its successor, the state. "I am confident," Plumer declared, "that the fact of the state's being the principal donor can be proved so as to remove the doubts of even an unwilling judge." In fact, when the university shared a selection of Wheelock's papers with President Brown, he instantly saw the risk they posed. "The written headings alone cover nine long pages," college lawyer Jeremiah Smith commented, with "numerous letters, records, and papers, including those in the matter of Landaff."

Brown informed Webster of his concerns: "They are going to attempt to show from the correspondence of Dr. Eleazar Wheelock that he considered the college to be altogether distinct from the school—the school, to be sure, being a private charity; the college, a public institution, and on a very different foundation. I presume no such evidence will be admitted. If it should be, the [subsequent] trial must be long, and it is impossible to conjecture what may be shown." If the documents showed that Wheelock had *not* been the college's first donor, then he could not be considered the founder (despite claims in the charter on this point). "In the attempt which they will make to prove this not to be a private eleemosynary corporation, they will probably bring in the lands and other donations given by the legislature," noted Brown. "May it not be of some consequence to ascertain these grants and obtain copies from the secretary's office?"

Brown went on to say the university lawyers would likely use their documents to compare Dartmouth with Oxford and Cambridge as civil (public) corporations: "They will attempt... to show a distinction between the universities in England and the colleges founded within them, the latter being admitted to be charities, the former not but designed for the purposes of regulation, government, etc., and [they will state that] Dartmouth College resembles the universities rather than the colleges in England, *ergo*, the legislature has a right to interfere. This, I doubt not, has occurred to you. They will make it, I think, their great point." He added: "They will endeavor to bring in as many things as can possibly be found to give to Dartmouth College the appearance of being what it is not: an institution of a public character, such as (it is admitted) the government may control."

On the comparison of Dartmouth with Oxford and Cambridge universities as public corporations, Webster seized a chance to make Justice Story aware of a recent debate in Parliament over the governance of the Oxbridge colleges. Lord Henry Brougham, a Whig reformer, had spearheaded a special investigation of charities for the education of the poor and had found evidence of widespread mismanagement. As historian Bruce Campbell notes, "His strongest criticism was directed at charities with 'special visitors' [in other words, trustees]," who routinely enriched themselves at the expense of the charities they were supposed to supervise and then hid behind the jurisdiction of corrupt (and juryless) royal courts of chancery. Brougham noted that English law regarded "the inheritance of the poor as a matter of public, not private, jurisdiction," yet too often England's private (eleemosynary) charities, including Oxbridge colleges, failed to fulfill their public functions.

The House of Lords disagreed. It said that under the sixteenth-century Statute of Charitable Uses private charities were immune to public oversight. Brougham's chief opponent, Lord Chancellor Eldon, maintained that "no 'honorable man' would become a charitable trustee in the future if trustees 'were to be exposed to suspicious and vexatious [probes] into all of the details of their duty.'" Eldon said that not only Parliament but also the courts "'ought to have nothing to do' with charities that had special visitors appointed by their founders... except where it was 'proved' that visitors had abused their trust." In the end, the House of Lords amended Brougham's reform bill to "[exempt] from investigation the universities of Oxford and Cambridge, the colleges of Westminster, Eton, and Winchester, and any 'charitable institution for the purposes of education, which have special visitors, governors, or overseers appointed by their founders.'"

Webster hoped the outcome of these debates would lead Justice Story to conclude that, if all the colleges of Oxford and Cambridge were immune to public investigation, then Dartmouth should be, too. "The universities and the great schools were excepted out of the provisions of the bill," Webster told Story in a two-point letter. "Its history shows that the English lawyers recognize a difference between charities having visitors [trustees] and such as have none. (Indeed, I did not observe until lately that the commissions issued under the Statute of Elizabeth do not extend to charities with visitors.)" Moreover, he added, the bill's authors held that Parliament had no power of "new-modelling, and directing to new uses, at its own pleasure, charitable funds arising from donations of individuals," such as those at Oxford, Cambridge, or... Dartmouth.

For the next several months, Webster continued to feed Story various "memoranda" on the *Dartmouth* litigation. He knew that if the university's lawyers could prove that Dartmouth was a public corporation founded by a grant from the Crown—and thus subject to public supervision—then his entire argument could fall apart. He therefore heaved a sigh of relief when, in Story's court at Exeter in October 1818, the university agreed that any new facts it had would be introduced later, when the US Supreme Court reconvened early the next year. "All things succeeded to a charm at Exeter," reported trustee Charles Marsh after both parties appeared. Webster added that, even if the university had new facts to offer, he would counter. He asked President Brown for whatever information he could locate to disprove the idea that Dartmouth's first donor was the Crown.

To present its new facts in court, the university recruited a new lawyer: William Pinkney of Maryland, who had served as James Madison's attorney general with great success from 1811 to 1814. To assist Pinkney with his preparations, the university dispatched Dr. Cyrus Perkins to

Baltimore with a trove of documents as well as the arguments presented by Sullivan and Bartlett in New Hampshire's Superior Court. The latter did not impress. "Mr. Pinkney is most prodigiously vexed with the management of the cause in New Hampshire," noted Perkins, "and says that, should it be lost, it will be lost by the very slovenly manner in which it has been conducted." He stressed that all the facts on Dartmouth's early donations *should* "have been found by the [Superior Court] in New Hampshire—and I know could have been [found] with such documents as we had at [our] command, but for the numbskulls we had for counsel." Perkins hoped Pinkney could do better.

When Justice Story heard that Pinkney had joined the university's side, he was excited to see him in action, for Pinkney had been retained to argue several cases before his court. "The next term of the Supreme Court will probably be the most interesting ever known," Story told a court reporter. "Several great constitutional questions—the constitutionality of the insolvent laws, of taxing the Bank of the United States, and of the Dartmouth College new charter—will probably be splendidly argued. Mr. Pinkney is engaged in these and several other very important questions sent from my circuit." He was not disappointed. Pinkney's very "first step" in the case showed "the genius of a commander," one historian notes. "He notified opposing counsel that he would move for reargument in *Trustees v. Woodward* and would argue it himself, if the court permitted."

Webster first heard of Pinkney's motion from Joseph Hopkinson, his cocounsel. "I suppose he expects to do something very extraordinary, as he says Mr. Wirt 'was not strong enough for it, has not back enough,'" Hopkinson wrote, aware that a reargument before the full court, with Pinkney in control of new facts, carried risks for the college. "It is most probable that Pinkney will succeed in his motion," Webster cautioned as the court's next session approached. Despite a one-day postponement to await three justices who had been delayed on their way to Washington, the session formally opened on February 2, 1819, and *Board of Trustees of Dartmouth College v. Woodward* led the docket. All rose as the justices filed into the courtroom, where, before the bench, Webster and Hopkinson were seated on the right and Pinkney and Wirt on the left, with Pinkney nearest the bar, eager for a chance "to open the battle with his motion for reargument."

CHAPTER 12

The Marshall Court Decides

When Chief Justice Marshall's gavel fell on February 2, 1819, a sense of eager anticipation filled the courtroom. "Pinkney had ... let it be known that he relished the chance of demolishing Webster's argument in the college case and thought little of Wirt's efforts," historian Joseph Burke notes. Pinkney stood poised to move the university's carefully gathered "new facts" into evidence ... but he never got a chance. "The instant the judges had taken their seats, the chief justice turned a 'blind ear' towards Pinkney (as tradition has it, and as Mills Olcott, one of the plaintiffs, used to relate it), and shut off his motion by announcing that he and his fellow justices had formed their opinions during the vacation," 5 to 1 in favor of the college. It was a total surprise. Marshall gave Pinkney no opportunity for reargument at all.

Marshall read the majority's decision from the bench. He began with a declaration that Dartmouth's charter was, in fact, a contract and therefore entitled to federal constitutional protection. "The charter is granted, and on its faith ... property is conveyed," he declared. "Surely, in this transaction, every ingredient of a complete and legitimate contract is to be found." Indeed, the conveyance of property was central to Marshall's interpretation of the Contract Clause, which, he wrote, "never has been understood to embrace other contracts than those which respect property, or some object of value, and confer rights which may be asserted in a court of justice." In this way, the charter of Dartmouth College was removed from any other purpose and reduced to a contract for control of the institution's original property.

And whose property did Marshall believe had founded Dartmouth College? "This is the point on which the cause essentially depends," the chief justice acknowledged. "If the funds of the college be public property, or if the state of New Hampshire, as a government, be alone interested in its transactions, the subject is one in which the legislature of the state may act according to its own judgment, unrestrained by any limitation of its power imposed by the constitution of the United States," he wrote. "But if this be a private eleemosynary institution, endowed with the capacity to take property for objects unconnected with government, whose funds are bestowed by individuals on the faith of the charter; if the donors have stipulated for the future disposition and management of those funds in the manner prescribed by themselves, there may be more difficulty in the case."

Marshall was not unaware of the institution's origins in Moor's Indian Charity School. "The origin of the institution was, undoubtedly, the Indian Charity School, established by Dr. Wheelock at his own expense," he recognized. "It was at his instance—and to enlarge this school—that contributions were solicited in England; the person soliciting these contributions was his agent; and the trustees who received the money were appointed by, and acted under, his authority. It is not too much to say that the funds were obtained by him [Wheelock], in trust, to be applied by him to the purposes of his enlarged school." But was the charter of incorporation granted for an "enlarged school" or for an entirely new (and propertyless) college? With no awareness of the "new facts" collected by the university—facts to prove that its first donor had been the Crown on behalf of the public—Marshall found that, with respect to property, the school and the college were one. As he put it: "The funds of the college consisted entirely of private donations."

In some ways, Marshall did not care whether the first donation to Dartmouth College had come from Eleazar Wheelock, Lord Dartmouth, John Wentworth, or King George III. "It is perhaps not very important who were the donors," he stated matter-of-factly. "The probability is that the Earl of Dartmouth and the other trustees in England were, in fact, the largest contributors"—an invalid assumption. Regardless of the source of the college's original donors, Marshall said the charter put its landed property solely in the hands of its trustees, who thereafter could do with it as they pleased. "As holders of the legal title and representatives of the equitable proprietors, the trustees could sell the land, because a sale would be an exercise of the owner's right," he asserted. Moreover, college lands, once vested in the board of trustees, were off-limits to public oversight. Why? Because, according to Marshall, "No part of the title, legal or equitable, is held by the state.... The legal title is in the trustees."

The university had contended that even if the institution's first donors *were* private individuals, its educational function gave it a public mission, subject to public supervision. But here too Marshall disagreed. "That education is an object of national concern and a proper subject of legislation, all admit," he wrote. "That there may be an institution founded by government and placed entirely under its immediate control, the officers of which would be public officers, amenable exclusively to government, none will deny. But is Dartmouth College such an institution? Is education altogether in the hands of government? Does every teacher of youth become a public officer and donations for the purpose of education necessarily become public property so far that the will of the legislature, not the will of the donor, becomes the law of the donation?" Marshall thought not. In his view, Wheelock never meant his institution to serve "the public" as such but only to serve the aims determined by his chosen trustees.

Marshall conceded that, under English law, Parliament could have altered the charter of Dartmouth College before the revolution. "Had Parliament, immediately after the emanation of this charter and the execution of those conveyances which followed it, annulled the instrument so that living donors would have witnessed the disappointment of their hopes, the perfidy of the transaction would have been universally acknowledged," but it would have been legal. He admitted, moreover, that similar powers had passed to New Hampshire's state legislature in the early years after the revolution. "A repeal of this charter at any time prior to the adoption of the present Constitution of the United States would have been an extraordinary and unprecedented act of power," Marshall noted, "but one which could have been contested only by the restrictions upon the legislature to be found in the constitution of the state." No such restrictions existed.

Yet according to Marshall, whatever powers the state once enjoyed with respect to charters, it lost them in 1789 when the US Constitution gave private contracts, and prior charters, a form of retroactive federal protection they did not originally have. Some might have said that prior charters were, in fact, altered or amended by this change, but Marshall did not. He believed the Constitution's framers wanted prior charters to fall under the protection of the new Contract Clause (just as land contracts before the first Northwest Ordinance did), even though such charters would have been written with no such possibility in mind. "The contract would at that time [1789] have been deemed sacred by all," he said, because *natural law* required adherence to contractual obligations. "The obligations ... created by the charter to Dartmouth College were the same in the new as they had been in the old government," he insisted ahistorically.

But if a charter from the Crown was a "contract" within the meaning of the Constitution, then who besides the Crown were the parties to it? Who had a "beneficial interest," or "consideration," in the contract? "The counsel for the defendant have insisted that the beneficial interest is in the people of New Hampshire," commented Marshall, which meant the "beneficial interest" extended to all people in the state—a proposition the chief justice found absurd. "The particular interests of New Hampshire never entered into the mind of the donors, never constituted a motive for their donation," he asserted (convinced "the donors" were private individuals). "The propagation of the Christian religion among the savages and the dissemination of useful knowledge among the youth of the country were the avowed and sole objects of their [donations]. In these, New Hampshire would participate, but nothing particular or exclusive was intended for her."

Marshall got it wrong. Given his incomplete knowledge of the institution's history, which could have been corrected by the university's new facts, he assumed Wheelock had relocated to New Hampshire because of a promise of *private* contributions, but in fact he relocated also—indeed mainly—because of a promise of *public* land grants. Marshall said Wheelock had obtained a charter from the royal governor in order to apply private funds to purposes of higher education in general. However, a charter was granted for the application of both private and public funds for education *in New Hampshire*—or in the language of the charter itself, "for the benefit of said province." A charter was not given for the benefit of Connecticut or Massachusetts or the colonies at large, but for the specific benefit of New Hampshire and its people. Even when John

Wheelock courted a connection with Vermont, it was to make Dartmouth a public college for two states, in exchange for public aid.

Whether or not Marshall knew these facts, he believed the only way for New Hampshire to control the property of Dartmouth College was for the original charter to have reserved that power explicitly for the colonial assembly. "The charter would have been ... repealable by the legislative power ... if that power ... had been expressly reserved," he remarked. But no such "reserve clause" appeared in the original charter. "The charter contains no exemption from repeal, and no clause or word capable of being understood as an allusion to the subject." And yet, the disputed Act of 1816 had given New Hampshire's legislators authority over Dartmouth's trustees with respect to college property. "This may be for the advantage of this college in particular, and may be for the advantage of literature in general," Marshall allowed, "but it is not ... the will of the donors, and [it] is subversive of that contract, on the faith of which their property was given."

With that, Marshall said the Act of 1816 had impaired Dartmouth's charter and infringed the private rights protected under its original contract and was, therefore, unconstitutional. "The management and application of the funds of this eleemosynary institution, which are placed by the donors in the hands of trustees named in the charter and empowered to perpetuate themselves, are placed by this Act under the control of the government of the state. The will of the state is substituted for the will of the donors in every essential operation of the college." In this way, he concluded, the state had overstepped its bounds. "It results from this opinion that the Acts of the legislature of New Hampshire ... are repugnant to the Constitution of the United States and that the judgment on this special verdict ought to have been for the plaintiffs. The judgment of the state court must therefore be reversed."

Marshall's decision has attracted volumes of analysis. According to historian Joseph Burke, the core of his decision rested on "a questionable version of the facts as supplied by Webster and on a questionable application of seventeenth-century English law of corporations to a nineteenth-century New England college." Marshall said the college's funds "consisted entirely of private donations," which made it a private corporation, immune to legislative oversight. "This statement ignored the fact that the original funds went to Moor's [Indian] Charity School and overlooked the many grants to the college from the colonial and state government of New Hampshire, including the land for its campus," Burke emphasizes. "In reality, Dartmouth College, like so many of the corporations of the day, was a 'mixed' corporation, founded and operated on both private and public funds."

Burke also questions Marshall's conclusion that Dartmouth's charter was a contract. On this point, even Marshall himself apparently had doubts. "He ... confessed that contracts such as the charter of 1769 were probably not in the minds of the framers of the Constitution," yet he felt their silence on this question did not mean they sought to exclude (prior) charters from the protection of the Contract Clause. He did not say how federal jurisdiction over charters was "implied" in the Constitution nor did he say how an unenumerated power could be taken away from the states (in apparent contravention of the Tenth Amendment). "In effect," Burke notes, "he asked counsel for [the university] to do the impossible: they had to demonstrate conclusively what the framers would have [said about whether charters were contracts] if a question they had not considered had been considered."

John Major Shirley offers a similar critique of Marshall's decision. "It is as remarkable for its omissions—for the coloring with which he invested and the fog-bank in which he enveloped the facts—as it is for the skill and subtle force of statement which enabled him to transfer it to the domain of abstract reasoning," Shirley writes. Or, as William Wirt said of Marshall's jurisprudence in general: "In a bad cause, his art consisted in laying his premises so remotely from the point directly in debate, or else in terms so general and specious, that a hearer, seeing no consequence which could be drawn from them, was just as willing to admit them as not." Indeed, the chief did not even carry all his colleagues with him. Justice Gabriel Duvall dissented, and Justice Bushrod Washington, in concurrence, hoped to "prevent any implied decision by this court of any other case than the one immediately before it."

Marshall's decision was slippery on several points. For example, he said the charter was a contract "to incorporate a religious and literary institution," but which institution? Dartmouth College or Moor's Indian Charity School (with a college later grafted onto an "enlarged school")?

The charter's preamble started with a description of the school and stressed the "necessity of a legal incorporation in order to [secure] the safety and well-being of said seminary." Yet as Shirley notes, the word "seminary" referred "with the utmost distinctness, not to what, in fact, had no existence [Dartmouth College] but to Moor's Indian Charity School, which had existed for years." On the date of the charter, Moor's Indian Charity School and Dartmouth College were two separate institutions—the former with property, the latter without—but Marshall's decision "confounds the two, makes them one, and treats them as identical."

In a way, Marshall betrayed his own misrepresentation of the facts when he admitted that Wheelock sought a charter for his original school on behalf of its donors. "Dr. Wheelock, acting for himself and for those who, at his solicitation, had made contributions to his school, applied for a charter as the instrument which should enable him, and them, to perpetuate their beneficent intention," he recounted. "An artificial, immortal being was created by the crown, capable of receiving and distributing forever, according to the will of the donors, the donations which should be made to it." Syntactically, the word "it" referred to Wheelock's "school," whose American trustees were obliged to consult the English trustees for any use of funds. "The corporation," Marshall wrote, "is the assignee of their rights, stands in their place, and distributes their bounty as they would themselves have distributed it, had they been immortal," with the word "their" a reference to the *school's* donors—because, in 1769, the college had received no donations whatsoever.

When the charter was proffered, the college had no donors and no donations. All the resources Wheelock had raised to date were for his Indian Charity School. The resources conferred on the college were given later, with the Landaff grant: the first college donation conveyed by the colonial governor on behalf of the Crown for the benefit of the public. Marshall wrote in his decision that "the funds of the college consisted entirely of private donations," but the initial Landaff grant was public. Indeed, when it was found in 1789 that Wentworth had appropriated private land on the mistaken assumption that it was public, the New Hampshire legislature replaced the original grant with a new one.

Legally, observes Shirley, the fact that Wentworth granted the Landaff township on behalf of the Crown made the corporation that received it a public corporation. "If the promise made by the governor is to be treated as made by the crown, [then] it would be a royal foundation, and Marshall concedes in his opinion that the revolution put the state in the place of the crown and Parliament, and this would make the state the visitor." In fact, Shirley notes, "If the proviso had been written into the charter that Parliament . . . might alter, amend, or repeal that charter at their pleasure, this proviso would have had . . . binding force." But the reason this provision was not written into the document in 1769 was that it was simply *assumed* that Parliament had the power to amend charters (as the Massachusetts Government Act, five years later, clearly demonstrated). "So far as the law of Great Britain was concerned," Shirley affirms, "such a clause would have been waste paper."

According to Marshall, the Crown—via the charter—had contracted away its right to alter the governance of the college, but could the Crown actually enter such a contract? Legal scholar Liam Seamus O'Melinn is doubtful, for the simple reason that royal charters were granted on the basis of a (royal) "concession" theory—not a (republican) "contract" theory of corporations. The Crown was not just a mere individual who bargained away private rights. On the contrary, "George III, one of the parties to the original Dartmouth 'contract,' was still alive in 1819, and had he been asked—and had he not been blind, deaf, and insane by this time—he would have denied vehemently that, by issuing the Dartmouth charter, he entered into any 'contract' [that abdicated his rights of visitation through his courts of chancery]." A king granted charters over which he retained absolute power; he did not enter contracts in which he abandoned legal, or visitatorial, authority.

What, indeed, had the king gotten from this "contract" if he were considered an individual party to it? What benefit, or "consideration"? None. "Where is the consideration?" O'Melinn asks. "According to Marshall, the consideration was the public benefit that would result from performance of the corporation's duties." But this view would render the people of New Hampshire, not the college trustees, the key party to the king's contract—an interpretation directly at odds with the one Marshall (and the college lawyers) advanced. Marshall wanted to make the charter a three-pronged contract between Wheelock, the Crown, and the college trustees, with none representing the public, but the idea of a royal "contract" for Dartmouth College made sense only if the king bargained on behalf of the public (his subjects), because a king never bargained as a mere individual.

As far as Marshall was concerned, the charter was a "contract made on a valuable consideration . . . for the security and disposition of property . . . on the faith of which real and personal estate" was "conveyed to the corporation." As historian Bruce Campbell remarks, however, "The most difficult problem in the case—the one, according to Marshall, 'on which more doubt has been entertained than on all that have been discussed'—was raised by the fact that the college trustees *alone* complained of the New Hampshire acts, yet they had no [individual] beneficial interest to be protected," because they were neither donors themselves nor designated as "visitors" by the original donor, the Crown. How then could the charter be a contract with valid "considerations" among each party? In essence, Marshall answered that George III entered a contract that shifted his absolute power as sovereign onto a merely local board of trustees who, as private individuals, received all the king's governance rights over the college . . . forever.

What led Marshall to decide the *Dartmouth* case the way he did? It was obvious that he did not want to dissolve all prerevolutionary charters or nullify all prerevolutionary contracts—a move that would carry such vast social, political, and commercial implications that it could be considered only with extreme legal care. Yet if prerevolutionary charters and contracts were to be protected, then it would have seemed that an essential feature of their creation—a basic right of public oversight—also would have to be preserved. Marshall appeared to want it both ways: he wanted to protect a prerevolutionary charter but preclude any prospect of public supervision. To some, the fact that Dartmouth's charter of 1769 named trustees but not "visitors" meant the Crown's ultimate authority over the corporation (via his royal governor) was implied. Marshall, however, gave all visitatorial rights exclusively to a board of twelve private individuals.

―――――

Marshall's decision stood in for a majority opinion, but three other justices offered concurrences. Justice William Johnson's concurrence, unwritten, fit a context in which Marshall often spoke for the court even when it was unclear whether his colleagues agreed with him. Early courts had followed an English practice where each judge gave an opinion "whenever he thought there was occasion for it," but this practice changed under Marshall, who increasingly spoke for all. In the Marshall court, historian Theodore White notes, it was common practice to make one judge (typically Marshall himself) the agent of the court: the one who assigned cases, wrote opinions, and read them in court, even when the opinions had the support of just three—or sometimes only two—judges if the rest were silent.

To ensure their views were heard, Johnson's colleagues Bushrod Washington and Joseph Story published their concurrences. Washington, the grandson of George Washington, offered a full analysis of the Contract Clause. "What is a contract?" he asked as he cited John Powell's two-volume *Essay upon the Law of Contracts and Agreements* (1790): "It may be defined to be a transaction between two or more persons in which each party comes under an obligation to the other and each reciprocally acquires a right to whatever is promised by the other. Under this definition,... the ingredients requisite to form a contract are parties, consent, and an obligation to be created or dissolved; these must all concur, because the regular effect of all contracts is on one side to acquire and on the other to part with some property or rights."

Washington agreed with Marshall that, in the case of Dartmouth College, the Crown had contracted with the individual college trustees to grant all the rights, privileges, and franchises of a charter in exchange for a promise to devote the college's property to higher education. "*King v. Pasmore* says that a grant of incorporation is a compact between the crown and a number of persons, the latter of whom undertake, in consideration of the privileges bestowed, to exert themselves for the good government of the place," Washington wrote. And once granted, the incorporation was irrevocable without the individual trustees' consent, unless the court found them derelict in their duties (as the court did in *King v. Pasmore*). "The charter of a corporation . . . may be forfeited through negligence or abuse of its franchises," Washington held, "in which case, the law judges that the body politic has broken the condition upon which it was incorporated, and thereupon the corporation is void."

In his concurrence, Washington said the charter of Dartmouth

College, granted by the Crown, was a contract between Wheelock and his American trustees, whose rights (absent proof of negligence) the Act of 1816 had unconstitutionally impaired. "Does not every alteration of a contract, however unimportant... impair its obligation?" the justice asked. "If the assent of all the parties to be bound by a contract be of its essence, [then] how is it possible that a new contract, substituted for, or engrafted on, another, without such assent, should not violate the old charter?" It never occurred to Washington that Dartmouth's charter was *itself* a new contract "engrafted" onto the agreements of the school's original English donors; rather, he said the college's (American) trustees were entirely within their rights to reject the new charter proffered by New Hampshire's legislature (even if Lord Kenyon, in *King v. Pasmore*, said a corporation was not free to reject a new charter offered by the Crown).

Justice Story, like Justice Washington, began his concurrence with the English law of corporations. He distinguished between civil (public) and charitable (private) corporations and, like Marshall, observed that even banks or hospitals could be public if wholly owned and operated by the state. "For instance, a bank created by the government for its own uses, whose stock is exclusively owned by the government is, in the strictest sense, a public corporation," he acknowledged. "But a bank whose stock is owned by private persons is a private corporation, even though it is erected by the government and its objects and operations partake of a public nature. The same doctrine may be affirmed of insurance, canal, bridge, and turnpike companies. In all these cases, the uses may in a certain sense be called public, but the corporations are private."

Story insisted that Dartmouth's (private) trustees were also its (public) visitors—despite the charter's silence on this point. "This visitatorial power... stands upon the maxim that he who gives his property has a right to regulate it in future," Story asserted, sure that Dartmouth's first donor was Eleazar Wheelock himself. "As founder, Dr. Wheelock and his heirs would have been completely clothed with the visitatorial power, but the whole government and control as well of the officers as of the revenues of the college being, with his consent, assigned to the trustees in their corporate character, the visitatorial power, which is included in this authority, rightfully devolved on the trustees," subject only to judicial review. "As visitors," he wrote, "their discretion was limited only by the charter and liable to no [external] supervision or control, at least unless it was fraudulently misapplied."

Having asserted the visitatorial power of trustees (a misapplication of English law, which said that corporate trustees could not also be visitors), Story asked whether the individual trustees of Dartmouth College had any personal stake ("beneficial interest" or "consideration") in the contract that allegedly empowered them. He answered that each trustee had an interest not only in the property but also in the privileges, or "franchises," attendant to membership in the corporation itself—privileges granted by the Crown that were thereafter irrevocable without their consent. "A grant of franchises is not, in point of principle, distinguishable from a grant of any other property," he argued. When the Crown gave Wheelock a charter, "There was an implied contract springing up and founded on a valuable consideration that the crown would not revoke or alter the charter or change its administration without the consent of the corporation."

According to Story, the charter signified an "implied contract" between Wheelock, the Crown, and the college trustees to "relinquish" the funds of Moor's Indian Charity School to a college:

> Is there not an implied contract by Dr. Wheelock, if a charter is granted, that the school shall be removed from his estate [in Connecticut] to New Hampshire? And that he will relinquish all control over the funds collected (and to be collected) in England under his auspices and subject to his authority? And that he will yield up the management of his charity school to the trustees of the college? [And] that he will relinquish all offers made by other American governments [in other words, other colonies] and devote his patronage to this institution?

Story thought so. "It will scarcely be denied that he gave up the right ... to maintain the charity school already established on his own estate and that funds collected for its use ... were yielded up by him as an endowment of the college."

While these sentences contained numerous misstatements, to Story they summarized the "implied contract" between Wheelock, the Crown, and the college trustees. Some had suggested the Crown was unable to contract with the college—not only because the sovereign never submitted to contracts with coequal parties but also because no "college" *existed* when the contract was made and thus could not be a party to it. Story, however, set this question aside on grounds that, in every case, a corporation had to be created before it could accept donations. "From the nature of things, the artificial person called a corporation must be created before it can be capable of taking anything," he argued, convinced that Dartmouth College (as opposed to Moor's Indian Charity School) had to be chartered *before* its designated trustees could receive any grants of property on its behalf.

But as historian Charles O'Kelley notes, the idea of a "contract" with an entity that did not yet exist was "tricky." While traditional jurisprudence might have said the king contracted with extant donors in order to establish corporations with certain rights and franchises, Story implied that George III contracted with an entirely new set of trustees in order to protect *future* donors' rights and franchises. In effect, he inverted the sequence of the corporation and its donations to suggest that corporate franchises had to be put in place before a corporation was able to receive any donations. As he put it (quasi-metaphysically), "When ... the corporation is to be brought into existence by some future acts [donations] of the corporators, the franchises remain in abeyance until such acts are done, and when the corporation is brought into life [by subsequent donations], the franchises instantaneously attach to it." It was the "grant of these franchises," not any specific donation, that constituted the contract—and *simultaneously* the creation of the corporation itself.

It was clear that Story did not want Dartmouth College—or any other corporation—to be subjected to external legislative supervision, which he identified with unhelpful partisanship. (If anything, he thought "public" legislators were even more likely than "private" trustees to impose politicized interests on a college.) To subject a corporation to public supervision would subject its property to popular seizure, he felt, and in an era when Federalists had lost to Republicans in state after state, this prospect struck fear into property holders like himself. Among those whose assets would be at risk were colleges, churches, and countless other corporations under Federalist control. These assets could be secure only if the legally irrevocable (and politically invulnerable) privileges of contract were upheld. Aside from all the finer legal points at stake in the *Dartmouth* case, for Story the protection of property was fundamental.

Story, like his colleagues, devoted significant attention to matters of "property" as the basis of contract law, but ultimately what set his opinion apart was his conclusion that, for contracts in the form of charters, what mattered was not the property conveyed so much as the corporate privileges, or franchises, bestowed on trustees vested with the governance of that property. "The franchises granted by the charter were vested in the trustees," he wrote; they were "the private demesnes [real property] of the corporation, held by it *not*, as the argument supposes, for the use and benefit of the people of New Hampshire, but, as the charter itself declares, 'for the use of Dartmouth College.'" Not given "for the benefit of said province" (as the charter also stated), these privileges, Story argued, were for the benefit of *the college trustees*. In his words, they were "to be devoted to the promotion of piety and learning not at large but in that college and in the establishments connected with it.... And the objects of it were left solely to the trustees."

Story understood why some had said that corporate privileges, or franchises, should not be included within the purview of contracts, typically limited to conveyances of material property. Still, he said (immaterial) corporate rights, or powers, had a special constitutional value, because they represented the legal authority to govern the use of corporate property. "The truth," he asserted, "is that all incorporeal hereditaments, whether they be immunities, dignities, offices, franchises, or other rights, are deemed valuable in law," even if they were not material goods that were traded, exchanged, or bargained in the market. Such were the privileges of corporate governance. "The right to be a freeman of a corporation is a valuable temporal right. It is a right of voting and acting in corporate concerns." A contract for the exercise of corporate rights was no less valuable than "a contract for the use and dominion of property."

Even if Dartmouth College's original property had come from the public—and not from private individuals—Story held that New Hampshire's Act of 1816 had impaired the incorporated privileges of the college trustees. "In my judgment, it is perfectly clear that any act of a legislature, which takes away any powers or franchises vested by its charter in a private corporation or its corporate officers, or which restrains or controls the legitimate exercise of them, or transfers them to other persons without its assent, is a violation of the obligations of that charter," he wrote. "If the legislature means to claim such an authority, it must be reserved in the grant [of the charter itself]. The charter of Dartmouth College contains no such reservation, and I am therefore bound to declare that the acts of the legislature of New Hampshire now in question do impair the obligations of that charter and are consequently unconstitutional and void."

Story's concurrence was known for its discussion of "reserve" clauses as the only way for a state to restrict the privileges of private corporations. Such clauses were not limited to charters for colleges; they had become increasingly common with the rise of "general incorporation laws." As early as 1789, for example, Connecticut had included a reserve clause in a charter for a business corporation, and by 1819 it had included such clauses in charters for at least forty businesses. All bank charters in Connecticut between 1796 and 1819 had reserve clauses, and every charter for an insurance firm after 1797 included such a clause. Massachusetts and New Hampshire followed suit. "Massachusetts was the first to reserve an unconditional power to regulate [financial] charges by a business corporation," Bruce Campbell notes. "In New Hampshire, most manufacturing company charters issued after 1808 reserved a legislative right to alter or . . . repeal [them]."

In the final lines of his concurrence, Story hinted that any state could limit the protections enjoyed by future corporations with "reserve clauses that gave the legislature the power to revise or even repeal their charters." An example was contained in the constitution of Story's own state. Massachusetts's constitution of 1780 gave the legislature the power to oversee the government of Harvard College in order to ensure its fidelity to its public mission. As historian R. N. Denham Jr. explains, "When the Constitution of Massachusetts was adopted, the [colonial] grant of 1636, under which Harvard was incorporated, was ratified and confirmed but with a right reserved to the legislature to [make] such alterations in the government of the [college] as might be done by the legislature of the [commonwealth]."

A similar right was reserved by Massachusetts's legislature in the charters of Williams and Bowdoin Colleges, incorporated in 1793 and

1794, respectively, "wherein the legislature reserved the power to 'alter, limit, annul, or restrain any powers vested by [these charters].'" The state had not hesitated to use this power. As recently as 1818, Phillips Academy in Andover, Massachusetts, had asked Williams College to join a merged institution to be located in Amherst, a proposal the college trustees welcomed. But objections arose on grounds that Williams's original charter had specified the college's location in Williamstown, so Massachusetts exercised its reserve powers and refused to charter the joint institution. Williams, the legislature argued, was not allowed to violate the explicit terms of its own charter. (Instead, a separate institution, Amherst College, was chartered a few years later.)

In some cases, legislatures required colleges to amend their charters with reserve clauses in order to become eligible for state aid. "For example," Campbell notes, "when Union College, chartered by the New York regents in 1795 with a self-perpetuating board of trustees of twenty-four individuals, sought permission [in 1804] to raise funds through a public lottery, the legislature conditioned its grant of [permission] on the college's acceptance of a charter amendment reducing the size of the board of trustees, adding a substantial number of state officials to the board, and allowing the [public] Regents to fill vacancies." Some felt the state had coerced the college into charter revisions that diminished its powers of self-government. Others said Union freely consented to revisions in exchange for aid. Story recognized the legality of these actions, but he warned—presciently—that legislative control was not always good for college governance.

CHAPTER 13

"New Facts"... and New Foundations

Story, whose concurrence had relied heavily on Webster's framework as well as college lawyer Jeremiah Mason's initial arguments before New Hampshire's Superior Court, expressed his gratitude to both. "I am exceedingly pleased with your argument in the Dartmouth College case," Story told Mason in a thank-you note. "I always had a desire that the question should be put upon the broad basis you have stated, and it was a matter of regret that we were so stinted in jurisdiction in the Supreme Court that half the argument could not be met and enforced." University lawyers George Sullivan and Ichabod Bartlett, meanwhile, were shocked by the court's decision. In particular, noted Webster, "The university people were dumbfounded—thunderstruck—when they found that Story had gone against them."

News of the court's written opinions elicited a mix of reactions. At the college, trustees, faculty, and students celebrated. (One account said they were "ecstatic.") "The students, most of whom had remained loyal to the college, fired a cannon in jubilation," historian John Whitehead recounts, though Webster "urged moderation" and told his colleagues he wanted "no flourish of trumpets." Aware that his related property cases were still unresolved in Story's circuit, Webster "did not want to alienate public opinion from the struggling college." And he was right to be concerned, because Republicans who had supported the university received the high court's decision with dismay. Republican editor Isaac Hill at the *New Hampshire Patriot* could hardly contain his disappointment.

Just two weeks after the court's decision, Hill reminded his readers that Justice Todd, a university ally, had been absent; that Justice Duvall had dissented; and that, during the eleven months between oral arguments and the final decision, Justice Story had been elected to Harvard's board of overseers, a possible conflict of interest. He added that Justices Livingston and Johnson had accepted honorary doctorates from

Harvard and Princeton, respectively, and that both college lawyers, Daniel Webster and Joseph Hopkinson, had accepted honorary degrees from Princeton—the upshot of which proved to Hill that Federalist colleges had used their influence to buy off the court. The majority, he concluded, had not reasoned "on the merits of justice in the case" but had "travel[ed] out the record" to reach a decision in favor of private interests.

Hill was not alone in his anger. William Allen, president of the university, received a letter from Dr. Cyrus Perkins, who had listened to Marshall read his decision from the bench. Perkins told Allen he detected a "most strange arrangement in this business—some monkery which perfectly astonishes all our friends here." He noted that Marshall's hasty decision and refusal to let Pinkney speak had meant the justices "could not be furnished with the necessary facts to put down the impudent falsehoods which were palmed on the court." The result, Hill told his readers, was that all the "funds of Dartmouth College, contributed by the people of New Hampshire," were now deemed the private property of the college trustees, "who had never contributed a cent to the institution." Hill urged the state, in response, to tax Dartmouth's assets "to the full extent of the law."

Hill's position had the support of Governor Plumer, who agreed that Marshall's decision had rendered "private" what previously had been "public" (not only the funds of the college but also education itself). "Marshall's reasoning appeared to the governor as another illustration of the court's alarming tendency toward restricting the powers of the states, and the haste in which the court disposed of the case only confirmed this suspicion," historian Francis Stites notes. Why had the justices been in such a hurry to conclude the case, especially since, a year earlier, they had postponed a decision to give the university a chance to gather "new facts"—facts the court never heard? Hill suspected a conspiracy (he called it a "combination") to strengthen private interests and weaken the power of legislatures to oversee colleges—and other corporations—everywhere.

In the meantime, Joseph Hopkinson wrote victoriously to President Brown at the college. "Our triumph ... has been complete," he announced. "Five judges ... concur not only in a decision in our favor but in placing it upon principles broad and deep, and which secure corporations of this description from legislative despotism and party violence for the future. The court goes all lengths with us, and whatever trouble these gentlemen may give us in the future in their great and pious zeal for the interests of learning, they cannot shake those principles which must and will restore Dartmouth College to its true and original owners." He added: "I would have an inscription [engraved] over the door of your building: 'Founded by Eleazar Wheelock, Refounded by Daniel Webster.'" Given the strategies Webster used to reframe the facts about the college's "founder" and "first donor," it was an epigraph with more than one meaning.

Hopkinson wished Brown "much happiness and success in promoting the usefulness of the institution and proving to the world that it has changed hands." Indeed, it had. As historian John Major Shirley recounts, "The [college] trustees did not wait for the [published] judgment in their favor but, as soon as the news of judge Marshall's opinion reached them, made the necessary arrangements, and, on February 8, 1819, took possession, by virtue of the law of the strongest, of the college buildings, etc., which, up to that time, had been held by president Allen and occupied by the officers and students of the university." Although several related cases were still in play in Story's circuit—at Webster's instigation—the college trustees declared the campus their rightful property and moved their supporters, more than one hundred undergraduates, back onto campus.

The handover did not go smoothly. It started when President Brown notified Allen that "the government of the college, after consulting gentlemen of legal information, have concluded to occupy the chapel tomorrow morning." The next day, Allen wrote in a public announcement, "The chapel, which was under lock and key, was entered and wrested from the university by force; in like manner have been taken the tutors' rooms and other apartments." He noted that such actions were premature when Story's circuit still had the college's own cases before it. "A suit against me, by way of a writ of ejectment, has been brought by Charles Marsh, Esq., of Vermont (the lessee of this very property)," he observed, and this suit was "pending in the Court of the United States" even as the college trustees pushed their way into the chapel pews.

Shortly after this exchange, Webster negotiated with the widow of secretary-treasurer William H. Woodward (who had died in August 1818) to return the college seal and records. He then pressed Allen for the return of the institution's library books and laboratory equipment, along with the rest of its campus structures. "I am happy to hear that Mrs. Woodward is so well advised as to be disposed to surrender the property," he assured Brown. "I should be equally happy to see the president of the university wise enough to deliver the books and apparatus and retire from the contest without giving anybody further trouble." He added: "The university folks should understand, very distinctly, that we are resolved to bring this controversy to an immediate end." Allen, who still hoped for a chance to present the university's new facts in court, was stunned.

So was New Hampshire congressman and university supporter William Hale, who looked for a way forward. "I do not yet despair," he wrote to Governor Plumer on March 29, 1819. "Upon the facts before it the court decided the old charter was a *contract* with the individuals who made the donations. If it should be found that the state made all—or nearly all—of the donations, some new foundation for such an opinion must be discovered. In my opinion, the court would go far to find it. What monstrous strides they made at the last term to restrict the power[s] of the states!" Plumer concurred. As historian Frederick Chase notes, he saw in the decision "the assumption of jurisdiction on the part of the court warranted neither by the Constitution nor state law and tending toward a consolidation [suppression] of the states. He believed [the decision] soon would be reversed."

The lawyers for Dartmouth University had one more chance to present their new facts to show that Dartmouth's original donations had come from the state. This chance arose when Story returned to his circuit in Portsmouth, New Hampshire, to hear the additional cases Webster had orchestrated with respect to interstate disputes over college property. Pinkney and Wirt said that "no final judgment should be entered until all the causes were fully heard," but with further arguments slated for May 1, Webster told President Brown he would do everything he could to block the new facts and, if possible, abandon his other cases. "In truth, I did not want a second argument," he confided to Jeremiah Smith—and he believed Story, given his robust concurrence, was on his side. "If I do not misjudge, we shall have no difficulty in the circuit court."

To have time for the collection of documents, the university asked Story for a six-month continuance. "Our papers were left at Washington," President Allen informed the college lawyers. "It is therefore to be hoped that you will not insist upon a trial until October," when all the new facts could be presented. College trustee Charles Marsh, however, said a delay was unacceptable: the college had won, and the university's new facts could not change that outcome. "Can you believe that the nature of a charter of fifty years' standing is now to be determined by something *ab extra*, which might have happened about the time it [was] issued, the evidence of which rests in loose, unrecorded, and indefinite narratives—letters or pamphlets to which the charter does not even refer," Marsh asked. "If I am correct in this, your papers would be of no consequence."

Marsh was right. That fall, after Story had seen the university's new facts, he decided they were irrelevant and dismissed the cases (as Webster himself wanted). He thereby ended the university's last hope for legal vindication. The Act of 1816 was officially rejected; the control of the institution's property, including its buildings and books, reverted back to the college trustees; and Dartmouth University was relegated to institutional oblivion. As Shirley notes: "Story's decision in the college causes, in effect, annihilated Dartmouth University; handed over the munificent bequest which John Wheelock had made to it to [Princeton Theological Seminary]; deposed William Allen, the president; and drove him from Hanover." The case was over, and the university—together with the state legislature as the legal representative of the people of New Hampshire and their concerns for public higher education—had lost.

Story's final disposition of the case meant that Dartmouth College was a private corporation, with both property and privileges vested in an independent board of trustees. Yet ironically, the board had very little property to oversee. Even if the college now controlled the lands granted by the state, its liquid assets did not equal its debts, and its legal costs alone nearly outstripped its annual income: $100 for Jeremiah Mason, $150 for Jeremiah Smith, and $1,000 for Daniel Webster and Joseph Hopkinson—liabilities that were modest in comparison with other debts. "The shrinkage of tuition fees from [the] diminution of students and the loss of rents of rooms and of lands were by far the most tangible [financial difficulties that faced the college]," Frederick Chase observes. In Wheelock, Vermont, for example, "No rents at all were collected for more than four years," and the college's tenants were "not easily brought again to payment."

With the college's total debts calculated at precisely $8,771.50, President Brown sought compensation from... the state. Huge costs had been incurred by the recent litigation, he wrote on June 14, 1819. "For a great part of these damages and expenditures, your memorialists deem themselves to have a good and valid claim against individuals," Brown explained, "but it would better accord with their wishes and, as they trust, with the honor and dignity of the state, that other provision should be made for remuneration," namely, "a committee to ascertain the amount of said damages and expenditures" to be paid by "the treasurer of the state, in favor of the treasurer of said college." Just as the legislature had loaned the university $4,000 to cover its legal costs after the superior court decision in 1818, so now the college wanted the state to cover its costs, too.

Before the finances of the college and university could be resolved, President Brown died and was replaced by Reverend Bennett Tyler, who promptly renewed his predecessor's requests for public assistance. John Church, a trustee, wrote to secretary-treasurer Mills Olcott: "I have no inclination to put the college under the control of the legislature... but if we can do anything to conciliate the government and secure the patronage of the state, I view it as important that it should be done." The state, however, rebuffed the college in favor of the university. Despite the effects of the Panic of 1819, which devastated New Hampshire's economy, it promised to compensate the university's suddenly jobless professors (although in most cases its payments came too late: James Dean left for a position at the University of Vermont; Nathaniel Carter became editor of the *New York Statesman*; and Thomas Searle died and left a family "in needy circumstances").

After the university closed, some of its former students transferred into other institutions, notably Union College, recognized for its modern curriculum (and modest admission standards). Others went to Bowdoin College, which had followed a Dartmouth-like path after the Republican legislature in Maine said the college should not receive public aid unless it accepted public oversight. This issue had become heated after 1807, when the—officially nonsectarian—college appointed Federalist-Congregationalist president Jesse Appleton, who (like Roswell Shurtleff at Dartmouth) led a series of revivals at the college. As conservative Federalist-Congregationalists deepened their control over Bowdoin's campus in Brunswick, liberal Republican-Dissenters decamped to Waterville, fifty miles north, to start a rival institution: the Maine Literary and Theological Institution (later Colby College).

Chartered in 1813 and opened in 1817 with a freer religious ethos, the new institution hoped for resources from its parent state, Massachusetts, which had funded both Harvard and Bowdoin through a tax on bank deposits. Republican-Dissenters in Maine had watched admiringly in 1816 as their copartisans in New Hampshire took Dartmouth College away from a Federalist-Congregationalist board and supported the new Dartmouth University with public funds. They wanted similar public aid for Waterville's "competing institution," but this idea was rejected by Federalist-Congregationalists on grounds that Massachusetts's bank tax already funded Maine's other college. So, even as Republican-Dissenters pushed for more religious pluralism, Federalist-Congregationalists protected Massachusetts's (and Maine's) "established church" and colleges, both subsidized by tax revenues.

This debate resurfaced three years later, however, when Maine became an independent state. As part of the deliberations over the Missouri Compromise—in which Missouri was opened to slavery and Maine became a (new) free state—the matter of Maine's separation from Massachusetts raised questions about the governance of both states' colleges. Massachusetts's constitution gave its legislature visitatorial rights over Harvard, Williams, and Bowdoin, but the Act of Separation, drafted in June 1819, sidelined public visitation and said Bowdoin's "president, trustees, and overseers" (all dominated by Federalist-Congregationalists) would henceforth "enjoy their powers and privileges in all respects, so the same shall not be subject to be altered, limited, annulled, or restricted except by judicial process, according to law." In other words, after separation, Massachusetts's public visitatorial rights would end, and Maine would not acquire them.

Four months later, when Maine drafted its new state constitution, Federalists and Republicans locked horns over whether Bowdoin should be subject to public visitation—and be eligible for public aid. Federalists wanted public aid to flow to all colleges in the new state, but Republicans said aid should flow only to colleges that submitted to legislative control. Aware of the *Dartmouth* case, one Republican legislator asked why public resources should go to colleges governed by private trustees under inalterable charters granted by another state. Why should Maine taxpayers fund Bowdoin, he asked, when the "management of our literary institutions is exclusively in the hands of individuals whose views may be adverse to the best interests of the government, and over whose conduct the state shall have no controlling power?"

Republicans in Maine refused to accept *Dartmouth*'s implication that a college founded by a state could later become immune to state oversight. As one Republican put it, *Dartmouth* was a bridge too far: "It goes to set up a literary institution beyond the reach or control of the laws of the state," he observed. "Let gentlemen be warned by this dangerous result. Let them never tolerate any power but that of the United States, within their jurisdiction, that shall be beyond their control. The time may come when creeds may be established, sects created, and parties built up, dangerous and destructive to the safety of the state and the liberties of the people.... Against such evils we ought to erect an effectual barrier." And so they did. By a vote of 151 to 18, the Republican majority in Maine said Bowdoin could not receive public aid unless the legislature had authority to "alter, limit, or restrain any of the powers vested" in the college's trustees.

Dartmouth clearly shaped Maine's deliberations. "By the highest judicial tribunal in our country," one Republican observed, "it is decided that literary institutions are independent of the government of the state in which they are situated, and which has founded and endowed them, and unless this convention engrafts onto the [state] constitution a provision to the contrary, it will be of binding force here." Delegates to Maine's constitutional convention thus inserted a "reserve clause" to ensure that "no donation, grant, or endowment shall at any time be made by the legislature to any literary institution established, or which may hereafter be established, unless at the time of making such endowment, the governor and council shall have the power of revising and negating the doings of the trustees and government of such institution, the selection of its officers, and the management of its funds."

Yet the chief obstacle to Maine's reserve clause was not the state's new constitution but the Act of Separation, which gave *Massachusetts's* legislature (dominated by Federalists) a veto over any law that affected colleges originally founded under Massachusetts's jurisdiction. Republicans in Maine resented this veto, which implied that Maine could not govern its own educational affairs. "Are we too ignorant even to be made sensible of the importance of knowledge?" one Republican asked. Indeed, so intense was the debate over Massachusetts's political and educational "shackles" that Bowdoin president Jesse Appleton—an early Dartmouth College graduate and close friend of Federalist-Congregationalists in Massachusetts—was overwhelmed by stress, contracted tuberculosis, and died. His successor, recruited by Republicans in Maine, was none other than William Allen, former president of the "public" Dartmouth University.

Allen was an obvious choice for those who had sought more public control over Maine's colleges. As historian Mark Douglass McGarvie explains, Allen believed "college and state shared an 'essential unity of... interests.'" He immediately launched a campaign to grant Bowdoin a new "public" charter so it could benefit from public aid. The college accepted. "By 1820," McGarvie notes, "the board of the college voted to accept legislative restructuring and petitioned the state for continuation of a $3,000 annual grant raised from [Massachusetts's] bank tax, 'and for such other donations as the legislature in its wisdom may be disposed to make.'" The legislature, in turn, pledged annual payments to Bowdoin for the next seven years, conditional on its assent to a new charter that guaranteed public oversight—a condition Allen welcomed.

Meanwhile, as Republicans in Maine took steps to make Bowdoin a "public" university, Federalists in Massachusetts took steps to *prevent* any such move at Harvard, an institution long subject to partisan dispute. For years, Federalists had treated Harvard as a quasi-public college, with ample public aid (most recently, the lion's share of the state's tax on banks). They granted this aid on the assumption that Federalists would retain a legislative majority (even if they knew from past experience that Federalist power was not permanent). Only after *Dartmouth*, when their grip on power again ebbed, did they look for ways to shift Harvard from a "public" to a "private" college. In 1820—after the Maine-Missouri deal and Massachusetts's need to revise its own constitution to accommodate the Act of Separation—the Federalists sought a way to make this shift official. The result altered the governance of Harvard ... and Bowdoin.

As early as January 1820, the Harvard-based *North American Review* had summarized a general shift toward "private" college governance after the *Dartmouth* case. "Perhaps no judicial proceedings in this country ever involved more important consequences or excited a deeper interest in the public mind than the case of Dartmouth College," the editors remarked. The "great question" in the case was, simply, "whether ... the corporation of Dartmouth College was public or private," and the answer was definitive: Dartmouth was private. "Within the last twenty years, we have seen the judicial department ... to be the strongest barrier against the tide of popular commotions or the usurping spirit of popular assemblies," the editors concluded. *Dartmouth* had proven that charters of incorporation, construed as constitutionally protected contracts, would be colleges' strongest protection against popular legislative intervention.

Significantly, the *North American Review* printed this summary of the *Dartmouth* case right before a review of Thomas Jefferson's so-called Rockfish Gap Report, written to secure public aid for his planned University of Virginia. From one point of view, it might have seemed that New Hampshire and Virginia had taken radically different approaches to this era's political economy of higher education: New Hampshire ended up with less state responsibility for higher education while Virginia sought more. Yet, from a different point of view, these cases were remarkably similar. In both, Republican majorities sought more public control over colleges (as well as churches) while Federalist minorities asked the courts to protect allegedly private colleges (and churches) from the encroachments of "the people"—often called "the mob."

Put simply, Republicans wanted a publicly managed system of secular higher education in which new state universities could benefit from state aid; Federalists wanted a privately managed system in which (sectarian) colleges, protected by corporate rights, would be guarded from state control. In a sense, *Dartmouth* served both interests. As historian Mark Douglass McGarvie has argued, "In delineating 'public' and 'private' spheres, the court effectively cut off public support for private religious education ... and encouraged [instead] the founding of [publicly supported] state schools with a secular curriculum. This was the Jeffersonians' goal all along, with no better model than that of the University of Virginia," an institution that welcomed public supervision in exchange for public support.

The ascendant political economy of higher education hinged on the idea that private colleges, as private corporations, had a constitutional right to govern themselves without state interference. As the Federalists often put it, perpetually appointed private trustees had a "right" to decide how institutions of higher education should operate. According to historian Gordon Wood, "Shrewder Federalists saw how they might be better off appropriating the 'rights talk' of their Jeffersonian opponents and using it ... against the popular power of state legislatures"—and they looked to federal courts for protection of private (corporate) rights. "In the United States, the laws of the land were not just what popular legislatures commanded," Wood notes; rather, "Many Federalists now argued that the laws of the land concerning individual rights belonged exclusively to the courts."

The courts' role in the sanctification of "corporate rights" had far-reaching consequences, for it recast a core assumption regarding the relationship between elected legislatures and public interests. *Dartmouth* seemed to suggest that elected majorities did not represent public interests as much as they ran a risk of violating private rights, and thus they needed to be checked by the courts. If anything, McGarvie notes, *Dartmouth* aligned with the market logic of this period to hint that "public interests were best fulfilled by the independent actions of private citizens," which, in turn, had to be guarded by the constitutional protection of contracts and upheld by federal courts. Like the contemporary push for general incorporation laws among banks and businesses (many of them protoindustrial firms), "The emerging law of contract, recognizing individuals as bound solely by their [private] commitments as expressions of their own wills, embodied this doctrine."

At its base, the law of contract was supposed to protect individual rights (notably property rights) from majority whim. "Large numbers of influential people, including John Marshall, were becoming increasingly disillusioned with democratic legislative politics in these years," Wood comments. Marshall was disgusted with a political culture in which "democracy and individual rights, public and private liberty, seemed at odds with one another." In his mind, "Since... representative legislatures were the source of the problem, not the solution, some other bulwark for individual rights would have to be found. This meant crucial issues of individual rights had to be taken out of the hands of popular legislatures and placed in the hands of some other institution, which turned out to be the courts."

Ironically, notes Wood, an early call for judicial protection from legislative "despotism" had come from *New Hampshire*, where in 1786, William Plumer had petitioned for the incorporation of minority religious sects and said judges were "the only body of men who [could] have an effective check upon a numerous assembly.'" Plumer asked the courts to guard private rights of conscience against legislative interference. "With the revolution, Americans had prepared the way for such a radical idea by their commitment to the right of religious freedom," Wood observes. "If formerly public ['established'] religious corporations created by the state became private entities immune from further state tampering, then why could not other formerly public corporations be treated in a like manner?" Plumer's defense of private corporate rights for dissenting churches laid the groundwork for Dartmouth's later defense of private corporate rights for colleges.

After the Congregationalists lost their status as New Hampshire's publicly supported "established" church in 1817, institutions once considered public (and subsidized by compulsory taxes) increasingly became private, funded by themselves. Moreover, with religion's disestablishment came a new conviction that, in the moral economy, as in the market economy, *private* corporations were the best way to serve *public* interests. As historian Kellen Funk notes, both colleges and churches "benefited from the legal assumption that the very existence of [private] corporations served the public good by making entrepreneurial opportunities more readily available to all" (just as early calls for the general incorporation of diverse religious sects had done). Of course, it remained to be seen whether this assumption was justified. As the editors of the *United States Law Journal* noted in 1822: "The great number of our corporate bodies, and the rapid manner in which they are increased by state legislatures, will yet render this branch of jurisprudence of [growing] importance and open a wide and fertile region of research." Indeed, it would.

CHAPTER 14

"A University ... under the Auspices and Control of the Legislature"

The idea that private colleges served public interests had been a subject of debate in 1820 when delegates to Massachusetts's constitutional convention took up the question of Harvard's governance and, specifically, whether that college, once quasi-public, should henceforth be considered private. Federalists in the state asserted that *Dartmouth* had recast colleges like Harvard as private corporations; Republicans answered that Harvard, like Bowdoin, had been subject to legislative oversight under the state constitution of 1780 and, indeed, had received annual subsidies under the state's bank tax since 1810. At the constitutional convention in 1820, Federalists became more determined than ever to detach Harvard from public control, while Republicans demanded various "alterations in the composition of Harvard's governing boards" to achieve "more legislative control" over the college's use of state resources.

As historian Harlow Walker Sheidley notes, Federalists approached the constitutional convention with four aims: (1) the autonomy of the judiciary (a strategy that "countervail[ed] majority rule, since the state bench was largely occupied by the elite of the eastern seaboard"); (2) the adoption of property requirements for seats in the senate (a strategy that "permitted the Federalist strongholds of Suffolk and Essex counties to command a third of the seats"); (3) the continuation of an "established" church, supported by state funds (a strategy that worked not only to aid Congregationalists but also to benefit "the conservatives' own Unitarian clergy"); and (4) the recognition of the corporate autonomy of Harvard (a strategy that "enabled this increasingly exclusive university to suit the needs of its elite constituency").

The conservatives' principal spokesman at the convention was Joseph Story, who labored alongside Daniel Webster to entrench Federalist power and, specifically, to establish Harvard's independence. "Story later confirmed that he acted with Webster 'in every important measure,'" including the work of a subcommittee to study Harvard governance led by state legislator and former congressman Josiah Quincy (later Harvard's president). Story claimed that his *Dartmouth* concurrence made it clear that Harvard was a "private" corporation with a right to govern itself. He was shocked by Republicans' suggestion that, precisely *because* of his concurrence, Massachusetts should consider a stronger "reserve" clause in a revised Harvard charter. When legislator George Blake said, "It was at least an open question whether the convention had 'a right to mould the government of ... [Harvard] into whatever form [it] pleased,' [Story] was horrified."

To establish Harvard's autonomy, Webster drafted a detailed *Report on the Constitutional Rights and Privileges of the Corporation of Harvard College*, which reexamined Harvard's early history to determine whether its first donor was the Massachusetts Bay Colony or, instead, private individuals. He cited Theophilus Parsons's consideration of this question from 1813 to note that, in 1636, the colony had given £400 "towards a school, or college"; that "twelve gentlemen were appointed a committee to have charge of the subject"; and that John Harvard, two years later, had "contributed liberally" to support the institution (which remained "the property of the colony"). In 1642 a public board of overseers was named, and in 1650 the college received a formal charter of incorporation from the colony, which created a board of fellows to govern the college's use of property—with the public overseers' consent.

Despite this history of public origins, Webster insisted the charter of 1650 was Harvard's foundational document, because it was the one that had established an independent corporation. "By these charters," Webster said, Harvard became a private corporation, since "all the property appertaining to the college became vested in the president and fellows for the purposes of the institution." Still, the governance structure in the charter of 1650 was complex. "All the powers of government—the whole management and control of the property and funds, and direction and instruction of the students—appear by this charter to have been conferred on the president and fellows," Webster noted, "with a provision, however, that the acts of the corporation should not take effect until the ... assent of the [public] overseers was obtained."

Harvard's charter was revised in 1657 to put the board of fellows ("the corporation") in charge of day-to-day affairs, but it still gave the public overseers the power to veto the corporation's actions. This structure was confirmed in 1691 and then again in 1780, after the revolution, when Massachusetts's new constitution said Harvard's public overseers must include ex officio the governor, lieutenant governor, leaders of both legislative chambers, and established Congregationalist ministers, with a provision that Massachusetts's legislature could "for the advantage of the college and the interest of letters, make alterations in its government in the same manner as they might have been made by the provincial [colonial] legislature." In other words, the public overseers still had veto power—a power reinforced in 1814 when the state gave the college a share of its bank-tax subsidy but added more legislators and clergy to its overseers (with their consent).

Still, according to Webster, it was not the original grant of public funds but the subsequent vestment of these funds in a private corporation that had made Harvard a private college. This process of collegiate "privatization" had not occurred in every state, however. Connecticut updated Yale's charter in 1818, 1819, and 1821 to *reaffirm* the public's role on the institution's board of trustees, as represented by the governor, lieutenant governor, and "six senior senators" (appointed by the governor). Why this reaffirmation? To ensure Yale's eligibility for state aid—though, after the Panic of 1819, the state had little to give. Indeed, even at Yale, notes historian Peter Dobkin Hall, the recession of the early 1820s, coupled with the *Dartmouth* case, led to pressures for privatization. When the college's requests for aid went unanswered, it "faced the challenge of diminished state support by turning for financial sustenance to its broadly dispersed alumni," who expected corporate protection for their private contributions.

Even as these debates unfolded at Harvard and Yale, the legislature in New Hampshire considered several requests to establish a wholly new public university in the state. As early as June 18, 1819, a legislative committee had been created to "consider the expediency and predictability of establishing a public literary institution." Two weeks later, the legislature had passed a resolution to put former Dartmouth University president William Allen in charge of a subcommittee "to consider . . . in what place it would be proper to locate the same; to ascertain what funds can be obtained for that purpose; to digest a plan for establishing and organizing said institution, and to report thereon to the legislature at their next session." Allen endorsed the idea but, then on his way to become president at Bowdoin, declined to chair the subcommittee himself.

Before he left, however, Allen suggested that perhaps Dartmouth College might accept public supervision—in the form of a public board of overseers in a revised charter—in exchange for public support. "It has occurred to me that, if a board of overseers could be constituted for Dartmouth College, consisting either of some of the principal officers of government or gentlemen chosen by the legislature, the result would be more favorable to the interests of literature and science than if a new college should be created," Allen wrote. "I should hope [Dartmouth's] trustees would now feel the importance of legislative patronage and would be willing that the state should acquire this control over the seminary, which has received repeated grants from the legislature, and which must need other grants."

A year later in 1820, as the recession deepened and the constitutional convention in neighboring Massachusetts got underway, New Hampshire governor Samuel Bell called again for public aid to "higher seminaries of education" in the state, and the subject was referred to another subcommittee, chaired by Isaac Hill (recently elected to a seat in the senate). Hopes ran high for a public university. "That such an institution will sooner or later go into operation under the high auspices of the people of New Hampshire cannot be doubted," Hill anticipated. "The . . . want of funds resulting from the peculiar times will not admit the commencement of such an institution at the present period, [but] prudent and enlightened legislators ought not to lose sight of the object." The next year, 1821, the legislature used a tax on banks to establish a "Literary Fund" with a proviso that it should never support any college not under state control.

It was not long before Dartmouth College stepped forward with a proposal to secure a share of this fund. That summer, the college's secretary-treasurer Mills Olcott (who also now held a seat in the legislature) told Daniel Webster that Dartmouth should request a piece of the public financial pie. "The friends of Dartmouth College who are here have thought her real interest might be subscribed by some legislative arrangement whereby . . . state funds should be obtained," he wrote as he suggested that, in exchange for part of the Literary Fund, the college should allow the legislature to name a twenty-member board of overseers to supervise its selection of future trustees. Webster, then involved with his defense of Harvard's independence, was dubious. "I should not think it expedient to move in the matter without much circumspection," he replied.

No matter how desperate the financial condition of the college, Webster felt the price to obtain state funds—a public board of overseers "to include the president of the senate, the speaker of the house, and others to be appointed by the governor and council"—was too high. "I do not believe the college could get a dollar from [the legislature]," he surmised. "They would be very likely to accept the proposition to appoint overseers, but as to the money part of the bargain I do not think they would give a cent." Besides, he added, "I do not think the present a favorable moment to create a board of overseers by executive appointment, with power afterwards of filling their own vacancies. It is easy to see what sort of men would be first appointed, and what sort of men they would perpetuate. . . . A board of overseers, such as would probably be appointed, would negative every important nomination of the trustees. Of this I have no sort of doubt."

Even as Webster rejected the idea of a legislative role in the selection of trustees, former governor William Plumer continued to believe that state oversight was best for colleges. As he observed during the *Dartmouth* litigation, "It has long been a subject of great regret to me that the name of 'Dartmouth University' has been considered as a political party question," for, in his mind, public colleges were less inclined toward partisanship than private ones. In 1821—as he launched a yearlong critique of private corporations in the *New Hampshire Patriot*—he recommended the establishment of public high schools (in emulation of Boston) "subject to control . . . of civil government." Once citizens saw the "salutary effects" of these schools, he promised, "The legislature will have an easy task to establish a public college, or university, on similar principles."

Four years later, in 1825, Republicans once again introduced a bill to create a "New Hampshire University," to be financed by the state's Literary Fund and overseen by the legislature. In response, Dartmouth College revived its bid for a share of public resources in exchange for public oversight. It offered an Act to Amend the Charter of Dartmouth College and Make an Appropriation for the Encouragement of that Institution, which said the legislature's constitutional responsibility to "cherish the interests of literature" required an equitable distribution of state resources. No doubt aware of the regional competition that Harvard faced after the incorporation of Amherst College earlier that year, Dartmouth argued that intrastate rivalry between a private college and a new public university "would rather tend to check than promote these great interests."

Republicans, meanwhile, said Dartmouth could share in the state Literary Fund only when it agreed to supplement its private board of trustees with a public board of overseers—a deal the college rejected. Bennett Tyler, president of the college, groused to Charles Marsh that Republican lawmakers were "unwilling to do anything for the college without a surrender of the charter," a demand he considered outrageous. "I found it impossible to obtain a grant to the college on any terms which the trustees would be likely to accept," Marsh wrote, but without state aid the college struggled. Its needs were so great that, in 1826, New Hampshire governor David Morrill (whose relative, US senator Justin Morrill of Vermont, later championed the idea of federal land grants to colleges) "implored the legislature to rescue [Dartmouth College]."

Morrill believed higher education in New Hampshire should be supported—but not supervised—by the state. But it was not to be. For the rest of the decade, Federalists continued to call for aid to Dartmouth, and Republicans countered with calls either for seats on Dartmouth's board or for a separate (public) university. In particular, Republicans said that Dartmouth's classical program was irrelevant to a rural state like New Hampshire, which needed a modern university with "an experimental farm and agricultural school," funded by public resources. In 1827, this idea passed the (Republican) senate but failed in the (Federalist) house. The next year, both sides tried again: Dartmouth renewed its call for a share of the Literary Fund, while its opponents called for a state-supported agricultural school. The result was stalemate.

In this context, Dartmouth, like other colleges, turned increasingly to private donors. In 1828, it sent members of its board abroad to repeat Wheelock's early solicitations. Pledges were to be collected, notes historian Frederick Chase, only if a "minimum of $30,000 was subscribed by August 25, 1829." But the day before that date, only $29,600 had been raised, so Dartmouth's president Nathan Lord (who had succeeded Tyler in 1828) added $400 to an earlier subscription of $300 "and thus saved the whole." This fund drive opened "a new era" for the college. "It did not remove all its difficulties or lift all its burdens, but it gave the relief that was necessary and helped morally as well as financially." Three years later, when the college paid off the last of its loans from John Wheelock, it was "for the first time . . . free of debt except to its own funds."

Meanwhile, as colleges solicited more private support, they also sought more corporate authority to manage private gifts. A crucial instance arose in the case of *Harvard College and Massachusetts General Hospital v. Amory* (1829), which involved the will of Boston merchant John McLean, husband of Ann (Amory) McLean, who had died in 1823 and had left $50,000 in trust for his wife, the interest to be paid to her during her life and the principal divided between Harvard and Massachusetts General Hospital after her death. Ann's brothers, as executor-trustees, invested her estate's principal with industrial corporations in which they held stock of their own. Harvard objected and said the Amory brothers used McLean's gift to enrich themselves via risky investments. Since the companies had limited liability, any bankruptcy could jeopardize Harvard's (future) share.

Harvard wanted the Amory brothers removed as trustees in order to protect its own stake in McLean's estate. "In effect," notes historian Peter Dobkin Hall, its lawyers asked the court to rule on two questions: "(1) how much discretion could trustees be permitted in making investment decisions; and (2) whether beneficiaries have a right to question the discretionary powers of trustees." On both fronts, Harvard lost. Massachusetts judge Samuel Putnam ruled that since no investment was completely safe from risk (and since McLean *himself* invested "nearly half of his property in manufacturing stock"), his executor-trustees had a right to decide where to put his financial legacy. When it came to fiduciary trusts, Putnam adopted the "prudent man" standard, which said trustees merely had to minimize any immediate (or "imprudent") loss of assets under their control.

Moreover, when they made investment choices, trustees were not required to consider the potential gains or losses of future beneficiaries (such as Harvard in this case). Any such requirement, said Putnam, might cause fiduciaries to avoid risk altogether, which served no one well. The upshot was that McLean's estate could be put into private companies—which is precisely what the region's manufacturers wanted. "Most importantly," Hall explains, "by sanctioning trustees' ability to invest in manufacturing, railroad, insurance, and other stocks, and by protecting them from threats of endlessly vexatious suits by disgruntled beneficiaries, the court . . . released family money into a common pool (making it available for rational investment in the broader economy)." Harvard, despite its loss in court, profited handsomely from a result that suggested private means could serve public ends.

The fact that Putnam ruled as he did was—indirectly—a result of the long-term effort that Joseph Story and others had made to give Massachusetts's courts more jurisdiction to decide cases involving wills, estates, and trusts. Back in 1810, when Story had led the legislature's committee to codify state laws of equity, he looked for ways to protect inherited wealth from legislative action. But even as Story and his colleagues pressed a conservative legal agenda in Massachusetts (to protect financial power from popular interventions), the US Supreme Court produced a more complex set of decisions. While the Marshall Court had long been a faithful ally of Federalists and their financial interests, two new justices—Smith Thompson and Robert Trimble (who had replaced Justices Livingston and Todd)—pushed the court in another direction.

Nowhere was this new direction more evident than it was in the landmark case of *Ogden v. Saunders* (1827), which unexpectedly prioritized the interests of debtors over creditors and, for the first time, put the high court's imprimatur on state insolvency laws (as long as they applied only to debts incurred *after* such laws were in place). Story joined Marshall in dissent, appalled by a decision they considered a first step down a slippery slope to dismantle the protection of contracts, destroy the "rights" of creditors, and ultimately disassemble a constitutional order in which private contracts (as well as charters) were off-limits to legislative interference. As far as Story and Marshall were concerned, an ill-advised majority in *Ogden v. Saunders* gave states unprecedented power to alter, amend, abridge, adjust, or even annul private contracts.

To grasp the significance of *Ogden v. Saunders*, one had to go back to 1819 when, just a few days after the court ruled in *Dartmouth v. Woodward*, it decided the case of *Sturges v. Crowninshield* on the constitutionality of state insolvency laws. This case had originated in 1811 when Massachusetts businessman Richard Crowninshield borrowed money from banker Josiah Sturges to support his mercantile ventures. Crowninshield later moved to New York, lost his money, and invoked New York's insolvency law of 1811 to be discharged from his debts. He obtained his discharge in February 1812, then moved back to Massachusetts, where he again prospered. Sturges, who still had not been paid, sued in Story's circuit in 1816 for the recovery of his original debt on grounds that Crowninshield had incurred his debt before the insolvency act was passed and thus was obliged to pay it.

Story and his fellow circuit judge, John Davis, agreed to disagree in their opinions so the full US Supreme Court would be able to consider two points: (1) whether state insolvency laws preempted a congressional prerogative to pass bankruptcy laws, and (2) whether such laws violated the Contract Clause. Article I, section 8, clause 4 of the Constitution gave Congress the sole power to make "uniform laws... on the subject of bankruptcies, throughout the United States," but Congress had not yet passed any such law. This gap led to split decisions at the circuit level. As historian Mark Killenbeck notes, "In *Golden v. Prince* (1814) in Pennsylvania, justice Bushrod Washington held that state laws on bankruptcy were invalid, but in *Adams v. Storey* (1817) in New York, justice John Livingston held that such laws—and specifically the law under which Sturges had sued—were valid."

In 1819, the high court produced a two-part decision in *Sturges v. Crowninshield*. First, it held that, since Crowninshield had contracted his debt before New York had passed its statute, he was obliged to pay. Second, however, the court struck down New York's insolvency law on grounds that it usurped a congressional prerogative to handle bankruptcy. In his opinion for the majority, Chief Justice Marshall combined both of these principles to hold that *any* law that released a debtor from an obligation represented an impairment of contract. With this argument, he almost went as far as to say that all insolvency laws were unconstitutional—as if the Contract Clause itself precluded any implementation of the Bankruptcy Clause—but his colleagues rejected this conclusion on grounds that it could render the Constitution internally contradictory.

The question in *Sturges v. Crowninshield* was not only whether state insolvency statutes were constitutional but also whether every contract was to be read solely in terms of the laws in place when it was granted (which could mean, for instance, that Dartmouth's charter should be read in terms of British colonial law). A similar question resurfaced in another case also decided in 1819, *McMillan v. McNeill*, when the court asked whether an insolvency law passed in one state could apply to debts later contracted in another. Marshall, given his opposition to all insolvency laws, considered this situation indistinguishable from the one presented in *Sturges* and ruled that states' authority to legislate in the area of contracts was extremely limited. But others disagreed, and this disagreement was on display eight years later in *Ogden v. Saunders*.

Ogden v. Saunders had gotten its start in September 1806 when Mr. Ogden of Louisiana contracted with Mr. Saunders of Kentucky via a bill of exchange. Ogden later relocated to New York and, in the wake of financial difficulties in 1824, sought a discharge of his debt under that state's insolvency law. When the case reached the US Supreme Court in 1827, it amounted to a rematch between William Wirt, who represented Ogden, and Daniel Webster, who represented Saunders (along with co-counsel Henry Wheaton) on three questions that came before the court: (1) whether Ogden's contract in Louisiana could be discharged under New York's insolvency law; (2) whether New York's insolvency law "impaired" the obligations of contract; and (3) whether *any* state had the authority to pass insolvency laws.

Webster's argument in *Ogden* repeated his argument in *Dartmouth*, namely, that a contract, once made, could not be unmade by any legislative act. It was obvious why he stuck with this argument: if he allowed in

Ogden that states could reserve a power to alter contracts in the future, then he could have allowed in *Dartmouth* that New Hampshire could inherit from Parliament a power to amend the charter of a college. Wirt countered that if a creditor entered a contract when a state had an insolvency law in place, then he was presumed to consent to the possibility of a debtor's future declaration of insolvency . . . just as Dartmouth College's trustees, when they accepted their charter in 1769, implicitly consented to Parliament's legally recognized authority to alter, amend, abridge, adjust, or annul that contract.

In the end, the court ruled 4 to 3 in favor of the debtor, Ogden, and said that New York's insolvency law was constitutional and that Ogden was therefore entitled to discharge a debt that had been contracted after that law was in place. In effect, the court held that state insolvency laws did not legally "impair" the obligations of future contracts, because these laws were presumed to be part of the original contract itself. (In other words, all parties acknowledged that a declaration of insolvency was possible when they entered the contract in the first place, just as Dartmouth's trustees would have acknowledged that amendments were possible when they accepted the royal charter for the college.) As historian James Ely notes, the *Ogden* majority said the Contract Clause barred "retroactive legislation" but "did not ban state laws relating to agreements made in the future."

Marshall and Story (as well as Duvall) dissented. For Justice Marshall, it was his only dissent in a major case—a sign of his waning influence on a rapidly evolving court. He continued to insist that, under the Constitution, every contract was inviolable and could not be altered without the consent of all parties. "Individuals do not derive from government their right to contract but bring that right with them into society," he asserted on natural-law grounds. Were it otherwise, a legislature could reserve to itself the authority to nullify *any* future contract at will. A legislative act "declaring that all contracts should be subject to legislative control and should be discharged as the legislature might prescribe [c]ould become a component part of every contract," he warned. "Thus, one of the most important features in the Constitution . . . would lie prostrate and be construed into an inanimate, inoperative, unmeaning clause."

Story's dissent, like Marshall's, held that only Congress had the authority to pass bankruptcy laws. (While of course a federal bankruptcy law undoubtedly could "impair" the obligations of contract as much as state insolvency laws, Story believed the explicit constitutional basis of a federal bankruptcy law made it acceptable.) Crucially, he feared that *Ogden* flew in the face of *Dartmouth*'s prohibition against state laws that altered private contracts. Indeed, had *Ogden* been a precedent when *Dartmouth* was heard, the outcome in *Dartmouth* could have been very different. Webster himself conceded as much. Shortly after *Ogden*, in a conversation with Dartmouth graduate Rufus Choate, he admitted: "There was a point which lay upon the surface of that case [*Dartmouth*], neither taken by counsel nor considered by the court. If it had been properly presented, the decision probably would have been the other way."

The principle that supported the *Ogden* decision—the states' authority to regulate (future) private contracts as part of their duty to protect the public interest—gained ascendance over time. "Little by little, the Supreme Court has whittled away at Marshall's conception of the 'contracts clause,' and the ideas of William Wirt played a role in this process of erosion," historian Joseph Burke notes. "Wirt argued in both the [*Dartmouth*] and the *Ogden* cases that the Contracts Clause did not prevent the state from regulating 'civil police.' . . . As part of these police powers, states [could] regulate [private corporations] 'affected with public interest.' The power of the states to regulate these 'quasi-public corporations' . . . recognized Wirt's contention in the [*Dartmouth*] case that the purpose of a corporation [its function], not the source of its endowment [its funds], determined whether it was public or private."

In the wake of its *Ogden* decision, the US Supreme Court grew more likely to uphold state laws that regulated private corporations. For example, in *Providence Bank v. Billings* (1830), it upheld a state tax on future bank deposits. Providence Bank called the new tax an impairment of contract, but the court upheld the measure on grounds that a state's necessary power of taxation could not be abridged by a bank charter and, moreover, that Providence Bank's charter had not exempted it from taxation. Many states used *Providence Bank* to give legislatures more explicit authority over charters. For example, Massachusetts said that "Every act of incorporation passed after [March 11, 1831] shall be subject to amendment, alteration, or repeal at the pleasure of the legislature." In this way, the state reserved a power to make or unmake private corporations in order to advance the public interest. Story was stunned.

CHAPTER 15

Colleges, Contracts, and the Common Good

In 1831, Story's attempts to shore up the law of contracts and corporations were put to a test in another case that revisited his *Dartmouth* concurrence. The case involved Bowdoin College president William Allen, formerly president of Dartmouth University and outspoken advocate for public control over colleges. Bowdoin's original charter from Massachusetts, granted in 1794, had put the institution under the authority of two bodies: a board of trustees comprised of the college president, treasurer, and eleven others; and a board of overseers comprised of various Massachusetts elected officials. Importantly, section 16 of the charter had reserved to Massachusetts's legislature the authority to "alter, limit, annul, or restrain any of the powers by this act vested in the corporation, as shall be judged necessary to promote the best interests of said college," but—crucially—the Act of Separation that had disconnected Maine from Massachusetts after the Missouri Compromise of 1820 had not passed this authority on to Maine's legislature.

Bowdoin College had opened to students in 1802, at which point the corporation had fixed the president's annual salary at $1,000 and had set his tenure in office to last "during good behavior." Two presidents—Joseph McKeen (1802–7) and Jesse Appleton (1807–19)—had served under these conditions before William Allen was elected in December 1819 in the wake of the *Dartmouth* litigation. Allen had taken office in May 1820 under a contract that included the same presidential salary and terms of tenure as his predecessors. In the interim, both the board of trustees and the board of overseers had voted to confirm Maine's new state constitution, which included a provision that shifted all rights "to enlarge, limit, or restrain the powers given by the charter" from the legislature of Massachusetts to the legislature of Maine (in contrast with the Act of Separation, which left such rights solely under *Massachusetts's* purview).

This state of affairs continued for the next decade, but on March 31,

{ 203 }

1831, Maine's legislature, dissatisfied with Allen's leadership, passed a statute that "no person shall be elected or re-elected to the office or place of president unless he shall receive, in each board, two-thirds of all the votes given on the question of his election; and every person elected to said office or place after the passing of this Act shall be liable to be removed at the pleasure of the board of trustees, or board of trustees and overseers." Bowdoin's two boards voted in September 1831 to "acquiesce in said act," then declined to reelect Allen, who immediately filed suit to collect his salary. He said his pay was a private contract, which the legislature's recent statute had altered. Even if Bowdoin's trustees and overseers had consented to new legislative rules of presidential election and tenure, he said he was still entitled to his promised salary.

The case went to Joseph Story's circuit, where Allen claimed that neither Maine's legislature nor Bowdoin's trustees or overseers had the authority to change the contractual terms of the presidency without his consent. It was the same question that had arisen in *Dartmouth*. Could a legislature change any part of a corporation's governance without all parties' consent? As historian John Major Shirley notes, Allen "undoubtedly took pleasure in compelling Story to decide in the case between him and Bowdoin the same question which he nominally had decided in May 1819 in the [*Dartmouth* case]." If he won, he got his salary, considered a private contract. If he lost, he would vindicate the right of legislatures to alter the governance of colleges as public corporations. All eyes focused on Story as he considered whether Bowdoin would be subject to legislative oversight.

John Sherbourne, the district court judge in Portland, Maine, sat in circuit with Story, but since he was a Bowdoin trustee, he recused himself, which meant Story heard Allen's case alone. Sherbourne hoped Story would protect the "private" governance rights of his fellow trustees, and his wish came true. Story sided with Bowdoin's trustees, ousted Allen (for a second time), and left his salary unpaid (despite his presidential contract). How did he reach this unexpected decision? He began with the Act of Separation that had detached Maine from Massachusetts fourteen years earlier. That act had affirmed Massachusetts's right to alter the charters of Maine's colleges, but *despite* provisions in Maine's new constitution, it had not reserved the same right for Maine's legislature, which meant that, while Massachusetts originally had the power to alter Bowdoin's charter, Maine had not inherited that power.

It was a decision written to reaffirm Story's basic view that, even if a charter had been subject to legislative (or Parliamentary) regulation at the start, it could be released from such regulation by a change of government (a revolution or separation of states), unless the new state's regulatory powers were explicitly reserved. Since the Act of Separation affirmed the powers of Bowdoin's independent board of trustees—but did *not* give Maine's legislature the power to oversee that board—the board's autonomy could not be abridged. It enjoyed all the privileges of collegiate governance, including the privilege to adjust the president's salary and terms of tenure. And since both the board of trustees and board of overseers had consented to Maine's legislation on presidential reelection at Bowdoin, it could fire Allen whenever it felt he fell short of its definition of "good behavior," with no obligation to pay his salary thereafter.

In his decision, Story had to do some fancy legal footwork to write an opinion that was compatible with his *Dartmouth* logic, for Bowdoin had been founded by a public entity (the state of Massachusetts) with public funds (land grants within then-Massachusetts territory), which ordinarily would have made the college a public corporation. As historian Bruce Campbell notes, "Although Marshall had stated in his opinion for the court in *Dartmouth* that a state could found an educational institution and place it under the state's control, Story held that it did not matter that Massachusetts had founded and initially endowed Bowdoin, because Bowdoin was otherwise private. The endowment was essentially a public subsidy to a private corporation." In this way, he set aside the rights of a first donor (rights, he argued, that Maine had not inherited from Massachusetts) and left Bowdoin's governance solely in the hands of its trustees.

Stephen Longfellow, a former Bowdoin overseer who had served as counsel for the state of Maine in the case (and whose son, the poet Henry Wadsworth Longfellow, had been a student at the college), said that under Bowdoin's charter the institution was a public corporation, subject as section 16 made clear to legislative amendment. Longfellow believed these "reserve" powers had transferred from Massachusetts to Maine with the Act of Separation—but Story disagreed. As historian George Thomas recounts, "Massachusetts had not given any of these powers to Maine when [they] split in 1820, which meant that Maine had no such powers with regard to Bowdoin College." According to Story, the prior Act of Separation trumped Maine's subsequent constitution and rendered its college-related "reserve" powers void.

Some have argued that Story's opinion in the Bowdoin case marked a conscious effort to roll back the "reserve" powers he outlined in his *Dartmouth* concurrence. While states had the authority to control the "public" corporations they created, "reserve" clauses were supposed to extend legislative oversight to otherwise private corporations, and in the years since *Dartmouth*, such clauses had become increasingly widespread. As legal historian Stephen Siegel observes, "Chancellor Kent wrote in 1827 that their insertion 'has become quite the practice, in all recent acts of incorporations,'" but Kent, like Story, was concerned about this proliferation. In his *Commentaries on American Law* (1826), the New York chancellor had asked "how far the exercise of [reserve-clause] power could be consistent with justice" and urged states to exercise this power "under the guidance of extreme moderation and discretion."

Story asserted in his Bowdoin decision that, while reserve-clause power were "certainly very broad," they were "not without limit." In his own three-volume *Commentaries on the Constitution of the United States* (1833), he contended that legislatures did not have unrestrained authority to amend charters—even if they had reserved the power to do so and even if a board of trustees had consented to such amendments. For example, he said, a state could not reserve a power to annul the charters it granted to independent boards, nor could it abridge their power to govern chartered institutions as they saw fit (a major qualification). As he wrote in *Allen v. McKean* on the role of Maine's legislature: "It is true that it is constituted the sole judge of 'what is the best interest of the college,' but still it cannot do anything pointedly destructive of that interest. . . . It cannot intermeddle with its property; it cannot extinguish its corporate existence."

Story acknowledged the awkwardness of his Bowdoin decision. "It is impossible . . . not to feel that the decision is full of embarrassment," he wrote. "If this court were permitted to have any choice as to the causes which should come before it, this one is among the last which it would desire to entertain. But no choice is left. This court is bound to a single duty, and that is to decide the causes before it according to law, leaving the consequences to fall as they may." In his view, the law said that, despite the original terms of Bowdoin's charter, Maine's legislature had inherited no governance rights. Bowdoin thus became a "private" college. He added, however, that it would be unfortunate if his decision led Bowdoin to become estranged from the public or be considered ineligible for public aid, which it, like other "private" colleges, desperately needed.

Some have said the case of *Dartmouth College Board of Trustees v. Woodward* laid the foundation of the modern American law of corporations because it defined charters as "contracts," protected them from legislative interference, and thus established corporations' rights of autonomous self-government and the freedom to pursue their own interests apart from public scrutiny. As historian Alyssa Penick notes, "*Dartmouth College* established the security of contract over custom and led charters to supersede any other legal framework for incorporation." And so it did. But while the court's decision may have freed private corporations—including private colleges—from many forms of legislative intervention, this emancipation had mixed effects. Dartmouth College may have won "independence" from state authority, but it continued to beg for state aid.

Indeed, despite Story's decision in *Allen v. McKean*, the Bowdoin trustees still courted public funds, as did others. Why? Because in the 1830s, private colleges increasingly had to compete with public alternatives, which received substantial public support in exchange for public supervision. Two years after Bowdoin's case, this support played a role in *University of Alabama v. Winston* (1833), which asked whether Alabama's sole university was "public" or "private." The state's high court said it was public—a corporation "originated . . . by legislative enactment, towards which no [individual] citizen has contributed one cent, either in money, other property, labor, or services, even as a trustee, without pecuniary remuneration." Even as many argued that higher education was better off in private hands, Alabama's legislature—which elected the university's board of trustees—retained a public right to oversee the governance of that institution.

Meanwhile, other universities received their own public charters of incorporation, along with public aid. While the charter of the University of Delaware (1833) was (somewhat ambiguously) "private," the University of Missouri (1839) was clearly "public" and soon was joined by the University of Iowa (1847), University of Wisconsin (1848), University of Mississippi (1848), University of Utah (1850), University of Minnesota (1851), and University of Florida (1853), as well as Pennsylvania State University and Michigan State University (both founded in 1855). Each received sizable land grants from its state in exchange for legislative oversight. The result was a set of public universities across the country. "While the *Dartmouth* decision provided the legal framework in which this development could occur," Bruce Campbell notes, public land grants and other forms of aid "were essential to the evolution of the system."

In some respects, these new state universities were the way of the future, and the courts defended their public role. In the 1852 case of *University of North Carolina v. Josiah Maultsby*, the court decided once and for all that the University of North Carolina was, constitutionally, "a public institution" and hence "subject to legislative control." The court affirmed its earlier decision in *University v. Foy* (1805) in which it ruled that public funds and public governance had made the university a public corporation. "It is admitted, and the court is prepared to hold, that charters of corporations founded by individuals on their own funds, either for their own emolument or for the purposes of education, or other general charity, are contracts of inviolable obligation," the court repeated in 1852. "But the University [of North Carolina] was founded by the state, on the public funds, and for a general public charity."

By contrast, whenever a charter gave a corporation's property and privileges to an independent and therefore "private" board of trustees, the corporation was considered a private entity. Such was the case in *Board of Trustees of Vincennes University v. State of Indiana* (1852), where the US Supreme Court ruled (ostensibly in line with *Dartmouth*) that, although Vincennes's first donation had come from a congressional land grant, the property had been vested in a private board and could not be redirected by the legislature to Indiana's public university. Similarly, in *Sage v. Dillard* (1854), where Kentucky legislators had claimed an implicit power to appoint new trustees at the Western Baptist Theological Institute, the court echoed *Allen v. McKean* when it said this action exceeded powers explicitly reserved in the Institute's charter. "Thus," notes historian Silas McCormick, "even the reservation clauses, to which states resorted after the 1819 ruling [in *Dartmouth*], were shown to have certain limitations."

The rights of private corporations resurfaced a year later in *City of Louisville v. the President and Trustees of the University of Louisville* (1855), wherein the city had endowed the university and had given it an independent board of trustees. When the city later imposed new trustees by popular election and gave them control over university property, the court recognized the university's initial public grant but repeated Story's premise in *Allen v. McKean* that, even if a state funded and chartered a university, it could not overrule trustees' use of property unless it had reserved that power specifically. As historian David Rabban writes, if Louisville wanted to control the university, "then it should have bargained for that power in the charter before it made [its] donation. Otherwise, the law treats donations to universities from municipal corporations no differently than donations from private individuals."

A century earlier, a public donation had implied public oversight. Virtually every American college of the colonial era and the early republic—Harvard, Yale, Columbia, the College of Philadelphia, the College of William and Mary, and countless others—had assumed that, under English law, public contributions brought public control. This assumption sat at the heart of New Hampshire's Act of 1816, which transformed Dartmouth College into Dartmouth University, as well as the decision of New Hampshire's Superior Court, which upheld that move on grounds that Dartmouth was a public corporation endowed with public funds. But when this case reached the US Supreme Court, the relationship between the college and the public was undone. What mattered was not the original public donation but the subsequent incorporation of an independent ("private") board of trustees to oversee the use of that donation in perpetuity.

The effects of this change were evident after Congress passed the Morrill Act of 1862, which directed federal land grants to northern colleges—both private and public—to support agricultural, mechanical, and military education. Yale and Brown received Morrill land grants, as did the Massachusetts Institute of Technology (which outflanked Harvard to get its state's grant). Dartmouth also benefited. In 1866, to accept eighty thousand acres of federal land in the West, New Hampshire incorporated a new College of Agriculture and the Mechanic Arts in Hanover, practically across the street from Dartmouth. "The institution was officially associated with Dartmouth College and was directed by Dartmouth's president," notes Bruce Campbell, but its charter provided for a separate board of nine trustees: five appointed by the governor and council and four by the Dartmouth College trustees.

The coexistence of Dartmouth College and the New Hampshire College of Agriculture and the Mechanic Arts continued for nearly a quarter century, until 1890, when Benjamin Thompson, a resident of Durham, New Hampshire, died and left his property for the establishment of a state agricultural college on the condition that it be located in his own city. The next year, Governor Hiram Tuttle signed legislation that accepted Thompson's bequest, and the board of the agricultural college agreed to move. While the state did not supplement Thompson's endowment for many years, the institution was renamed the University of New Hampshire under a new charter and new board in 1923. Supported by public funds, the university became the state's first institution to challenge the 154-year higher-education monopoly of Dartmouth College.

Even after the incorporation of the University of New Hampshire in Durham, the state's "private" college in Hanover continued to seek public aid—with the caveat that any public funds would fall under the purview of its private trustees. This pursuit of public aid was no surprise. Despite the arguments that had prevailed in court a century earlier, Dartmouth College had been founded with a public land grant, and public grants were its principal source of income for many years (much to its trustees' chagrin when, for decades, its lands produced little if any revenue). Inasmuch as Dartmouth was founded with public aid, its dependence on such aid was to be expected, and its repeated protestations that its private trustees served "the public interest" were part and parcel of a larger political economy of American higher education.

What made the *Dartmouth* case historically and constitutionally significant was not only the fact that college attorney Daniel Webster cleverly masked the college's first grant of public lands but also, ironically, the fact that subsequent jurisprudence minimized the importance of many of the arguments Webster had mustered to win in court. Webster built his case on grounds of trustees' property rights (thus his specious claim that all the college's initial property came from private donations), but later cases had less to do with corporations' *property* rights than with claims of the *privileges* of corporate governance. Marshall in his majority opinion and Story in his concurrence stressed that charters were contracts because they gave the members of a corporation specific franchises that could not be altered, amended, or annulled without their consent. Later cases affirmed this view.

The conveyance of privileges, or franchises, even more than any conveyance of property, made a charter of incorporation a "contract" within the meaning of the Constitution. Indeed, as Story's later decisions stressed, the rights, privileges, and franchises of corporate governance were so permanent—so paramount—that not even a board of trustees *itself* could abdicate them without a fundamental abandonment of its charter obligations. Just as governments could not legally contract away their basic right to exist (even by a process of constitutional amendment), neither could a private board of trustees contract away its corporate existence or its responsibility to carry out the original purposes of its charter. Should it attempt such a move, the nation's highest court, responsible for the defense of all charters as contracts, would have to intervene to prevent it. (This constitutional duty to defend corporations from their own boards was grounded in James Wilson's view of the US government as a "corporation of corporations." Just as government could not abdicate its legislative powers, or its powers of corporate governance, neither could it let any other corporate trustees do so.)

In the case of Dartmouth College and its charter of incorporation, two interrelated questions competed for supremacy. One was the question of who received the "beneficial interest" of the charter: the private board or the public itself? The other was the question of why the Crown had granted a charter in the first place: to serve the private interests of the board or the public interests of the colony (or the state)? As early as the sixteenth century, the Elizabethan Statute of Charitable Uses had presumed that charters of incorporation ensured that private assets would serve public interests and that, when charters granted privileges of corporate governance to private boards in perpetuity, those boards would use their privileges to serve publicly desirable ends. Since a charter never would be granted to advance publicly undesirable ends, a corporation would not be allowed to betray the ends for which it was established. And who ensured this fidelity to public ends? The courts.

Dartmouth established the inviolability of private charters as well as the authority of corporate governance under private boards of trustees, but it did not render corporations *entirely* immune from public oversight. Corporations were still obliged to obey "the laws of the land"; they could not commit illegal acts or compromise public safety. They were, therefore, subject to some measure of public supervision to ensure their fidelity to publicly desirable ends. *Dartmouth*, in this sense, left open the question of whether the interests of higher education were best served by private or public oversight. New Hampshire's legislature had said that Dartmouth's trustees were too preoccupied with private interests to be trusted with the supervision of higher education, but Dartmouth's trustees said precisely the same thing about New Hampshire's legislature. Neither side had any faith in the other to advance genuinely public ends—and, for better or worse, both had plenty of historical evidence to support their respective points of view.

CONCLUSION

Most observers today associate "corporate" law not with colleges but with companies—that is, business corporations—though sometimes colleges and companies have been connected in unexpected ways. Take for example the US Supreme Court's decision in *Charles River Bridge v. Warren Bridge* (1837), a case that had its origin at Harvard nearly two centuries before litigation began. In 1650, when Harvard got its charter, the Massachusetts Bay Colony got a royal grant to run a ferry across the Charles River from Boston to Charlestown. The college operated this ferry until 1785, whereafter it allowed the proprietors of the Charles River Bridge Company to replace the ferry with a bridge. The company acquired rights to collect bridge tolls for the next forty years in exchange for payments to Harvard of £200 a year. In 1792, Massachusetts extended the company's original charter by thirty years, for a total of seventy years of tolls and payments to the college.

Over time, as the City of Boston grew, the Charles River Bridge Company defended its chartered toll rights. But in 1793, after the state had extended its charter, the legislature chartered a second corporation, the West Boston Bridge Company, to build another bridge over the river. Then a decade later, calls arose for a third bridge, and in 1828 a proposal surfaced for a fourth bridge, to be operated by the Warren Bridge Company and located only 260 feet away from the Charles River Bridge on the Charleston side. The original Charles River Bridge Company cried foul, as did Harvard, which noted that, after the six-year charter of the Warren Bridge Company expired, that bridge would become toll-free and thus render the Charles River Bridge Company's right to collect tolls "essentially worthless." To protect its privileges, the Charles River Bridge Company filed suit on grounds of an unconstitutional impairment of its original contract.

When the case reached the US Supreme Court in 1831, it represented yet another rematch between Daniel Webster as the lead attorney for the Charles River Bridge Company (assisted by Warren Dutton) and William Wirt for the Warren Bridge Company (unassisted). Webster argued that his client had exclusive commercial rights under its charter that "could not be revoked without the consent of that company, or just compensation." Wirt responsed that, in fact, the original charter of the Charles River Bridge Company included no explicit provision for a monopoly on bridge tolls. He asserted that charters should be "construed most favorably to the people" and cited the recent English case of *Stourbridge Canal v. Wheeley* (1831), wherein the canal's profits had been lessened by the construction of a railroad. Britain's courts said the railroad did not violate the charter of the canal and, moreover, that governments had a right to meet society's expansive transportation needs.

Various delays prevented a decision in *Charles River Bridge v. Warren Bridge*, and in 1837 the case was reargued. Webster and Dutton reappeared for the Charles River Bridge Company, but Wirt had died and was replaced by John Davis and Simon Greenleaf, who repeated his arguments. In the interval, Chief Justice John Marshall also had died and was replaced by Roger Taney, who ultimately crafted the majority opinion. Taney accepted Wirt's public-interest argument. He considered the Charles River Bridge Company's original charter a public franchise and said that "state-granted franchises should be construed strictly in favor of the state." Since the words of the charter did not confer exclusive commercial rights, the court would not "infer" such rights. Moreover, he added, if the Charles River Bridge Company had been granted a monopoly, then all of Boston would be "obliged to stand still until the claims of the old turnpikes shall be satisfied." Not only the Charles River Bridge Company but also Harvard was disappointed in Taney's decision.

Joseph Story, who considered this decision a direct assault on chartered rights, dissented. He reminded his colleagues that *Fletcher v. Peck* (which he argued in 1810) held that a state could not revoke the contracts it made or the chartered franchises it granted. He asked: "If it cannot [revoke] or resume the franchise itself, can it take away its whole substance and value?" Common-law precedent had long held that bridge charters were protected against competition; why should the charter of the Charles River Bridge Company be any different? Story cited Justice Bushrod Washington's concurrence in *Dartmouth* (which in turn drew on Blackstone's *Commentaries*) to suggest the Charles River Bridge Company's original charter was an exclusive royal—public—contract. With revenue for Harvard at stake, he concluded: "I stand upon the old law established more than three centuries ago . . . in resisting any encroachment on the rights and liberties of the citizens, secured by public grants."

Of course, it was precisely the *public* nature of the grant that opened it to alteration.

Story detected in the *Charles River Bridge* decision a constitutional sea change, a new era in which contracts and charters would become less secure. "The old constitutional doctrines are fading away, and a change has come over the public mind from which I augur little good," he complained. "I am the last of the old race of judges," he later told his friend Harriet Martineau in London. "Do you remember the story of the last dinner of a club who dined once a year? I am in the predicament of the last survivor." Eight years on, this conviction was complete. "I have long been convinced that doctrines and opinions of the old court were daily losing ground, and especially those on great constitutional questions," he wrote in April 1845 (a year after the court had decided several cases on corporate rights). "I am the last member now living of the old court, and I cannot consent to remain where I can no longer hope to see those doctrines recognized and enforced." Five months later he retired.

He did so just in time, because in 1848, when the northern West River Bridge Company went to court to defend its presumed corporate rights against Vermont's use of eminent domain to permit the construction of a turnpike near the bridge, the court again ruled in favor of the state. The decision (which cited *Dartmouth*) explained that "the act of incorporation in this case was a contract . . . between the state and its members" and insisted that Vermont's actions were not "violations of the obligation of any contract made by it with the corporation." Two years later, in *Perrine v. Chesapeake and Delaware Canal Company* (1850), the court again echoed *Charles River Bridge* when it said a company had no exclusive right to canal tolls, because such a right was not specified in the charter, and in *Piqua Branch of the State Bank of Ohio v. Knoop* (1854) the court said a tax on banks was permissible, because such a tax *was* specified in the charter.

While these decisions limited corporate privileges, they aligned with Story's concurrence in *Dartmouth* in their insistence that corporate rights extended only as far as the explicit terms of a charter. Indeed, the court ruled again on this question in *Dodge v. Woolsey* (1855), which held that if a charter set a specific rate for a state tax on banks, then not even a new state constitution, ratified by the people, could raise that rate until the original charter expired. One dissenter cited *Dartmouth* to contend that even if legislatures could not alter charters, the sovereign people could.

"This court has not, till now, impugned the sovereignty of the people of a state over these artificial bodies called into existence by their own legislatures," the dissent argued. But no court had said that *private* contracts were alterable. And even *public* contracts were unalterable unless explicit rights of amendment were reserved.

Taxes were a subject of constant litigation between states and corporations (including colleges) during the mid-nineteenth century. In *Washington University v. Rouse* (1869), the court upheld the university's permanent contractual exemption from taxes and said that its exemption would apply no matter how much wealth the university acquired in pursuit of its ("public") educational objects. In the court's words, "The exemption from taxation became one of the franchises of the corporation, of which it could not be deprived by any species of state legislation." While dissenters questioned the state's right to "bargain away" its powers of taxation forever, lest "rich corporations" strike legislative deals to exempt themselves from taxes in perpetuity, the court's majority replied that a right to bargain was fundamental to a state's powers of incorporation, and in this case, the bargain applied to a single university—not in general.

Even as the court protected the explicit terms of corporate charters, however, it also upheld states' use of "reserved powers" to regulate corporations in the public interest. After the Civil War—a conflict that highlighted the need for congressional authority to enforce the original "contract" accepted by the states—the court revisited Story's reserved-powers doctrine in the *Pennsylvania College Cases* (1871). When the Pennsylvania legislature used its reserved powers of amendment to permit Washington College and Jefferson College to combine into one institution, the change was accepted by requisite majorities of each board of trustees but rejected by others who disliked the new trustees' use of funds. The court responded that "persons making contracts with a private corporation know that the legislature, even without the assent of the corporation, may amend . . . their charters in all cases where the power to do so is reserved in the charter."

In subsequent years, the balance of "chartered rights" and "reserved powers" surfaced in *Miller v. State* (1872), *Edwards v. Kearzey* (1877), and

Farrington v. Tennessee (1878), the last of which, citing *Dartmouth*, affirmed that, in the absence of powers reserved explicitly for a legislature, the court would uphold private corporate rights. But what if, as part of its chartered functions, a private corporation offended public interests, or public health or safety? This question arose in *Fertilizing Company v. Hyde Park* (1878), where the wealthy Chicago suburb of Hyde Park declared itself off-limits to railroad cars that carried offal (the discarded entrails of dead animals), which the charter of the Fertilizing Company had permitted it to ship in the vicinity. The court sided with Hyde Park and said the city's transportation ordinance was "a police regulation of health and comfort." After this case, the court increasingly upheld the use of state and municipal "police" powers to regulate corporations in the interest of public welfare.

Another case from this period, decided at the state level, attributed the state's authority of regulation not to its "police" powers alone but also to its "visitatorial" powers over corporate operations. All corporations were subject to public visitation to ensure compliance with "the laws of the land," and in *Attorney General v. Chicago and Northwestern Railroad Company* (1874), the Supreme Court of Wisconsin said the state could enforce statutory restrictions on railroad freight charges. The state's attorney general asserted his visitatorial power to enforce this law "on behalf of the public," and the court upheld his actions. "The grounds on which [visitatorial] jurisdiction rests are ancient," it noted, "but the extent of its application has grown rapidly of late years, until a comparatively obscure and insignificant jurisdiction has become one of great magnitude and public import."

States' use of their police powers to regulate corporations was particularly evident in *Stone v. Mississippi* (1880), where a lottery company's privileges were rescinded for the protection of "public morals." This case originated when state legislators granted the Mississippi Agricultural, Educational, and Manufacturing Aid Society a twenty-five-year charter to fund its operations via a lottery (and directed part of the proceeds to a planned university to demonstrate the lottery's advancement of a public good). When voters later said lotteries were immoral, a subsequent legislature used its police powers to amend the charter—a move the court upheld *not* on grounds of any specifically "reserved powers" but rather on grounds that lotteries were a "pestilence" curable by state law. "No legislature can bargain away public health or public morals," the court said as it quoted Marshall's decision in *Dartmouth*. "The Constitution did not intend to restrain states in the regulation of their civil institutions, adopted for internal government."

Stone v. Mississippi stressed that states had a right to regulate the property and privileges of the corporations they chartered. "They may create [private] corporations and give them, so to speak, a limited citizenship," the court allowed, "but, as citizens limited in their privileges . . . these creatures of governmental creation are subject to such rules and regulations as may, from time to time, be ordained and established for the preservation of health and morality." The court went on to say that states could not contract away their fundamental rights and responsibilities of governance. "The contracts which the Constitution protects are those that relate to property rights, not governmental [rights and responsibilities]," it held. "Certainly, the right to suppress [lotteries] is governmental, to be exercised at all times by those in power at their discretion. Anyone, therefore, who accepts a lottery charter does so with the implied understanding that the people, in their sovereign capacity, and through their properly constituted agencies, may res[cind] it at any time when the public good shall require."

The state's power to regulate corporate property resurfaced in *Douglas v. Kentucky* (1897), where trustees of Shelby College turned over lottery privileges to a third party, who complained when the state later withdrew those privileges. While the court recognized the state's authority to end the lottery, it also recognized the complainant's right of contract and required the state to repay his losses. The court confessed to some embarrassment for this decision, given *Stone v. Mississippi*, but said that charters for immoral activities were not constitutionally protected. If they were, then a state's "duty of protecting and fostering the honesty, health, morals, and good order of the state would be cast into the winds, and vice and crime would triumph in their stead." Indeed, the court averred, "The essential principles of self-preservation forbid that [any legislature] should possess a power so revolting, because [it would be] destructive of the main pillars of government."

Acceptable corporate regulation—whether under "police," "reserved," or "visitatorial" powers—continued in the new century, not only in *City of Owensboro v. Cumberland Telephone and Telegraph Company*

(1913), where a reserved power of amendment was found, but also in *Atlantic Coast Line Railroad Company v. City of Goldsboro* (1914), where even though no such power was found, a municipal ordinance that required freight transfers at railway terminals rather than city streets was upheld via police powers. A similar justification prevailed in *Louisville Bridge Company v. United States* (1917), where again, in the absence of explicit reserved powers, the court upheld bridge height requirements on grounds of the secretary of war's responsibility to regulate commerce in relation to public safety. Just a year later, however, in *Hammer v. Dagenhart* (1918), the court rejected federal child labor regulations on grounds that "powers not expressly delegated to the national government are reserved [to states, or the people]."

Each of the aforementioned decisions cited *Dartmouth*—either on the chartered rights of corporations or the reserved powers of states. A landmark case that did not cite *Dartmouth* was *Home Building and Loan Association v. Blaisdell* (1934), which affirmed federal efforts to alter mortgage contracts during the depression. In this case, the court held that, while the Constitution appeared to prohibit "any" impairment of contracts, this prohibition was not "absolute," particularly in cases of national economic crisis. The same year, in *W. B. Worthen Company v. Thomas* (1934), the court said that any contract amendments must be "precisely and reasonably designed to meet a grave temporary emergency in the interest of the general welfare." A year later, in the related case of *Hopkins Federal Savings and Loan Association v. Cleary* (1935)—a case that did cite *Dartmouth*—the court held that, once a state had chartered a public loan corporation, it could not be rechartered as a federal corporation against its will.

During the depression, with state police powers seemingly ascendant over claims of corporate autonomy, it appeared to some that *Dartmouth* had run its legal course. But then came a line of argument that revived mid-nineteenth-century interpretations that equated "corporations" with "citizens" and said they should enjoy the same powers and privileges as "natural persons." This line of argument emerged in *United States v. Scophony Company of America* (1948), which held that a multinational corporation, initially chartered in England but engaged in business via agents in the United States, could be sued wherever it was "found" and thus had "citizenship." Questions about the "citizenship" of corporations had arisen in many previous cases—*Bank of the United States v. Deveaux* (1809), *Trustees of Philadelphia Baptist Association v. Hart's Executors* (1819), *Ex parte Schollenberger* (1877), *Neirbo Company v. Bethlehem Shipbuilding Corporation* (1939)—but *Scophony* prompted Justice Felix Frankfurter to caution that claims of corporate "personhood" or "citizenship" were constitutionally perilous and should be "narrowly watched, lest they be abused and fail in their service to reason."

Frankfurter was right to worry, for *Scophony* foreshadowed a shift in jurisprudence during the second half of the twentieth century from attempts to balance chartered rights with reserved powers on grounds that corporations were legal "creations" toward a rapid expansion of corporate rights on grounds that corporations were legal "citizens." This shift was evident when, in *Virginia State Board of Pharmacy v. Virginia Citizens Consumer Council* (1976) and *First National Bank of Boston v. Bellotti* (1978), the court decided that a corporation was a legal person, or citizen, whose First Amendment speech rights extended to "issues that materially affect its business, property, or assets" (a decision aligned with *Stone v. Mississippi*'s assertion that any "contracts which the Constitution protects are those that relate to property rights, not governmental [rights]"). *Bellotti* took for granted that corporations were legal persons and posed the question: What kinds of speech rights should this corporate person enjoy?

The majority in *Bellotti* found that limits on property-related corporate speech did not serve any important or narrowly tailored government interest and that corporations were therefore free to speak on behalf of their shareholders as long as they followed their internal governance rules (or "procedures of corporate democracy"). A strong dissent from Chief Justice William Rehnquist, however, cited *Dartmouth* to say that "the mere creation of a corporation does not invest it with all the liberties enjoyed by natural persons." Rehnquist quoted Marshall's observation that a corporation had only those rights "incidental to its very existence," that is, necessary to fulfill the essential purpose for which it was chartered. "Although the Court has never explicitly recognized a corporation's right of commercial speech [for example, via product ads]," he noted, "such a right might be considered necessarily incidental to the business of a commercial corporation."

But even if *commercial* speech was necessary for a company—or *educational* speech was necessary for a college (both in light of their status as corporate persons)—*political* speech was another matter. "So long as the judicial branches of the state and federal governments remain open to protect the corporation's interest in its property, it has no need (though it may have the desire), to petition the political branches for similar protection," Rehnquist wrote. "Indeed, the states might reasonably fear that corporations [once endowed with rights of political speech] would use their economic power to obtain further benefits beyond those already bestowed [in their charters]." According to Rehnquist, political speech rights were to be enjoyed *only* by "natural persons." (His interpretation may have been a reaction to Justice William Douglas's dissent in *Sierra Club v. Morton* [1972], which suggested that silent entities such as mountains could assert personhood to qualify for corporate protections.)

Questions of corporate speech and corporate personhood returned a decade later in *Austin, Michigan Secretary of State v. Michigan State Chamber of Commerce* (1990), wherein the court upheld a narrowly tailored state law that prohibited the use of general corporate funds to pay for campaign ads. This decision cited *Dartmouth*, as did an opposite decision two decades later in *Citizens United v. Federal Elections Commission* (2010), wherein the high court put forward a particularly expansive definition of corporate speech rights ("electioneering communications") on grounds of corporate personhood. A blockbuster ruling, *Citizens United* overturned *Austin*, struck down a federal law that had prohibited the use of general corporate funds to pay for campaign broadcasts, and, controversially, equated "corporate speech" (that is, corporate expenditures for political speech) with "citizens' speech."

The majority in *Citizens United* said that state restrictions on corporate speech "interfered with the 'open marketplace' of ideas" and that regulatory limits imposed a form of "censorship" that was "vast in its reach, suppressing the speech of both for-profit and non-profit, both small and large, corporations." The majority pledged that corporate speech would "not give rise to corruption or the appearance of corruption" in American politics and that any resultant "appearance of influence or access will not cause the electorate to lose faith in this democracy" (with "democracy" characterized by a marketplace of ideas where both "natural" or "artificial" persons were coequal participants). But this opinion provoked a strong response. The court's four dissenters saw a clear distinction between corporations and citizens. Unlike the latter, they said, the former had "no consciences, no beliefs, no feelings, no thoughts, no desires" and were not "members of 'We, the People,' by whom and for whom our Constitution was established."

The dissenters reminded the majority of Marshall's definition of a "corporation" in *Dartmouth*: "Being the mere creature of law, it possesses only those properties which the charter of its creation confers upon it." Thus, unless political speech rights were explicitly conferred upon a corporation, it could not claim such rights. The dissenters recalled the many decisions in which the court had upheld state regulations of corporate speech on grounds of public interest. For this reason, they said, the majority's conclusion that "the societal interest in avoiding corruption and the appearance of corruption does not provide an adequate justification for regulating corporate expenditures on candidate elections" rested on "an incorrect description of that interest, along with a failure to acknowledge the relevance of established facts and the considered judgments of state and federal legislatures over many decades."

Citizens United was not the only twenty-first-century decision to expand the parameters of corporate personhood. *Burwell v. Hobby Lobby Stores* (2014) also expanded these parameters when it granted corporations not only First Amendment speech protections but also First Amendment *religious* protections. When the federal Affordable Care Act required employers to provide women's contraception, Hobby Lobby Stores refused on grounds that such a requirement violated its (corporate) faith. Since churches were exempt from the requirement, Hobby Lobby said, other corporations should be, too. The majority agreed, but the same justices who had dissented in *Citizens United* also dissented in this case. They noted that corporate religious exemptions might enable corporations to evade otherwise relevant statutes and, indeed, that no prior case had ever "recognized a for-profit corporation's qualification for a religious exemption from a generally applicable law." Why not? Because "the exercise of religion is characteristic of natural persons, not artificial legal entities."

The dissenters argued that churches differed from companies because their members were presumably united under a single religious belief system, but in fact the "corporate" nature of a church did not rely on members' unity of belief. It relied on their joint control of property, and it was this justification that Hobby Lobby used to claim its First Amendment religious freedoms as corporate (not individual) rights. As the court had repeatedly held, the laws of corporations were rooted in property claims, and Hobby Lobby's claim to control property as it chose was rooted in religious principles—just as, nearly two centuries earlier, Dartmouth's board of trustees claimed to control the use of college property in part on the basis of religious principles. In a sense, when *Hobby Lobby* equated companies with churches, it brought full circle a series of nineteenth-century debates over the legal privileges and protections of churches (and colleges) as corporations.

American corporations have followed a circuitous legal path. Marshall, in his landmark opinion, drew on ancient jurisprudence to define a corporation as "an artificial being, invisible, intangible, and existing only in contemplation of law," and he drew on British precedent to say that charitable (private) corporations should be governed by trustees, subject to judicial review to ensure compliance with the laws of the land. But times change. In 1819, when Marshall issued his decision, it would have been inconceivable that private corporations, as legal "citizens," would hold political speech rights apart from state regulation, just as it would have been inconceivable in 1769 that Dartmouth College was a completely private corporation, independent of governmental oversight. Over the past two and a half centuries, American corporate law has evolved, and the consequences of this evolution may take centuries more to be revealed.

RELEVANT CASES

Phillips v. Bury (1694)
Bentley v. Bishop of Ely (1729)
Eden v. Foster (1744)
King v. Bishop of Chester (1747)
Green v. Rutherford (1750)
King v. Bishop of Ely (1756)
St. John's College v. Todington (1757)
King v. Vice Chancellor of Cambridge (1765)
King v. Pasmore (1789)
Bracken v. The Visitors of William and Mary College (1790)
Attorney General ex. rel. Bishop of London v. College of William and Mary (1790)
Ware v. Hylton (1796)
Kelley v. Bean (1798)
Muzzy v. Wilkins (1803)
Turpin v. Lockett (1804)
Trustees of the University of North Carolina v. Foy (1805)
Wales v. Stetson (1806)
Bank of the United States v. Deveaux (1809)
Fletcher v. Peck (1810)
Brown v. Penobscot Bank (1812)
Golden v. Prince (1814)
Terrett v. Taylor (1815)
Town of Pawlet v. Clarke (1815)
Inhabitants of the Fourth School District v. Wood (1816)
Stetson v. Kempton (1816)
Martin v. Hunter's Lessee (1816)
Adams v. Storey (1817)
Eustis v. Parker (1818)
Hatch v. Lang (1818)
Marsh v. Allen (1818)
Pierce ex dem. Lyman v. Gilbert (1818)
Trustees of Philadelphia Baptist Association v. Hart's Executors (1819)
McMillan v. McNeill (1819)

Bullard v. Bell (1819)
Sturges v. Crowninshield (1819)
Trustees of Dartmouth College v. Woodward (1819)
Ogden v. Saunders (1827)
Harvard College and Massachusetts General Hospital v. Amory (1829)
Providence Bank v. Billings (1830)
Allen v. McKean (1833)
University of Alabama v. Winston (1833)
Charles River Bridge v. Warren Bridge (1837)
Perrine v. Chesapeake and Delaware Canal Company (1850)
University of North Carolina v. Josiah Maultsby (1852)
Board of Trustees of Vincennes University v. State of Indiana (1852)
Sage v. Dillard (1854)
Piqua Branch of the State Bank of Ohio v. Knoop (1854)
Dodge v. Woolsey (1855)
City of Louisville v. the President and Trustees of the University of Louisville (1855)
Washington University v. Rouse (1869)
Pennsylvania College Cases (1871)
Miller v. State (1872)
Attorney General v. Chicago and Northwestern Railroad Company (1874)
Ex parte Schollenberger (1877)
Edwards v. Kearzey (1877)
Farrington v. Tennessee (1878)
Fertilizing Company v. Hyde Park (1878)
Stone v. Mississippi (1880)
Douglas v. Kentucky (1897)
City of Owensboro v. Cumberland Telephone and Telegraph Company (1913)
Atlantic Coast Line Railroad Company v. City of Goldsboro (1914)
Louisville Bridge Company v. United States (1917)
Hammer v. Dagenhart (1918)
Home Building and Loan Association v. Blaisdell (1934)
W.B. Worthen Company v. Thomas (1934)
Hopkins Federal Savings and Loan Association v. Cleary (1935)
Neirbo Company v. Bethlehem Shipbuilding Company (1939)
United States v. Scophony Company of America (1948)

Sierra Club v. Morton (1972)
Virginia State Board of Pharmacy v. Virginia Citizens Consumer Council (1976)
First National Bank of Boston v. Bellotti (1978)
Austin, Michigan Secretary of State v. Michigan State Chamber of Commerce (1990)
Falwell v. Miller (2002)
Citizens United v. Federal Elections Commission (2010)
Burwell v. Hobby Lobby Stores (2014)

CHRONOLOGY

1636	Harvard College is established with donation of £400 from the Massachusetts Bay Colony.
1638	Harvard College accepts donation from John Harvard.
1642	Harvard College accepts increased legislative representation on a new board of overseers.
1650	Harvard College adds board of fellows (the "corporation"), comprised of the president, faculty, and tutors.
1657	Harvard College amends the composition of its boards of fellows and overseers.
1673	Harvard College receives enlarged board of fellows without the consent of the existing corporation.
1693	College of William and Mary is chartered.
1694	*Philips v. Bury* codifies the law of charitable (eleemosynary) corporations such as Exeter College, Oxford.
1711	Eleazar Wheelock is born in Windham, Connecticut.
1733	Eleazar Wheelock graduates from Yale College.
1744	Eleazar Wheelock opens his Indian Charity School in Lebanon, Connecticut.
1745	Connecticut's assembly grants a new charter to Yale College.
1754	New York's assembly charters King's College under Anglican leadership.
1754	Joshua Moor donates land to Eleazar Wheelock's Indian Charity School.
1755	Eleazar Wheelock and others sign a deed of trust for the governance of the Indian Charity School in Lebanon, Connecticut.
1758	Joshua Moor dies, and his widow transfers control of his land donation to Eleazar Wheelock personally.
1763	New Hampshire governor Benning Wentworth offers Eleazar Wheelock a charter to relocate his Indian Charity School.
1766	Yale College president Thomas Clap resigns after governance dispute with colonial assembly.
1766	Eleazar Wheelock sends Samson Occom and Nathaniel Whitaker abroad to raise money for his Indian Charity School.

{ 229 }

1767	Lord Dartmouth becomes president of the English board of trustees of the Indian Charity School.
1767	Eleazar Wheelock receives offer of land for his Indian Charity School from New Hampshire governor John Wentworth.
1768	Eleazar Wheelock tells John Wentworth that relocation of his Indian Charity School from Connecticut to New Hampshire will require approval from his English board of trustees.
1768	To appease his English board of trustees, Eleazar Wheelock revises his will to replace Nathaniel Whitaker as his successor to lead the Indian Charity School.
1769	John Wentworth grants a charter that creates a board of trustees for "Dartmouth College" and names Eleazar Wheelock as founder (December 13).
1770	John Wentworth grants the Landaff township to Dartmouth College (January 25).
1770	Eleazar Wheelock says "My Indian Charity School... is become a body corporate and politic under the name of Dartmouth College."
1770	Eleazar Wheelock moves to Hanover, New Hampshire; he uses school money to build a new edifice on college land.
1770	The English board of trustees objects to any use of its school funds to support a college.
1770	Eleazar Wheelock leads spiritual revival at Dartmouth College.
1776	Eleazar Wheelock receives money from the Continental Congress to support his school but not his college activities.
1778	Eleazar Wheelock joins other Hanover residents who seek to secede from New Hampshire and become annexed to Vermont.
1778	Vermont's assembly votes to bring the "University of Dartmouth" under state patronage.
1779	Eleazar Wheelock dies and names his son John Wheelock to succeed him as president of the Indian Charity School and Dartmouth College.
1779	Pennsylvania's legislature seizes the College of Philadelphia and reassigns all its assets to a public "University of the State of Pennsylvania."
1779	Virginia's governor Thomas Jefferson leads successful effort to amend the statutes of the College of William and Mary.

1780	Massachusetts's legislature asserts its authority over Harvard College board of overseers in new state constitution.
1784	New York's legislature recharters King's College as Columbia, part of a publicly governed "University of the State of New York."
1787	New York's legislature returns Columbia College to independent governance under its original charter.
1788	John Wheelock offers to make Dartmouth College the public University of Vermont.
1789	New Hampshire replaces the original colonial grant of the Landaff township with a new land grant for Dartmouth College under the governance of both the college trustees and the legislature.
1789	John Phillips makes his first donation toward a professorship of divinity at Dartmouth College.
1789	US Constitution is ratified.
1790	John Marshall successfully defends the College of William and Mary against John Bracken's claim that its reorganization by the college visitors in 1779 was an illegal act.
1790	Pennsylvania's legislature restores the original charter of the College of Philadelphia.
1791	The College of Philadelphia consents to a new charter as the University of Pennsylvania.
1793	Massachusetts's legislature charters Williams College and reserves several rights of public oversight.
1796	Virginia's legislature forcibly renames Washington Academy as Washington College and imposes new trustees.
1796	Connecticut's legislature increases public aid to Yale College.
1799	New Hampshire's legislature suggests a new charter to merge Dartmouth College and the Indian Charity School, but John Wheelock refuses.
1804	Dartmouth College trustees request legislative review of school and college finances.
1804	Revivalist tutor Jonathan Shurtleff joins the Dartmouth College faculty as Phillips Professor of Divinity.
1804	Virginia court in *Turpin v. Lockett* upholds a legislative seizure of colonial land grants to Anglican church.

1805	North Carolina court rules in *Trustees of the University of North Carolina v. Foy* that a university named in the state constitution and founded with public funds is a public corporation, even if governed by a self-perpetuating board of trustees originally named by the legislature.
1807	New York legislators attempt to revise the charter of Columbia College to place it under public authority.
1807	Dartmouth College trustees seek new charter to merge the college and the Indian Charity School in exchange for a new land grant (to replace the original Landaff grant of 1770 and the later grant of 1789).
1808	John Wheelock successfully objects to merger of Dartmouth College and Indian Charity School.
1809	John Wheelock rejects Roswell Shurtleff's requests to preach in Hanover's town church, but the college trustees defend Shurtleff's right to do so.
1810	Federalist legislators in Massachusetts add members to Harvard College board of overseers to undermine Republican influence.
1812	Republican legislators in Massachusetts charter the Massachusetts General Hospital and reserve a right of legislative oversight.
1813	Federalist legislators in Massachusetts revise the charter of Massachusetts General Hospital to remove legislative oversight.
1813	Federalist legislators in New Hampshire dismantle the state judiciary and set up a parallel (and partisan) court.
1814	Republican legislators in New Hampshire revive the state judiciary; Governor William Plumer appoints new judges.
1814	Dartmouth College board of trustees restricts John Wheelock's instructional role.
1815	John Wheelock publishes *Sketches of the History of Dartmouth College and Moor's Charity School*.
1815	New Hampshire's legislature agrees to John Wheelock's request for an investigation of Dartmouth College board of trustees.
1816	New Hampshire governor William Plumer makes legislative supervision of Dartmouth College a campaign issue.

1816	New Hampshire legislature passes the Act of 1816 to amend the charter of Dartmouth College as "Dartmouth University" (June 27).
1816	New Hampshire's legislature passes so-called Penal Acts to bring Dartmouth College faculty and trustees under state authority.
1816	Dartmouth College trustees file a suit for "trover" of institutional records in the court of common pleas of Grafton County; suit is referred to New Hampshire's Superior Court.
1817	John Wheelock dies; the college trustees name Francis Brown to succeed him as president of both Dartmouth College and the Indian Charity School; meanwhile, Dartmouth University names William Allen as president.
1817	President James Monroe attends commencement festivities at both Dartmouth College and Dartmouth University.
1817	*Trustees of Dartmouth College v. Woodward* is heard in New Hampshire's Superior Court; Jeremiah Mason and Jeremiah Smith argue for the college; George Sullivan and Ichabod Bartlett argue for the university/the state.
1817	New Hampshire's Superior Court decides for the university/the state; decision read by Chief Justice William Richardson.
1817	Dartmouth University, victorious in court, attempts to seize the property of Dartmouth College, including the libraries of its student literary societies.
1817	US Supreme Court justice Joseph Story is (mistakenly) suspected of bias in favor of Dartmouth University.
1817	Justice Story appears to advise lawyers for Dartmouth College on alternate legal strategies.
1817	Daniel Webster files three parallel lawsuits in Justice Story's circuit in an effort to prove the "private" property rights of Dartmouth College trustees.
1817	Justice Henry Livingston decides *Adams v. Storey*; upholds New York insolvency law that permits abrogation of future debt contracts, a decision at odds with Justice Bushrod Washington's decision in *Golden v. Prince* (1814).
1818	*Trustees of Dartmouth College v. Woodward* is heard in the US Supreme Court; Daniel Webster and Joseph Hopkinson argue for

	the college; John Holmes and William Wirt argue for the university/the state.
1818	US Supreme Court postpones decision in *Dartmouth v. Woodward* for a year.
1818	Daniel Webster prints his *Argument in the Case of the Trustees of Dartmouth College v. William H. Woodward* for distribution to judges.
1818	New York chancellor James Kent, a close friend of Justices William Johnson and Henry Livingston, appears to side with the university/the state, then reverses to support the college.
1818	Henry Brougham conducts parliamentary investigation to reveal abuse of charitable trusts in England; fails to win greater public authority to supervise Oxbridge colleges, etc.
1818	Dartmouth University lawyers assemble "new facts" to prove that Dartmouth College's first donor was Governor John Wentworth on behalf of the colony of New Hampshire.
1819	Dartmouth University hires William Pinkney to present its "new facts" before the US Supreme Court; his argument is never heard.
1819	US Supreme Court decides *Trustees of Dartmouth College v. Woodward* with a 5–1 ruling in favor the college.
1819	Dartmouth College reclaims the campus occupied for two and a half years by Dartmouth University.
1819	Justice Story dismisses Daniel Webster's three additional lawsuits intended to prove the property rights of Dartmouth College trustees; all related cases are now closed.
1819	New Hampshire's legislature contemplates a public "New Hampshire University," but the Panic of 1819 and subsequent economic recession thwart its plans.
1820	Dartmouth College president Francis Brown dies and is replaced by Bennett Tyler.
1820	The Missouri Compromise instigates the separation of the new state of Maine from the state of Massachusetts.
1820	The separation of Maine from Massachusetts requires new state constitutions, with new provisions for the governance of colleges; Daniel Webster and Joseph Story collaborate to

	minimize the collegiate oversight of Massachusetts's legislature; Maine's legislature does not inherit such oversight.
1821	New Hampshire uses a bank tax to create a Literary Fund to support a new public university; Dartmouth College discusses the creation of a public board of overseers in exchange for a share of this fund.
1825	Massachusetts charters Amherst College with no public aid.
1825	New Hampshire resumes consideration of a public university supported by the state Literary Fund; again, Dartmouth College seeks a share of this fund.
1827	US Supreme Court rules in *Ogden v. Saunders* that state insolvency laws are constitutional; Justices Marshall, Story, and Washington dissent on grounds that financial contracts, once made, cannot be unmade.
1833	Justice Story decides in *Allen v. McKean* that Bowdoin College, founded with public funds, is nonetheless a private corporation, because its charter had created an independent board of trustees and the Act of Separation that created the state of Maine did not explicitly reserve a right of legislative supervision; this decision reverses core principles of Story's concurrence in *Dartmouth*.
1862	Congress passes the Morrill Act to provide northern states federal land grants to support higher education.
1866	To receive a Morrill land grant, New Hampshire charters a College of Agriculture and the Mechanic Arts, attached to Dartmouth College but governed by a separate board of trustees.
1890	New Hampshire moves its College of Agriculture and the Mechanic Arts from Hanover to Durham.
1923	New Hampshire recharters the College of Agriculture and the Mechanic Arts as the public University of New Hampshire.

BIBLIOGRAPHIC ESSAY

Over two centuries have passed since the court ruled in *Trustees of Dartmouth College v. Woodward*, and during those years the case has attracted considerable scholarly attention. For early histories and collections of documents related to the case, see for example David McClure and Elijah Parish, *Memoirs of the Rev. Eleazar Wheelock, D.D.* (Newburyport, MA: Edward Little, 1811); *Documents Relative to Dartmouth College* (Concord, NH: by order of the legislature, 1816); Timothy Farrar, *Report of the Case of the Trustees of Dartmouth College Against William H. Woodward, Argued and Determined in the Superior Court of Judicature of the State of New Hampshire, November 1817, and on Error in the Supreme Court of the United States, February 1819* (Portsmouth, NH: J. W. Foster, 1819); Baxter Perry Smith, *The History of Dartmouth College* (Boston: Houghton, Osgood, 1878); John Major Shirley, *The Dartmouth College Causes and the Supreme Court of the United States* (St. Louis: G. I. Jones, 1879); Frederick Chase, *A History of Dartmouth College and the Town of Hanover, New Hampshire*, 2 vols. (Cambridge, MA: J. Wilson, 1891–1913; the second volume is John King Lord, *A History of Dartmouth College, 1815–1909* [1913]); Leon B. Richardson, *History of Dartmouth College*, 2 vols. (Hanover, NH: Dartmouth College Publications, 1932); and James Dow McCallum, *Eleazar Wheelock: Founder of Dartmouth College*, Dartmouth College manuscript series, no. 4 (Dartmouth College Publications, 1939). For histories of the case and the college written since the mid-twentieth century, see Ralph Nading Hill, ed., *The College on the Hill: A Dartmouth Chronicle* (Hanover, NH: Dartmouth Publications, 1964); Henry J. Friendly, "The Dartmouth College Case and the Public-Private Penumbra: A Lecture Delivered on May 10, 1968, at Dartmouth College," supplement to the *Texas Quarterly* 12, no. 2 (1969); Francis Stites, *Private Interest and Public Gain: The Dartmouth College Case, 1819* (Amherst: University of Massachusetts Press, 1972); John S. Whitehead, *The Separation of College and State: Columbia, Dartmouth, Harvard, and Yale, 1776–1876* (New Haven, CT: Yale University Press, 1973); Bruce Campbell, *Law and Experience in the Early Republic: The Evolution of Dartmouth College Doctrine, 1780–1819* (unpublished PhD dissertation, Michigan State University, 1973); Jürgen Herbst, *From Crisis to Crisis: American College Government, 1636–1819* (Cambridge, MA: Harvard University Press, 1982); and Dick Hoefnagel,

Eleazar Wheelock and the Adventurous Founding of Dartmouth College (Hanover, NH: Hanover Historical Society, 2002).

Aside from these book-length works, a number of studies on the *Dartmouth* case have appeared in scholarly journals and law reviews. For articles from the late nineteenth and early twentieth centuries, see for example Aldace Walker, "A Legal Mummy, or, the Present Status of the Dartmouth College Case: An Address Delivered at the Annual Meeting of the Vermont Bar Association, at Montpelier, Vt., October 28, 1885" (Argus and Patriot Book and Job Printing House, 1886); Charles J. Doe, "A New View of the Dartmouth College Case," *Harvard Law Review* 6, no. 4 (November 5, 1892): 161–183, and vol. 6, no. 5 (December 15, 1892): 213–222; W. S. G. Noyes, "Webster, His Debt to Mason, in the Dartmouth College Case," *American Law Review* 28 (1894): 356–367; Alfred Russell, "Status and Tendencies of the Dartmouth College Case," *American Law Review* 30, no. 3 (1896): 321–356; William Trickett, "The Dartmouth College Paralogism," *Forum* 10, no. 7 (1906): 147–158; Robert Sprague Hall, "The Dartmouth College Cases," *Green Bag* 20 (1908): 244–247; R. M. Denham, "An Historical Development of the Contract Theory in the Dartmouth College Case," *Michigan Law Review* 7, no. 3 (January 1909): 201–225; Jesse F. Orton, "Confusion of Property with Privilege: The Dartmouth College Case," *The Virginia Law Register* (1909): 417–427; Charles Warren, "An Historical Note on the Dartmouth College Case," *American Law Review* 46, no. 5 (September–October 1912): 665–675; James C. Jenkins, "Should the Dartmouth College Decision Be Recalled," *American Law Review* 51 (1917): 711–751; Horace H. Hagan. "The Dartmouth College Case," *Georgetown Law Journal* 19, no. 4 (May 1931): 411–426; Hugh E. Willis, "The Dartmouth College Case—Then and Now," *St. Louis Law Review* 19, no. 3 (April 1934): 183–200; Gordon R. Clapp, "The College Charter," *Journal of Higher Education* 5, no. 2 (February 1934): 79–87; and William Gwyer North, "The Political Background of the Dartmouth College Case," *New England Quarterly* 18, no. 1 (1945): 181–203.

For a sample of journal essays and law review articles published since the mid-twentieth century, see Maurice G. Baxter, "Should the Dartmouth College Case Have Been Reargued?" *New England Quarterly* 33, no. 1 (1960): 19–36; Merle Borrowman, "The False Dawn of the State University," *History of Higher Education Quarterly* 1, no. 2 (June 1961): 6–22; Richard W. Morin, "Will to Resist: The Dartmouth College Case,"

Dartmouth Alumni Magazine (April 1969); Jere Daniell, "Eleazar Wheelock and the Dartmouth College Charter," *History of New Hampshire* (1969): 33–45; Steven J. Novak. "The College in the Dartmouth College Case: A Reinterpretation," *New England Quarterly* 47, no. 4 (December 1974): 550–563; Bruce Campbell, "John Marshall, the Virginia Political Economy, and the Dartmouth College Decision," *American Journal of Legal History* 19, no. 1 (1975): 40–65; Bruce A. Campbell, "*Dartmouth College* as a Civil Liberties Case: The Formation of Constitutional Policy," *Kentucky Law Journal* 70, no. 3 (Summer 1982): 643–706; Eldon L. Johnson, "The Dartmouth College Case: The Neglected Educational Meaning," *Journal of the Early Republic* 3, no. 1 (Spring 1983): 45–67; Mary Frampton Beach, "An Analysis of the Dartmouth College Case and Its Impact on the Founding of American Colleges and Universities Between 1819 and 1839" (unpublished PhD dissertation, Boston College, 1990); Elizabeth Brand Monroe, "The Influence of the Dartmouth College Case on the American Law of Educational Charities," *Journal of Supreme Court History* 32, no. 1 (March 2007): 1–21; Peter Jaros, "A Double Life: Personifying the Corporation from *Dartmouth College* to Poe," *Poe Studies* 47 (2014): 4–35; Jane Fiegen Green, "'An Opinion of Our Own': Education, Politics, and the Struggle for Adulthood at Dartmouth College, 1814–1819," *History of Education Quarterly* 52, no. 2 (May 2012): 173–195; Ernest A. Young, "*Dartmouth College v. Woodward* and the Structure of Civil Society," *University of New Hampshire Law Review* 18, no. 1 (November 2019): 41–61; David M. Rabban, "From Impairment of Contracts to Institutional Academic Freedom: The Enduring Significance of the Dartmouth College Case," *University of New Hampshire Law Review* 18, no. 1 (November 2019): 9–25; Alyssa Penick, "From Disestablishment to *Dartmouth College v. Woodward*: How Virginia's Fight over Religious Freedom Shaped the History of American Corporations," *Law and History Review* 39 (2021): 479–512; Margaret M. Blair, "How *Trustees of Dartmouth College v. Woodward* Clarified Corporate Law," *Vanderbilt University Law School Legal Studies Research Paper Series*, working paper no. 21–19 (2021), https://perma.cc/GDZ6-K6SS; and Charles R. T. O'Kelley, "What Was the *Dartmouth College* Case Really About?" *Vanderbilt Law Review* 74, no. 6 (November 2021): 1645–1726.

Several biographies, memoirs, and collections of correspondence have been published on central figures in Dartmouth College history. For example, on Samson Occom and Nathaniel Whitaker, see William

D. Love, *Samson Occom and the Christian Indians of New England* (Boston: Pilgrim, 1899); Harold W. Blodgett, *Samson Occom* (Hanover, NH: Dartmouth College Publications, 1935); Leon Burr Richardson, ed., *An Indian Preacher in England, Being Letters and Diaries Relating to the Mission of the Reverend Nathaniel Whitaker to Collect Funds in England for the Benefit of Eleazar Wheelock's Indian Charity School, from Which Grew Dartmouth College* (Hanover, NH: Dartmouth College Publications, 1933); Colin G. Calloway, *The Indian History of an American Institution: Native Americans and Dartmouth* (Hanover, NH: Dartmouth College Press; University Press of New England, 2010); Jessica Lauren Criales, "'My Obligation to the Doctor for His Paternal Care': Eleazar Wheelock and the Female Students at Moor's Indian Charity School, 1761–1769," *Social Sciences and Missions* 30, nos. 3–4 (2017): 279–297; and Ivy Schweitzer, ed., "Occom's Circle," a digital collection of works by and about Samson Occom that can be found at https://www.dartmouth.edu/~occom/, accessed 28 October 2024. On New Hampshire governors Benning and John Wentworth, see Lawrence Shaw Mayo, *John Wentworth, Governor of New Hampshire, 1767–1775* (Cambridge, MA: Harvard University Press, 1921); Jere R. Daniell, "Politics in New Hampshire under Governor Benning Wentworth, 1741–1767," *William and Mary Quarterly* 23, no. 1 (1966): 76–105; Jess G. Hayes, *Boots and Bullets: The Life and Times of John W. Wentworth* (Tucson: University of Arizona Press, 1967); Paul W. Wilderson, *Protagonist of Prudence: A Biography of John Wentworth, The King's Last Governor of New Hampshire* (1977); Brian Cuthbertson, *The Loyalist Governor: Biography of Sir John Wentworth* (Halifax, NS: Petheric Press, 1983); Bobby Wright, "'For the Children of the Infidels'? American Indian Education in the Colonial Colleges," *American Indian Culture and Research Journal* 12, no. 3 (1988): 1–14; and Paul W. Wilderson, *Governor John Wentworth and the American Revolution: The English Connection* (Halifax, NS: Petheric, 1994). On Governor William Plumer, see William Plumer Jr., *Life of William Plumer* (Boston: Phillips, Sampson, 1857) and Lynn W. Turner, *William Plumer of New Hampshire, 1759–1850* (Chapel Hill: University of North Carolina Press, 1962); on Isaac Hill, see Cyrus P. Bradley, *Biography of Isaac Hill of New Hampshire* (Concord, NH: J. F. Brown, 1835); on William Allen, see Egbert C. Smyth, *Three Discourses upon the Religious History of Bowdoin College During the Administrations of Presidents M'Keen, Appleton, and Allen* (Brunswick, ME: J. Griffin, 1858). For broader works on Dartmouth's establishment in historical context, see Craig Steven Wilder, *Ebony and Ivy: Race, Slavery, and the Troubled History of America's Universities* (New York: Bloomsbury, 2013); and Steve Pincus, "Dartmouth College and Patriot State Building" in *Dartmouth and the World: Religion and Political Economy circa 1769*, ed. Henry C. Clark (Vancouver, BC: Fairleigh Dickinson University Press, 2023), 39–64.

Of course, Daniel Webster has received extensive biographical treatment. See, for example, Charles Lanman, *The Private Life of Daniel Webster* (New York: Harper & Brothers, 1852); Samuel P. Lyman, *The Public and Private Life of Daniel Webster, Including Most of His Great Speeches, Letters From Marshfield, etc.*, 2 vols. (Philadelphia: J. E. Potter, 1852); George Ticknor Curtis, *Life of Daniel Webster* (New York: D. Appleton, 1870); Henry Cabot Lodge, *Daniel Webster* (New York: Houghton, Mifflin, 1883 and 1911); Samuel W. McCall, *Daniel Webster* (Boston: Houghton, Mifflin, 1902); John B. McMaster, *Daniel Webster* (New York: D. Appleton-Century, 1902); F. Webster, *The Writings and Speeches of Daniel Webster* (Boston: Little, Brown, 1903); Everett P. Wheeler, *Daniel Webster: The Expounder of the Constitution* (New York: G. P. Putnam's Sons, 1905); Allen L. Benson, *Daniel Webster* (New York: Cosmopolitan Book, 1929); Claude Moore Fuess, *Daniel Webster*, 2 vols. (Boston: Little, Brown, 1930); Maurice G. Baxter, *Daniel Webster and The Supreme Court* (Amherst: University of Massachusetts Press, 1966); R. Kent Newmyer, "Daniel Webster as Tocqueville's Lawyer: The Dartmouth College Case Again," *American Journal of Legal History* 11, no. 2 (April 1967): 127–147; Alfred S. Konefsky and Andrew J. King, eds., *The Papers of Daniel Webster*, 3 vols. (Hanover, NH: Published for Dartmouth College by the University Press of New England, 1982–89); and Robert V. Remini, *Daniel Webster: The Man and His Time* (New York: W. W. Norton, 1997). See also Burton A. Konkle, *Joseph Hopkinson, 1770–1842: Jurist, Scholar, Inspirer of the Arts, Author of Hail Columbia* (Philadelphia: University of Pennsylvania Press, 1931).

Joseph Story, too, has attracted significant historical attention. See, for example, Joseph Story, *The Opinion of Judge Story in the Case of William Allen v. Joseph McKeen, Treasurer of Bowdoin College: Decided in the Circuit Court of the United States at the May Term at Portland* (Boston: Printed at the office of the *Daily Advertiser and Patriot*, 1833); William W. Story, ed., *Life and Letters of Joseph Story, Associate Justice of the Supreme Court of the United States and Dane Professor of Law at Harvard University*, 2 vols. (Boston: Little,

Brown, 1851); Gerald T. Dunne, "Mr. Justice Story and the American Law of Banking," *American Journal of Legal History* 5 (1961): 205–229; Gerald T. Dunne, "Joseph Story: The Middle Years," *Harvard Law Review* 80, no. 8 (June 1967): 1679–1709; Gerald T. Dunne, *Joseph Story and the Rise of the Supreme Court* (New York: Simon & Schuster, 1970); Craig T. Friend, *Joseph Story, Bankruptcy, and the Supreme Court*, in *Encyclopedia of Historic U.S. Court Cases, 1690–1990*, ed. John W. Johnson (New York: Garland, 1992), 340–343; Morgan Dowd, "Justice Joseph Story: A Study of the Contributions of a Jeffersonian Judge to the Development of American Constitutional Law" (unpublished PhD dissertation, University of Massachusetts, 1964); James McClellan, *Joseph Story and the American Constitution: A Study in Political and Legal Thought with Selected Writings* (Norman: University of Oklahoma Press, 1971); Gerald T. Dunne, "Justice Story and the Modern Corporation—A Closing Circle?" *American Journal of Legal History* 17 (1973): 262–270; R. Kent Newmyer, "Justice Joseph Story, the Charles River Bridge Case, and the Crisis of Republicanism," *American Journal of Legal History* 17 (1973): 232–245; R. Kent Newmyer, "Justice Joseph Story's Doctrine of 'Public and Private Corporations' and the Rise of the American Business Corporation," *DePaul Law Review* 25 (1976): 825–841; R. Kent Newmyer, *Supreme Court Justice Joseph Story: Statesman of the Old Republic* (Chapel Hill: University of North Carolina Press, 1985); Alan Watson, *Joseph Story and the Comity of Errors: A Case Study in Conflict of Laws* (Athens: University of Georgia Press, 1992); and David Lynch, *The Role of Circuit Courts in the Formation of United States Law in the Early Republic: Following Supreme Court Justices Washington, Livingston, Story, and Thompson* (Portland, OR: Hart, 2018). On Justice Story's colleague Gabriel Duvall, see David P. Currie, "The Most Insignificant Justice: A Preliminary Inquiry," *University of Chicago Law Review* 50, no. 2 (1983): 466–480; and Frank H. Easterbrook, "The Most Insignificant Justice: Further Evidence," *University of Chicago Law Review* 50, no. 2 (1983): 483–503.

John Marshall, a titan of American judicial history, has numerous first-rate biographies. Among the most useful are Albert J. Beveridge, *The Life of John Marshall*, 4 vols. (New York: Houghton Mifflin, 1929); David Loth, *Chief Justice: John Marshall and the Growth of the Republic* (New York: W. W. Norton, 1949); Saul K. Padover, "The Political Ideas of John Marshall," *Social Research* 26, no. 1 (Spring 1959): 47–70; W. Melville Jones, *Chief Justice John Marshall: A Reappraisal* (Ithaca, NY: Published for the

College of William and Mary by Cornell University Press, 1956); Florian Bartosic, "With John Marshall from William and Mary to Dartmouth College," *William and Mary Law Review* 7 (1966): 259–266; C. Peter Magrath, *Yazoo: Law and Politics in the New Republic: The Case of Fletcher v. Peck* (Providence, RI: Brown University Press, 1966); Robert K. Faulkner, *The Jurisprudence of John Marshall* (Westport, CT: Greenwood, 1968); Stanley Kutler, *John Marshall* (Englewood Cliffs, NJ: Prentice-Hall, 1972); Bruce A. Campbell, "John Marshall, the Virginia Political Economy, and the *Dartmouth College* Decision," *American Journal of Legal History* 19 (1975): 40–65; Leonard Baker, *John Marshall: A Life in Law* (New York: Macmillan, 1974); William F. Swindler, "Another Early College Charter Case," *Yale Bulletin of Supreme Court History* (1977); William F. Swindler, *The Constitution and Chief Justice Marshall* (New York: Dodd, Mead, 1978); Francis N. Stites, *John Marshall: Defender of the Constitution* (Boston: Little, Brown, 1981); George L. Haskins, *Foundations of Power: John Marshall 1801–1815* (New York: Macmillan, 1981); G. Edward White, "The Working Life of the Marshall Court, 1815–1835," *Virginia Law Review* 70 (1984): 1–52, and *The Marshall Court and Cultural Change, 1815–1835* (New York: Macmillan, 1988); Charles F. Hobson, *The Great Chief Justice: John Marshall and the Rule of Law* (Lawrence: University of Kansas Press, 1996); Charles F. Hobson, "John Marshall and the Fairfax Litigation: The Background of Martin v. Hunter's Lessee," *Journal of Supreme Court History*, 1996, no. 2 (1996): 36–50; Jean E. Smith, *John Marshall: Definer of a Nation* (Lawrence: University Press of Kansas, 1996); Herbert A. Johnson, *The Chief Justiceship of John Marshall, 1801–1835* (Columbia: University of South Carolina Press, 1997); Stephen A. Siegel, "Rebalancing Professor Ely's Reappraisal of the Marshall Court and Property Rights," *John Marshall Law Review* 33, no. 4 (Summer 2000): 1165–1174; R. Kent Newmyer, *John Marshall and the Heroic Age of the Supreme Court* (Baton Rouge: Louisiana State University Press, 2001); James W. Ely Jr., "The Marshall Court and Property Rights: A Reappraisal," *John Marshall Law Review* 33 (2002): 1023–1197; Christopher Wolfe, "'An Artificial Being': John Marshall and Corporate Personhood," *Harvard Journal of Law and Public Policy* 40, no. 1 (Winter 2017): 201–235; John R. Paul, *Without Precedent: John Marshall and His Times* (New York: Riverhead Books, 2018); and David S. Schwartz, *The Spirit of the Constitution: John Marshall and the 200-Year Odyssey of McCulloch v. Maryland* (New York: Oxford University Press, 2019). See also Oliver Schroeder Jr., "The

Life and Judicial Work of Justice William Johnson, Jr.," *University of Pennsylvania Law Review* 95, no. 3 (February 1947): 344–386.

Several of the lawyers involved with the *Dartmouth* case have received their own biographical treatments. On Jeremiah Smith, see John H. Morison, *Life of the Hon. Jeremiah Smith, LL. D., Member of Congress During Washington's Administration, Judge of the United States Circuit Court, Chief Justice of New Hampshire* (Boston: C. C. Little and J. Brown, 1845). On Jeremiah Mason, see *Proceedings in Massachusetts and New Hampshire on the Death of the Hon. Jeremiah Mason* (Boston: John Wilson, 1849); George S. Hillard, *Memoir and Correspondence of Jeremiah Mason* (Cambridge: Riverside, 1873); and Jeremiah Mason, *Memoir, Autobiography, and Correspondence of Jeremiah Mason* (Kansas City, MO: Lawyers' International, 1917). On judge William Richardson, see Charles H. Bell, *Life of William M. Richardson, LL.D.: Late Chief Justice of the Superior Court in New Hampshire* (Concord, NH: Israel S. Boyd and William White, 1839). On William Wirt, see Samuel Southard, *A Discourse on the Professional Character and Virtues of the Late William Wirt* (Washington, DC: Gales and Seaton, 1834); John P. Kennedy, *Memoirs of the Life of William Wirt, Attorney General of the United States*, 2 vols. (Philadelphia: Lea and Blanchard, 1849); Joseph Burke, "William Wirt: Attorney General and Constitutional Lawyer" (unpublished PhD dissertation, Indiana University, 1965); and Steven M. Klepper, "The Elite Federal Bar in Baltimore, 1818–1834," *The Federal Lawyer* (July 2011): 31–36. On William Pinkney, see William Pinkney, *Some Account of the Life, Writings, and Speeches of William Pinkney* (New York: J. W. Palmer, 1826); William Pinkney, *The Life of William Pinkney* (New York: D. Appleton, 1853); and Robert M. Ireland, "William Pinkney: A Revision and Re-emphasis," *American Journal of Legal History* 14, no. 3 (1970): 235–246, and *The Legal Career of William Pinkney, 1764–1822* (New York: Garland, 1986).

For works on some of the other legal figures in the *Dartmouth* case, see, for example, Lucien H. Alexander, *James Wilson, Nation-Builder, 1742–1798* (Boston: Boston Book, 1907); William F. Obering, *The Philosophy of Law of James Wilson, Associate Justice of the United States Supreme Court, 1789–1798; A Study in Comparative Jurisprudence* (Washington, DC: Issued by the Office of the Secretary of the American Catholic Philosophical Association, Catholic University of America, 1938); Page Smith, *James Wilson, Founding Father, 1742–1798* (Chapel Hill: University of North Carolina Press for the Institute of Early American History and Culture, 1956); Jean-Marc Pascal,

The Political Ideas of James Wilson, 1742–1798 (New York: Garland, 1991); and Mark David Hall, *The Political and Legal Philosophy of James Wilson, 1742–1798* (Columbia: University of Missouri Press, 1997). On Chancellor James Kent, see John Duer, *A Discourse on the Life, Character, and Public Services of James Kent, Late Chancellor of the State of New-York, Delivered by Request, before the Judiciary and Bar of the City and State of New-York, April 12, 1848* (New York: D. Appleton, 1848); William Kent, *Memoirs and Letters of James Kent, LL.D.: Late Chancellor of the State of New York* (Boston: Little, Brown, 1898); Macgrane Coxe, "Chancellor Kent at Yale, 1777–1781," *Yale Law Journal* 17, no. 5 (March 1908): 311–337 and "Chancellor Kent at Yale, Part II," *Yale Law Journal* 17, no. 8 (June 1908): 553–572; John T. Horton, *James Kent: A Study in Conservativism 1763–1847* (New York: D. Appleton-Century, 1939); and Joseph Dorfman, "Chancellor Kent and the Developing American Economy," *Columbia Law Review* 61, no. 7 (November 1961): 1290–1317. On Theophilus Parsons, see Isaac Parker, *A Sketch of the Character of the Late Chief Justice Parsons: Exhibited in an Address to the Grand Jury, Delivered at the Opening of the Supreme Judicial Court, at Boston, on the Twenty-third Day of November, 1813, after the Usual Charge* (Boston: John Eliat, 1813); Theophilus Parsons, *The Law of Contracts*, 2 vols. (Boston: Little, Brown, 1853); and Theophilus Parsons, *Memoir of Theophilus Parsons, Chief Justice of the Supreme Judicial Court of Massachusetts; With Notices of Some of His Contemporaries* (Boston: Ticknor and Fields, 1859).

On the law of contracts and the rise of US business corporations, see Samuel Williston, "History of the Law of Business Corporations before 1800: I," *Harvard Law Review* 3 (October 1888): 105–124 and Samuel Williston, "History of the Law of Business Corporations before 1800: II," *Harvard Law Review* 4 (October 1888): 149–166; Joseph Stancliffe Davis, *Essays in the Earlier History of American Corporations*, vol. 1 (Cambridge, MA: Harvard University Press, 1917); Adolf Berle and Gardiner Means, *The Modern Corporation and Private Property* (New York: Macmillan, 1932); Joseph G. Blandi, *Maryland Business Corporations, 1783–1852* (Baltimore: Johns Hopkins University Press, 1934); Robert A. East, *Business Enterprise in the American Revolutionary Era* (Gloucester, MA: P. Smith, 1938); James J. Robbins, "Private Corporation: Its Constitutional Genesis," *Georgetown Law Journal* 28, no. 2 (November 1939): 165–183; George Herberton Evans Jr., *Business Incorporations in the United States, 1800–1943* (New York: National Bureau of Economic Research, 1948); William C. Kessler, "A Statistical

Study of the New York General Incorporation Act of 1811," *Journal of Political Economy* 48, no. 6 (December 1940): 877–882; William C. Kessler, "Incorporation in New England: A Statistical Study, 1800–1875," *Journal of Economic History* 8 (1948): 43–62; John W. Cadman Jr., *The Corporation in New Jersey: Business and Politics, 1791–1875* (Cambridge, MA: Harvard University Press, 1949); Edwin Merrick Dodd, *American Business Corporations until 1860, with Special Reference to Massachusetts* (Cambridge, MA: Harvard University Press, 1954); James Willard Hurst, *The Legitimacy of the Business Corporation in the Law of the United States, 1780–1970* (Charlottesville: University of Virginia Press, 1970); Ronald E. Seavoy, "Laws to Encourage Manufacturing: New York Policy and the 1811 General Incorporation Statute," *Business History Review* 46, no. 1 (1972): 85–95; Ronald E. Seavoy, "The Public Service Origins of the American Business Corporation," *Business History Review* 52 (1978): 31–60; Ronald E. Seavoy, *The Origins of the American Business Corporation, 1784–1855: Broadening the Concept of Public Service during Industrialization* (1982); Gregory A. Mark, "The Personification of the Business Corporation in American Law," *University of Chicago Law Review* 54, no. 4 (1987): 1441–1483; Herbert Hovenkamp, "The Classical Corporation in American Legal Thought," *Georgetown Law Journal* 76, no. 5 (June 1988): 1593–690 and *Enterprise and American Law, 1836–1937* (Cambridge, MA: Harvard University Press, 1991); David Shelledy, "Autonomy, Debate, and Corporate Speech," *Hastings Constitutional Law Quarterly* 18, no. 3 (Spring 1991): 541–585; Daniel B. Klein and John Majewski, "Economy, Community, and the Law: The Turnpike Movement in New York, 1797–1845," *Law and Society* 26 (1992): 469–512; Susan Pace Hamill, "From Special Privilege to General Utility: A Continuation of Willard Hurst's Study of Corporations," *American University Law Review* 49 (1999): 81–180; Ron Harris, *Industrializing English Law: Entrepreneurship and Business Organization, 1720–1844* (Cambridge: Cambridge University Press, 2000); Henry Hansmann and Reinier Kraakman, "The End of History for Corporate Law," *Georgetown Law Journal* 89 (2001): 439–468; Margaret M. Blair, "Locking In Capital: What Corporate Law Achieved for Business Organizers in the Nineteenth Century," *UCLA Law Review* 51 (2003): 387–455; Kenneth Lipartito and David B. Cicila, eds., *Constructing Corporate America: History, Politics, Culture* (Oxford: Oxford University Press, 2004); Howard Bodenhorn, "Bank Chartering and Political Corruption in Antebellum New York: Free Banking as Reform," working paper 10479 (Cambridge, MA: National Bureau of Economic Research, 2004); John Majewski, "Toward a Social History of the Corporation: Shareholding in Pennsylvania, 1800–1840," in *The Economy of Early America: Historical Perspectives and New Directions*, ed. Cathy D. Matson (University Park: Pennsylvania State University Press, 2006); Andrew M. Schocket, *Founding Corporate Power in Early National Philadelphia* (DeKalb, IL: Northern Illinois University Press, 2007); Eric Hilt, "When Did Ownership Separate from Control? Corporate Governance in the Early Nineteenth Century," *NBER*, working paper 13093 (2007); Eric Hilt, "Corporate Law and the Shift Toward Open Access in the Antebellum United States," *NBER*, working paper 21195 (2015); Qian Lu and John Joseph Wallis, "Banks, Politics, and Political Parties: From Partisan Banking to Open Access in Early Massachusetts," *NBER*, working paper 21572 (2015); Mark R. Killenbeck, "M'Culloch in Context," *Arkansas Law Review* 72, no. 1 (Summer 2019): 35–77; Elizabeth Pollman, "The History and Revival of the Corporate Purpose Clause," *Texas Law Review* 99 (2021): 1423–1452; Elizabeth Pollman, "Corporate Personhood and Limited Sovereignty," *Vanderbilt Law Review* 74, no. 6 (November 2021): 1727–1754; and Saule Omarova, "The 'Franchise' View of the Corporation: Purpose, Personality, Public Policy," in *Research Handbook of Corporate Purpose and Personhood*, eds. Elizabeth Pollman and Robert B. Thompson, Cornell Legal Studies Research Paper no. 21-18 (July 2021), available at https://ssrn.com/abstract=3887478, accessed 28 October 2024; among others.

On the law of contracts and corporations in relation to charitable activity, including wills, trusts, and estates, see Irvin G. Wyllie, "The Search for an American Law of Charity, 1776–1844," *The Mississippi Valley Historical Review* 46, vol. 2 (September 1959): 203–221; W. K. Jordan, *Philanthropy in England, 1480–1660* (London: George Allen and Unwin, 1959); Howard S. Miller, *The Legal Foundations of American Philanthropy, 1776–1844* (Madison: State Historical Society of Wisconsin, 1961); Gareth Jones, *History of the Law of Charity, 1532–1827* (Cambridge: Cambridge University Press, 1969); Margaret Gerteis, "The Massachusetts General Hospital, 1810–1855: An Essay on the Political Construction of Social Responsibility" (unpublished PhD dissertation, Tufts University, 1985); Bruce A. Campbell, "Social Federalism: The Constitutional Position of Nonprofit Corporations in Nineteenth Century America," *Law and History Review* 8, vol. 2 (Autumn 1990): 149–188; Conrad Edick Wright, *The Transformation of Charity in Postrevolutionary New England* (Boston: Northeastern University Press, 1992); Peter Dobkin Hall, *Inventing the Nonprofit Sector and Other Essays on Philanthropy, Voluntarism, and Nonprofit Organizations* (Baltimore: Johns Hopkins University Press, 1992); Peter Dobkin Hall, "What the Merchants Did with Their Money: Charitable and Testamentary Trusts in Massachusetts, 1780–1880," in *Entrepreneurs: The Boston Business Community, 1700–1850*, eds. Conrad Edick Wright and Katheryn P. Viens (Boston: Massachusetts Historical Society; distributed by Northeastern University Press, 1997), 365–422; Norman I. Silber, *A Corporate Form of Freedom: The Emergence of the Modern Nonprofit Sector* (Boulder, CO: Westview, 2001); Kathleen D. McCarthy, *American Creed: Philanthropy and the Rise of Civil Society, 1700–1865* (Chicago: University of Chicago Press, 2003); Johann Neem, "Politics and the Origins of the Nonprofit Corporation in Massachusetts and New Hampshire, 1780–1820," *Nonprofit and Voluntary Sector Quarterly* 32, no. 2 (September 2003): 344–365.

On the relationship between the law of corporations and religious disestablishment, see Patrick J. Dignan, *History of the Legal Incorporation of Catholic Church Property in the United States, 1784–1932* (New York: P. J. Kenedy and Sons, 1935); Charles B. Kinney, Jr., *Church and State: The Struggle for Separation in New Hampshire* (New York: Teachers College of Columbia University, 1955); Norman Allen Baxter, *History of the Freewill Baptists: A Study in New England Separatism* (Rochester, NY: American Baptist Historical Society, 1957); Mark deWolfe Howe, *The Garden and the Wilderness: Religion and Government in American Constitutional History* (Chicago: University of Chicago Press, 1965); John D. Cushing, "Notes on Disestablishment in Massachusetts, 1780–1833," *William and Mary Quarterly* 26 (April 1969): 172–185; Kirk Gilbert Alliman, "The Incorporation of Massachusetts Congregational Churches, 1692–1833: The Preservation of Religious Autonomy" (unpublished PhD dissertation, University of Iowa, 1970); William G. McLoughlin, *New England Dissent, 1630–1833: The Baptists and the Separation of Church and State*, 2 vols. (Cambridge, MA: Harvard University Press, 1971); Paul G. Kauper and Stephen S. Ellis, "Religious Corporations and the Law," *Michigan Law Review* 71, no. 8 (August 1973): 1499–1574; Leonard W. Levy, *The Establishment Clause: Religion and the First Amendment* (New York: Macmillan, 1986), chs. 2–3; Thomas J. Curry, *The First Freedoms: Church and State in America to the Passage of the First Amendment* (New York: Oxford University Press, 1986); Randolph A.

Roth, *The Democratic Dilemma: Religion, Reform, and the Social Order in the Connecticut River Valley of Vermont, 1791–1850* (Cambridge: Cambridge University Press, 1987); Thomas Buckley, "Evangelicals Triumphant: The Baptists' Assault on the Virginia Glebes, 1786–1801," *William and Mary Quarterly* 45, no. 1 (1988): 33–69; Nathan O. Hatch, *The Democratization of American Christianity* (New Haven, CT: Yale University Press, 1991); Kelly Olds, "Privatizing the Church: Disestablishment in Connecticut and Massachusetts," *Journal of Political Economy* 102, no. 2 (1994): 277–297; Thomas E. Buckley, S.J., "After Disestablishment: Thomas Jefferson's Wall of Separation in Antebellum Virginia," *Journal of Southern History* 61, no. 3 (August 1995): 445–480; John C. DeBoer and Clara Merritt DeBoer, "The Formation of Town Churches: Church, Town, and State in Early Vermont," *Vermont History* 64 (1996): 69–88; Thomas E. Buckley, "The Use and Abuse of Jefferson's Statute: Separating Church and State in Nineteenth-Century Virginia," in *Religion in the New Republic: Faith and the Founding of America*, ed. James H. Hutson (Lanham, MD: Rowman and Littlefield, 1999); Michael W. McConnell, "The Supreme Court's Earliest Church-State Cases: Windows on Religious-Cultural-Political Conflict in the Early Republic," *Tulsa Law Review* 37, no. 1 (2001): 7–44; Philip Hamburger, *Separation of Church and State* (Cambridge, MA: Harvard University Press, 2002); Douglas G. Smith, "The Establishment Clause: Corollary of Eighteenth-Century Corporate Law?" *Northwestern University Law Review* 98, no. 1 (2003): 239–302; Mark Douglass McGarvie, *One Nation under Law: America's Early National Struggles to Separate Church and State* (DeKalb, IL: Northern Illinois University Press, 2004); Shelby Balik, "The Religious Frontier: Church, State, and Settlement in Northern New England, 1780–1830" (unpublished PhD dissertation, University of Wisconsin-Madison, 2006), chs. 1–2; Jewel Spangler, *Virginians Reborn: Anglican Monopoly, Evangelical Dissent, and the Rise of the Baptists in the Late Eighteenth Century* (Charlottesville: University of Virginia Press, 2008); Shelby M. Balik, "Equal Rights and Equal Privilege: Separating Church and State in Vermont," *Journal of Church and State* 50, no. 1 (Winter 2008): 23–48; John Ragosta, *Wellspring of Liberty: How Virginia's Religious Dissenters Helped Win the American Revolution and Secured Religious Liberty* (New York: Oxford University Press, 2010); Sarah Barringer Gordon, "The Landscape of Faith: Religious Property and Confiscation in the Early Republic," in *Making Legal History: Essays in Honor of William E. Nelson*, eds. Daniel J.

Hulsebosch and R. B. Bernstein (New York: New York University Press, 2013), 13–48; Sarah Barringer Gordon, "The First Disestablishment: Limits on Church Power and Property before the Civil War," *University of Pennsylvania Law Review* 162, no. 2 (January 2014): 337–372; Sara Barringer Gordon, "The African Supplement: Religion, Race, and Corporate Law in Early National America," *William and Mary Quarterly* 72, no. 3 (2015): 385–422; Kellen Funk, "Church Corporations and the Conflict of Laws in Antebellum America," *Journal of Law and Religion* 32, no. 2 (2017): 263–284; and Amanda Porterfield, *Corporate Spirit: Religion and the Rise of the Modern Corporation* (New York: Oxford University Press, 2018).

On the Contract Clause and the relationship between charters, contracts, and constitutions, as well as the city as a corporation and the many directions of corporate-law jurisprudence, see, for example, Benjamin F. Wright, *The Contract Clause of the Constitution* (Cambridge, MA: Harvard University Press, 1938); Gerald E. Frug, "The City as a Legal Concept," *Harvard Law Review* 93, no. 6 (1980): 1057–1154; James L. Kainen, "Nineteenth-Century Interpretations of the Federal Contract Clause: The Transformation from Vested to Substantive Rights against the State," *Buffalo Law Review* 31, no. 2 (Spring 1982): 381–480; Michael Phillips, "The Life and Times of the Contract Clause," *American Business Law Journal* 20, no. 2 (Summer 1982): 139–178; Hendrik Hartog, *Public Property and Private Power: The Corporation of the City of New York in American Law* (Chapel Hill: University of North Carolina Press, 1983); Elizabeth Mensch, "Hartog's New York and the Ideology of Public and Private," *Wisconsin Law Review* 1986 (1986): 571–584; Pauline Maier, "The Revolutionary Origins of the American Corporation," *William and Mary Quarterly* 50, no. 1 (1993): 51–84; Christine Desan, "The Constitutional Commitment to Legislative Adjudication in the Early American Tradition," *Harvard Law Review* 111, no. 6 (April 1998): 1381–1504; Daniel J. Hulsebosch, "*Imperia in Imperio*: The Multiple Constitutions of Empire in New York, 1750–1770," *Law and History Review* 16, no. 2 (1998): 319–379; Gordon S. Wood, "The Origins of Vested Rights in the Early Republic," *Virginia Law Review* 85, no. 7 (1999): 1421–1445; Liam Seamus O'Mellin, "The Sanctity of Association: The Corporation and Individualism in American Law," *San Diego Law Review* 37, no. 1 (2000): 101–165; Stephen Innes, "The Corporate Roots of American Government: From Corporation to Commonwealth" in *Colossus: How the Corporation Changed America*, ed. Jack Beatty (New York:

Broadway Books, 2001); Liam Seamus O'Mellin, "Neither Contract nor Concession: The Public Personality of the Corporation," *George Washington Law Review* 74 (2006): 201–259; Mary Sarah Bilder, "The Corporate Origins of Judicial Review," *Yale Law Journal* 116, no. 3 (2006): 502–567; Jason Kaufman, "Corporate Law and the Sovereignty of States," *American Sociological Review* 73, no. 3 (June 2008): 402–425; Robert E. Wright, "Rise of the Corporation Nation" in *Founding Choices: American Economic Policy in the 1790s*, eds. Douglas A. Irwin and Richard Sylla (Chicago: University of Chicago Press, 2010), 217–258; Geoffrey P. Miller, "The Corporate Law Background of the Necessary and Proper Clause," *George Washington Law Review* 79, no. 1 (2010): 1–32; Margaret M. Blair, "Corporate Personhood and the Corporate Persona," *University of Illinois Law Review* 2013, no. 3 (2013): 785–820; Naomi Lamoreaux, "Revisiting American Exceptionalism: Democracy and the Regulation of Corporate Governance in Nineteenth-Century Pennsylvania," *NBER*, working paper (2014); Jeff Lingwall, "Education Clauses in Corporate Charters: How Child Welfare Law Confronted the Industrial Revolution," *Journal of Law and Education* 43, no. 2 (Spring 2014): 189–224; Ruth Bloch and Naomi Lamoreaux, "Voluntary Associations, Corporate Rights, and the State: Legal Constraints on the Development of American Civil Society, 1750–1900," in Naomi Lamoreaux and John Joseph Wallis, *Organizations, Civil Society, and the Roots of Development* (Chicago: University of Chicago Press, 2017), 231–290; David Ciepley, "Is the U.S. Government a Corporation? The Corporate Origins of Modern Constitutionalism," *American Political Science Review* 111, no. 2 (2017): 418–435; Margaret M. Blair and Elizabeth Pollman, "The Supreme Court's View of Corporate Rights: Two Centuries of Evolution and Controversy" and Eric Hilt, "Early American Corporations and the State" in *Corporations and American Democracy*, eds. Naomi Lamoreaux and William Novak (Cambridge, MA: Harvard University Press, 2017), 245–285 and 37–73; Gregory Ablavsky, "Empire States: The Coming of Dual Federalism," *Yale Law Journal* 128, no. 7 (2019): 1792–1869; and David S. Schwartz, "Mr. Madison's War on the General Welfare Clause," *UC Davis Law Review* 56, no. 2 (December 2022): 887–957.

On the shift from commonwealth republicanism to democratic capitalism, or political liberalism in relation to contracts, corporations, and a new market orientation, see Oscar Handlin, "Laissez-Faire Thought in Massachusetts, 1790–1880," *Journal of Economic History* 3, no. 1 (1943):

55–65; Oscar Handlin and Mary Handlin, *Commonwealth: A Study of the Role of Government in the American Economy: Massachusetts, 1774–1861* (New York: New York University Press, 1947); Louis Hartz, *Economic Policy and Democratic Thought: Pennsylvania, 1776–1860* (Cambridge, MA: Harvard University Press, 1948); Nathan Miller, *The Enterprise of a Free People: Aspects of Economic Development in New York State during the Canal Period, 1792–1838* (Ithaca, NY: Cornell University Press, 1962); Gordon S. Wood, *The Creation of the American Republic, 1776–1787* (Chapel Hill: University of North Carolina Press, 1969); Donald B. Cole, *Jacksonian Democracy in New Hampshire, 1800–1851* (Cambridge, MA: Harvard University Press, 1970); Jere R. Daniell, *Experiment in Republicanism: New Hampshire Politics and the American Revolution, 1741–1794* (Cambridge, MA: Harvard University Press, 1970); Jon C. Teaford, *The Municipal Revolution in America: Origins of Modern Urban Government, 1650–1825* (Chicago: University of Chicago Press, 1975); Drew R. McCoy, *The Elusive Republic: Political Economy in Jeffersonian America* (New York: Norton, 1980); Andrew R. L. Cayton, "The Fragmentation of 'A Great Family': The Panic of 1819 and the Rise of the Middling Interest in Boston, 1818–1822," *Journal of the Early Republic* 2, no. 2 (Summer 1982), 143–167; Joyce Appleby, *Capitalism and a New Social Order: The Republican Vision of the 1790s* (New York: New York University Press, 1984); H. N. Butler, "Nineteenth-Century Jurisdictional Competition in the Granting of Corporate Privileges," *Journal of Legal Studies* 14, no. 1 (1985): 129–166; Joan Williams, "The Development of the Public/Private Distinction in American Law," *Texas Law Review* 64, no. 1 (August 1985): 225–250; John Henry Culley, "People's Capitalism and Corporate Democracy: An Intellectual History of the Corporation" (unpublished PhD dissertation, University of California-Santa Barbara, 1986); Randolph A. Roth, *The Democratic Dilemma: Religion, Reform, and the Social Order in the Connecticut River Valley of Vermont, 1791–1850* (Cambridge: Cambridge University Press, 1987); R. Kent Newmyer, "Harvard Law School, New England Legal Culture, and the Antebellum Origins of American Jurisprudence," *The Journal of American History* 74, no. 3 (December 1987): 814–835; George M. Thomas, *Revivalism and Cultural Change: Christianity, Nation Building, and the Market in the Nineteenth-Century United States* (Chicago: University of Chicago Press, 1989); Harlow Walker Sheidley, "Preserving 'The Old Fabrick': The Massachusetts Conservative Elite and the Constitutional Convention of 1820–1821," *Proceedings of the*

Massachusetts Historical Society 103 (1991): 114–137; Joyce Appleby, *Inheriting the Revolution: The First Generation of Americans* (Cambridge, MA: Harvard University Press, 1991); Joyce Appleby, *Liberalism and Republicanism in the Historical Imagination* (Cambridge, MA: Harvard University Press, 1992); Gordon Wood, *The Radicalism of the American Revolution* (New York: Vintage Books, 1993); William Novak, *The People's Welfare: Law and Regulation in Nineteenth-Century America* (Chapel Hill: University of North Carolina Press, 1996); Johann Neem, *Creating a Nation of Joiners: Democracy and Civil Society in Early National Massachusetts* (Cambridge, MA: Harvard University Press, 2008); Gordon S. Wood, *Empire of Liberty: A History of the Early Republic, 1789–1815* (New York: Oxford University Press, 2009); John Lauritz Larson, *The Market Revolution in America: Liberty, Ambition, and the Eclipse of the Common Good* (New York: Cambridge University Press, 2010); and Naomi Lamoreaux, "Corporate Governance and the Expansion of the Democratic Franchise: Beyond Cross-Country Regressions," *Scandinavian Economic History Review* 64, no. 2 (2016): 103–121.

On the broader history of American higher education during the colonial and early national periods, including useful institutional histories, see Josiah Quincy, *The History of Harvard University*, 2 vols. (Boston: Crosby, Nichols, Lee, 1860); Elmer Ellsworth Brown, *The Origins of American State Universities* (Berkeley: University of California Press, 1903); Kemp P. Battle, *History of the University of North Carolina from Its Beginning to the Death of President Swain, 1789–1868*, 2 vols. (Raleigh, NC: Printed for the author by Edwards & Broughton Printing, 1907–1912); Howard R. Burnett, "Early History of Vincennes University," *Indiana Magazine of History* 29, no. 2 (1933): 114–121; Donald Tewksbury, *The Founding of American Colleges and Universities before the Civil War, with Particular Reference to the Religious Influences Bearing upon the College Movement* (New York: Teachers College, Columbia University, 1932); David Spence Hill, *Control of Tax-Supported Higher Education in the United States* (New York: The Carnegie Foundation for the Advancement of Teaching, 1934); Samuel Eliot Morison, *Three Centuries of Harvard, 1636–1936* (Cambridge, MA: Harvard University Press, 1936); Edward C. Elliott and M. M. Chambers, *The Colleges and the Courts: Judicial Decisions Regarding Institutions of Higher Education in the United States* (New York: Carnegie Foundation for the Advancement of Teaching, 1936); Roscoe Pound, "Visitatorial Jurisdiction over Corporations in Equity," *Harvard Law Review* 49, no. 3 (1936):

369–395; Henry Lefavour, "The Proposed College in Hampshire County in 1762," *Proceedings of the Massachusetts Historical Society* 66 (1936): 53–79; Lawrence A. Cremin and R. Freeman Butts, *A History of Education in American Culture* (New York: Holt, 1953); Richard Hofstadter and Walter P. Metzger, *The Development of Academic Freedom in the United States* (New York: Columbia University Press, 1955); Louis Leonard Tucker, "President Thomas Clap and the Rise of Yale College, 1740–1766," *The Historian* 19, no. 1 (November 1956): 66–81; Malcolm Moos and Francis E. Rourke, *The Campus and the State* (Baltimore: Johns Hopkins University Press, 1959); Blackwell P. Robinson, *The History of Escheats at the University of North Carolina, 1789–1955* (Chapel Hill: University of North Carolina Press, n.d.); Louis L. Tucker, *Puritan Protagonist: President Thomas Clap of Yale College* (Chapel Hill: University of North Carolina Press for the Institute of Early American History and Culture, 1962); Frederick Rudolph, *The American College and University: A History* (New York: Knopf, 1962); Theodore Crane, *The Colleges and the Public, 1787–1862* (New York: Teachers College, Columbia University, 1963); David Tyack, *George Ticknor and the Boston Brahmins* (Cambridge, MA: Harvard University Press, 1967); Ruth A. White, "Vignettes of Library History: No. 1: The Library That Saved a University," *Journal of Library History* 1, no. 1 (January 1966): 66–69; Lawrence A. Cremin, *American Education: The Colonial Experience, 1607–1783* (New York: Harper & Row, 1970); Douglas Sloan, *The Scottish Enlightenment and the American College Ideal* (New York: Teachers College Press, Columbia University, 1971); David F. Allmendinger Jr., "The Strangeness of the American Education Society: Indigent Students and the New Charity, 1815–1840," *History of Education Quarterly* 11, no. 1 (1971): 3–22; David Potts, "American Colleges in the Nineteenth Century: From Localism to Denominationalism," *History of Education Quarterly* 11, no. 4 (1971): 363–380; Robert Polk Thomson, "The Reform of the College of William and Mary, 1763–1780," *Proceedings of the American Philosophical Society* 115, no. 3 (June 1971): 187–213; Howard H. Peckham, "Collegia Ante Bellum: Attitudes of College Professors and Students toward the American Revolution," *Pennsylvania Magazine of History and Biography* 95, no. 1 (January 1971): 50–72; John S. Brubacher, *The Courts and Higher Education* (New York: Jossey-Bass, 1971); David E. Swift, "Yankee in Virginia: James Marsh at Hampden-Sydney, 1823–1826," *The Virginia Magazine of History and Biography* 80, no. 3 (July 1972): 312–332; Natalie Naylor, "The

Antebellum College Movement: A Reappraisal of Tewksbury's Founding of American Colleges and Universities," *History of Education Quarterly* 13, no. 3 (Fall 1973): 261–274; Ronald Story, "Harvard and the Boston Brahmins: A Study in Institutional and Class Development, 1800–1865," *Journal of Social History* 8, no. 3 (1975): 94–121; David F. Allmendinger Jr., *Paupers and Scholars: The Transformation of Student Life in Nineteenth-Century New England* (New York: St. Martins, 1975); Jürgen Herbst, "The American Revolution and the American University," *Perspectives in American History* 10 (1976): 279–354; David C. Humphrey, *From King's College to Columbia, 1746–1800* (New York: Columbia University Press, 1976); Howard Miller, *The Revolutionary College: American Presbyterian Higher Education, 1707–1837* (New York: New York University Press, 1976); J. E. Morpurgo, *Their Majesties' Royall Colledge: William and Mary in the Seventeenth and Eighteenth Centuries* (Williamsburg, VA: College of William and Mary, 1976); Steven J. Novak, *The Rights of Youth: American Colleges and Student Revolt, 1798–1815* (Cambridge, MA: Harvard University Press, 1977); David Potts, "'College Enthusiasm!' as Public Response, 1800–1860," *Harvard Educational Review* 47, no. 1 (1977): 28–42; J. W. Bridge, "The Rev. John Bracken v. The Visitors of William and Mary College: A Post-Revolutionary Problem in Visitatorial Jurisdiction," *William and Mary Law Review* 20, no. 3 (1978): 415–440; Kathryn McDaniel Moore, "The War with the Tutors: Student-Faculty Conflict at Harvard and Yale, 1745–1771," *History of Education Quarterly* 18, no. 2 (Summer 1978): 115–127; Lawrence Cremin, *American Education: The National Experience, 1783–1876* (New York: Harper & Row, 1980); David W. Robson, "College Founding in the New Republic, 1776–1800," *History of Education Quarterly* 23, no. 3 (Autumn 1983): 323–341; Natalie A. Naylor, "'Holding High the Standard': The Influence of the American Education Society in Antebellum Education," *History of Education Quarterly* 24, no. 4 (Winter 1984): 479–497; David W. Robson, *Educating Republicans: The College in the Era of the American Revolution, 1750–1800* (Westport, CT: Greenwood, 1985); John F. Roche, *The Colonial Colleges in the War for American Independence* (Port Washington, NY: Associated Faculty, 1986); Louise L. Stevenson, *Scholarly Means to Evangelical Ends: The New Haven Scholars and the Transformation of Higher Learning in America, 1830–1890* (Baltimore: Johns Hopkins University Press, 1986); Jack C. Lane, "The Yale Report of 1828 and Liberal Education: A Neo-Republican Manifesto," *History of Education Quarterly* 27, no. 3 (1987): 325–338; Mark Noll, *Princeton and the Republic,*

1768–1823: The Search for Enlightenment in the Era of Samuel Stanhope Smith (Princeton, NJ: Princeton University Press, 1989); George M. Marsden, *The Soul of the American University: From Protestant Establishment to Established Nonbelief* (New York: Oxford University Press, 1994); Dennis Henry Holtschneider, "Institutional Aid to New England College Students, 1740–1800" (unpublished PhD dissertation, Harvard University, 1997); Mark Douglass McGarvie, "Creating Roles for Religion and Philanthropy in a Secular Nation: The Dartmouth College Case and the Design of Civil Society in the Early Republic," *Journal of College and University Law* 25, no. 3 (Winter 1999): 527–568; Edwin Duryea and Donald T. Williams, *The Academic Corporation: A History of College and University Governing Boards* (New York: Routledge, 2000); Roger Geiger, "The Reformation of the Colleges in the Early Republic, 1800–1820," *History of Universities* 16, no. 2 (2001): 129–182; J. David Hoeveler, *Creating the American Mind: Intellect and Politics in the Colonial Colleges* (Lanham, MD: Rowman & Littlefield, 2002); Daniel Walker Howe, "Church, State, and Education in the Young American Republic," *Journal of the Early Republic* 22, no. 1 (Spring 2002): 1–24; Silas Lee McCormick, "Transylvania University: 'Public' Higher Education in Kentucky, 1780–1878" (unpublished PhD dissertation, University of Illinois, 2007); Howard F. McMains, "The Indiana Seminary Charter of 1820," *Indiana Magazine of History* 106, no. 4 (December 2010): 356–380; Rodney A. Smolla, "The Public and Private Sphere" in *The Constitution Goes to College: Five Constitutional Ideas That Have Shaped the Americana University* (New York: New York University Press, 2011); Roger L. Geiger, *The History of American Higher Education: Learning and Culture from the Founding to World War II* (Princeton, NJ: Princeton University Press, 2014); George Thomas, "Rethinking the Dartmouth College Case in American Political Development: Constituting Public and Private Educational Institutions," *Studies in American Political Development* 29, no. 1 (April 2015): 23–39; George Thomas, "The Founders and the Idea of a National University: Constituting the American Mind," *Journal of the Early Republic* 37, no. 2 (Summer 2017): 370–373; Alan Taylor, *Thomas Jefferson's Education* (New York: W. W. Norton, 2019); Timothy V. Kaufmann-Osborn, *The Autocratic Academy: Reenvisioning Rule within America's Universities* (Durham, NC: Duke University Press, 2023); Michael Banerjee, "California's Constitutional University: Private Property, Public Power, and the Constitutional Corporation, 1868–1900,"

California Legal History 18 (January 2024): 215–271; and Adam R. Nelson, *Exchange of Ideas: The Economy of Higher Education in Early America* (Chicago: University of Chicago Press, 2023), and *Capital of Mind: The Idea of a Modern American University* (Chicago: University of Chicago Press, 2024).

INDEX

Academy of Philadelphia, 14
Act for Establishing Religious Freedom, 72
Act of 1816: appellate review of, 123, 132, 137; college property and, 129; initial passage of and response to, 91–94, 97, 100–101, 104; New Hampshire Superior Court and, 119, 209; Joseph Story and, 125–126; U.S. Supreme Court review of and decision on, 140, 165, 171, 174, 181
Adams, Ebenezer, 97
Adams, John, 45
Allen, William, 96, 120, 122, 129, 150, 178–181, 185, 193, 203–205
Ames, David, 121
Amherst College, 176, 195, 245
Amory, Francis, 196
Amory, Jonathan, 196
Andover Theological Seminary, 125, 150
Anglican Church, 14–15, 17, 19, 43, 45, 47, 58, 60, 72–73, 103, 133, 155, 239, 242
Appleton, Jesse, 183, 185, 203
Archbishop of Canterbury, 15
Articles of Confederation, 53
Ashurst, Lord, 117
Atlantic Coast Line Railroad Company v. City of Goldsboro, 219
Attorney General ex. rel. Bishop of London v. College of William and Mary, 60, 142
Attorney General v. Chicago and Northwestern Railroad Company, 217
Austin, Michigan Secretary of State v. Michigan State Chamber of Commerce, 221

bank, 5, 53, 55, 65, 111, 171, 175, 183, 185–187, 190, 192–193, 201, 215

Bank of North America, 53, 55
Bank of the United States, 160
Bank of the United States v. Deveaux, 118, 137, 160, 220
bankruptcy, 56, 155–156, 196, 198–199, 201
Bankruptcy Clause, 156, 199
Baptists, 70, 72, 209, 220
Bartlett, Ichabod, 101, 111–114, 126, 142, 160, 177
Bell, Samuel, 116, 141, 193
beneficial interest, or contractual benefit: and Bowdoin College, 185; Dartmouth College or its trustees, 43, 48, 49, 51, 107, 109–110, 113, 118, 136, 142, 164, 167–169, 172, 174, 211; and *First National Bank of Boston v. Bellotti*, 221; and in the law of corporations, 75, 89; and Moor's Indian Charity School, 35, 37, 48; of New Hampshire, 33–34, 89, 110, 118, 135–136, 142, 144, 164, 167–169, 174, 211. *See also* private benefit and public benefit
beneficiaries, 196–197
Bentley v. Bishop of Ely, 62
Bishop of Exeter, 23–24
Bishop of London, 17, 31–32, 60, 142
Bishop of Oxford, 23
Bishop of Winchester, 22
Blackstone, William, 73, 75, 100, 109, 118, 214
board of overseers, 22, 105, 134–135, 159; and Bowdoin, 183, 203–205; and College of William and Mary, 61; and Dartmouth, 90–92, 95, 126, 193–195; and Harvard, 45, 75–77, 90, 99, 135, 177, 191–192; and Williams, 64; and Yale, 20, 45

{ 259 }

Board of Trustees of Vincennes University v. State of Indiana, 208
Boston Massacre, 35
Boston Repertory, 83
Boston Tea Party, 39
Bowdoin College, 48, 97, 124, 150, 175, 183–186, 190, 193, 203–207
Boyle, Robert, 60, 142
Bracken, John, 58, 60–63
Bracken v. the Visitors of William and Mary College, 60–63
Brainerd, David, 12, 13
Brown, Francis, 88, 90, 93, 96, 97, 111, 121–125, 127, 145, 150–152, 157–159, 178–180, 182, 209
Brown v. Penobscot Bank, 111
Brougham, Henry, 158
Bullard v. Bell, 116
Burroughs, Eden, 48, 67–68
Burwell v. Hobby Lobby Stores, 222
Bury, Arthur, 23–24

Cambridge University. *See* University of Cambridge
Camm, John, 45
Carter, Nathaniel, 120–122, 182
Chandler, Colonel, 30
charitable corporation. *See* corporation, charitable
Charles River Bridge v. Warren Bridge, 213–215
church, vii, 3–4, 6–7, 21, 54, 56–57, 173, 186, 188, 222–223; Anglican or Episcopalian, 14–15, 17, 45, 47, 60, 72–74, 103–104, 155; Congregationalist, 11–13, 18, 67–74, 183; and Dartmouth College, 67–72, 81, 83, 86; "established," 5, 11, 14–15, 69–74, 83, 103–104, 133, 183, 188, 190; and Maine, 183; and Massachusetts, 183; and New Hampshire, 133, 188; and New York, 133; Presbyterian, 16, 67–74; and Vermont, 133; and Virginia, 72–74
Church, John, 182
Church of Christ at Dartmouth College (aka the College Church), 67–69
Choate, Rufus, 201
Citizens United v. Federal Elections Commission, 221–222
City of Louisville v. the President and Trustees of the University of Louisville, 209
City of Owensboro v. Cumberland Telephone and Telegraph Company, 218
civil corporation. *See* corporation, civil
Civil War, 216
Clap, Thomas, 12–13, 19–20, 25, 45
Clinton, DeWitt, 151–152, 154–155
Clinton, George, 50
"Clintonians," 154–155
Coke, Sir Edward, 20
Colby College. *See* Maine Literary and Theological Institution
College of New Jersey, 14. *See* also Princeton
College of Philadelphia (later the University of Pennsylvania), 14, 44, 54, 56–58, 209
College of Physicians (Boston), 77
College of Physicians and Surgeons. *See* New York College of Physicians and Surgeons
College of William and Mary, 44–45, 58–63, 133, 142, 209
Colmier, John, 23
colonial government (colonial governor, legislature, assembly, etc.), 140; charters and, 5, 16–18, 26–27, 98, 199; colleges and, 6, 12–13, 209; established church and, 11–13, 17; New Hampshire and "first donor"

to Dartmouth College, 2, 21–26,
11–12, 16, 18, 21, 31, 33–34, 40–41, 69,
92, 97, 106, 109, 113, 144, 164–167, 172,
211; Massachusettts and, 39, 77, 175,
191–192; New York and, 14–15, 18, 41,
152; Vermont and, 133; Virginia and,
59, 61–62, 72; Yale, Connecticut,
and, 12–13, 16–21, 25, 36, 45, 112
colony. *See* colonial government
Columbia College, 46–47, 151, 153–155,
209
Commentaries on American Law, 206
Commentaries on the Constitution of the United States, 206
Commentaries on the Laws of England, 73, 75, 100, 214
common law, 73–74, 214
commonwealth republicanism. *See* republicanism
company, vii, 3–7, 21–22, 42, 102–103, 171, 175, 196–197, 213–215, 217–221, 223
Concord, New Hampshire, 90
Concord Gazette, 85
Congregationalist Church, 11–14, 17–19, 68, 70–71, 82–85, 124, 183, 185, 188, 190, 192
Congress (U.S.), 53, 102, 116, 124, 155–156, 198, 201, 209
consent (or assent), and contracts or charters, 3, 28, 38, 53–58, 75, 100, 132, 137, 152–154, 170–172, 176, 185; and American Revolution, 39; and Bowdoin College, 204–206; and contested public seizure of the College of Philadelphia, 44; corporate trustees and, 64, 66, 76–78, 91–92, 95, 97–104, 112, 117, 132, 191–192, 211, 213; and the Crown, 73; and Dartmouth College, 38, 130, 132, 144, 170–172, 200; *King v. Pasmore* and, 112; and Lord Dartmouth, 35;

and the New Hampshire Grants, 42; James Wilson on, 53–57
constitution (state or federal), 114, 162, 215; of England, 73; of Maine, 184–185, 203–204, 206; of Massachusetts, 45, 75–77, 183, 186, 190, 192; of New Hampshire, 70, 95, 117, 137, 140, 163, 175; of New York, 152; of North Carolina, 74–75; of Pennsylvania, 57–58; of Vermont, 43, 47; of Virginia, 45
Constitutional Convention (Maine), 184
Constitutional Convention (Massachusetts), 190, 193
Constitutional Convention (United States), 55
Continental Congress, 39–41, 43–44
Contract Clause, vii, 3, 55, 102, 104, 118–119, 137, 161, 164, 166, 170, 198–201
contracts, views on charters of incorporation as, vii, 3–4, 20, 53, 74, 76, 92, 104, 118–119, 127, 134, 155–156, 161, 165–166, 168, 174, 180, 207–208, 211, 215; constitutional protection for, 55–57, 102–104, 109, 118–119, 127–128, 135, 137, 163–164, 166, 169–170, 173, 186–187, 198–201, 211, 213–216, 218, 220; employment contracts, 60, 203–204; equity law and, 127; grants of land, property, or privileges as, 50, 101–104, 126, 128–129, 136, 142, 161, 165, 174; implied, 172; loans as, 53, 65, 155–156, 198–201, 213–216, 219; obligations of, 3, 57–58, 104, 118, 127, 141, 144, 164, 171, 208, 214; parties to, vii, 109, 117, 135–137, 142, 144, 168–173, 216; private, 4, 54–56, 65, 74, 92, 103, 117, 127, 136–137, 155–156, 163–165, 187, 198–201, 204, 216; public legislation and constitutions as, 54, 56–57, 136, 140–141, 144, 163–164, 216, 218; vs. royal concessions, 168–171, 173, 214

{ *Index* } 261

corporation, charitable (private, including eleemosynary and "closed"), 3, 44, 65, 72, 135, 150, 154, 211; charitable, 5, 21, 24, 134–135; civil, 21, 105; "closed," 42; eleemosynary, 23, 61–63, 100–101, 105–106, 113, 121, 133, 138, 151, 157–158, 162, 165; municipal, 21, 42, 99–100, 209; "open," 42; private, vii, viii, 4, 6, 23, 26, 42, 58, 60–61, 63–64, 71, 73–75, 78, 82, 85, 89, 92, 99–101, 105, 107, 110–111, 115, 117–118, 133, 144, 152, 171, 175, 181, 187–188, 190–192, 194, 201–202, 205–207, 209, 216–218, 223; public, viii, 6–7, 19, 42, 45, 58, 60–63, 69–70, 73–76, 81, 91, 95, 99–100, 103, 106, 110–111, 113–114, 117–119, 133–134, 144, 152, 155, 157–159, 167, 171, 188, 201, 204–206, 208–209

Council of Revision (also Court of Errors, New York), 151–152, 154–155

court of chancery. *See* court of equity

court of equity, 22, 25, 109, 126–127, 197. *See also* equitable property

Court of King's Bench, 23

Crown (as supreme head of monarchical government): and charters of incorporation, as for colleges, 2, 3, 14–17, 21, 23, 26–27, 30, 59, 63, 100, 112, 117, 136, 140, 142, 153, 164, 167–172, 211; colonial governor or government in relation to, 1, 27, 45, 59, 113; and concession vs. contract theory of charters, 118, 136; and donations, including of land, 41, 63, 72, 106, 109, 113–114, 117, 128, 142, 144, 157, 159, 162, 167, 169; jurisdictional powers and prerogatives of (including visitatorial powers), 14, 22, 24, 73, 114, 162, 169; replaced by state and federal governments after the revolution, 114, 140, 144, 153, 168

Crowninshield, Richard, 198

Daggett, David, 141, 145
Dana, Samuel, 116
Dane, Nathan, 55
Dartmouth, New Hampshire (independent district; also Dartmouth, Vermont), 41–44
Dartmouth University: Act of 1816's designation of, 91, 111, 132, 183, 194–195, 209; board of trustees, 93–94, 96–98, 112, 116, 208; and Bowdoin College or William Allen, 185, 192, 203; and controversy over library books, 96, 120–122, 180; and *Dartmouth* litigation, 98, 101, 108, 116–117, 120–123, 126, 134, 139, 143, 145, 149–151, 157–164, 166, 177–183; and disputes over property ownership, 96–97, 110, 120, 128–130, 133, 180; and donations from John Wheelock, 96–97, 104; and "new facts," 157–159, 161–162, 164, 178, 180; students at, 122, 179, 183; and visit of James Monroe, 97–98

Dartmouth v. Woodward, vii, 1, 7, 23–24, 103, 116, 141; and disputes over "first donors," 20; historical context of, 68, 194; and law of corporations, viii, 4–5, 74; and New Hampshire Superior Court, 82, 103, 116; and "privatization" of colleges, 192; and role of corporate trustees and visitors, 24, 63; subsequent references to, 184, 186, 194, 198–200, 203–205, 208–210, 214–215, 218, 222; and US Supreme Court, 132, 139, 149, 159–160, 169, 174, 177, 201, 203–204; William Woodward as named defendant in, 41, 93

262   { *Index* }

Davenport, James, 12
Davis, John, 198, 214
Dean, James, 120–122, 182
Delaney, James, 14
disestablishment (religious, church), 71–72, 103, 188
dissenters (religious), 12, 14, 22, 34, 70, 74, 183
Dodge v. Woolsey, 215
Duane, James, 46
Dunham, Josiah, 85, 150
Dutton, Warren, 213–214
Duvall, Gabriel, 157, 166, 177, 200
Dwight, Timothy, 64

Earl of Dartmouth (also Lord Dartmouth), 2, 26, 28, 35, 132–133, 162
Eden v. Foster, 24, 106
Edwards v. Kearzey, 216
Eldon, Lord Chancellor, 158
eleemosynary corporation. *See* corporation, eleemosynary
eminent domain, 110, 215, 227
English Society for the Propagation of the Gospel in Foreign Parts, 18
Episcopal Church, 72–74, 104
equitable property (or equitable estate), 107, 137, 142, 162–163
established church. *See* church, "established"
Eton College, 159
Eustis v. Parker, 99
evangelicalism (or evangelicals), 7, 12–13, 15, 34, 67, 69
Exeter College, Oxford, 23, 100
Ex parte Schollenberger, 220

Farrington v. Tennessee, 217
Federalist Party, 6, 82, 124, 150, 178, 187, 197; and John Holmes, 139; and James Kent, 150; in Maine, 183–186;

in Massachusetts, 76–78, 102, 123, 183–186, 190; in New Hampshire, 71, 81–85, 88, 95–96, 105, 116, 124, 178, 186, 195; in New York, 153–154; and Joseph Story, 126, 173; in Virginia, 186
fellows (faculty and collegiate governance), 13, 22–25, 45, 76–77, 191–192
Fertilizing Company v. Hyde Park, 217
"first donor" (as "founder"), and Dartmouth, 2–3, 34, 84, 105–106, 108–109, 113–114, 117, 128, 130, 132–136, 143–144, 157, 159, 162–163, 171, 179; and Bowdoin, 205; and College of William and Mary, 58–60; in Elizabethan Law, 19, 21–22, 58, 105, 133–134; and Harvard, 191; and Oxford and Cambridge, 23–24, 100; and Yale, 19
First National Bank of Boston v. Bellotti, 220
Fletcher, Robert, 102
Fletcher v. Peck, 102, 129, 214
"founder." *See* "first donor"
franchise, 22, 47, 110, 118, 136–138, 141–142, 170, 172–174, 211, 214, 216
Franklin, Benjamin, 14
Franklin, Samuel, 50

general incorporation, 71, 74, 175, 187–188
Gilbert, Benjamin, 124, 129
glebes (lands), 43, 47, 72–75, 103
Glorious Revolution (1688), 22
Goodrich, Chauncey, 132
Gore, Christopher, 123
"grafted" foundations (or "engrafted" or "enlarged" foundations), 2, 19, 76–77, 91, 95, 112, 135, 143–144, 162, 166, 171, 184, 203
Grafton County, 94
Grafton Presbytery, 67

Great Awakenings (First and Second), 11–14, 67, 69, 70
Greenleaf, Simon, 214
Green v. Rutherford, 63
Gresham, Sir Thomas, 98
Gresham College, London, 98

Hale, William, 139–140, 143, 145, 180
Halifax, Lord, 17
Hamilton College, 97
Hammer v. Dagenhart, 219
Hanover, New Hampshire, 1, 85–86, 120, 141, 145, 150, 181; aligned with revolutionary patriots, 39, 40; attempt to secede from New Hampshire; chosen as site of Wheelock's school, 34–36, 97, 113; 42–44; medical school in, 78; and New Hampshire College of Agriculture and the Mechanic Arts, 210; religious revivals, church taxes, and sectarian and partisan conflict in, 67–69, 72, 81, 83, 98
Harvard, John, 76
Harvard College, 47, 97, 116, 124–125, 127, 150, 177–178, 183, 209–210; as beneficiary, 196–197; and Charles River Bridge, 213–214; and charter disputes, 75–78, 99, 185–186, 190–195; and established Congregationalist church, 11; incorporation of, 22, 45, 65, 90, 92, 112, 114, 135; and Massachusetts constitution of 1780, 175, 183
Harvard Law School, 55, 149
Harvard Medical School, 77–78
Hatch, Horace, 129
Hatch v. Lang, 129
Henry St. George Tucker, 72–73
Hill, Isaac, 84, 88, 124, 177–178, 193
Hillsborough Bank, 116

Holmes, John, 139–141, 145, 149
Holt, John, 23–24, 219
Home Building and Loan Association v. Blaisdell, 219
Hopkins Federal Savings and Loan Association v. Cleary, 219
Hopkinson, Joseph, 123, 125–126, 141, 143–145, 160, 178–179, 182
Horrocks, James, 59
House of Lords, 23, 158–159
Hutchinson, Henry, 120–121
Hutchinson, Thomas, 39

implied contract, 172
implied powers (or implied rights), 53, 104, 166, 169, 172, 208–209, 218
Indian Charity School. *See* Moor's Indian Charity School
Inhabitants of the Fourth School District v. Wood, 99
insolvency, 155–156, 160, 197–201

Jay, James, 41
Jay, John, 41
Jefferson, Thomas, 45, 58, 60–61, 63, 71, 72, 89, 98
Jefferson College, 216
Johnson, Samuel, 15
Johnson, William, 151, 157, 177
judicial review (of corporate governance), 15, 25, 55, 62, 92, 104–105, 107, 115, 135, 172, 184, 186, 188, 221, 223

Kelley v. Bean, 70
Kent, James (Chancellor), 150–155, 206
Kenyon, Lord, 112, 171
King, Rufus, 55
King Charles I, 111
King George III, 26, 41–42, 111, 162, 168–169, 173
King James II, 22–23

King's College, 14–15, 41, 44, 46
"Kingsland," 41, 44, 133
King v. Bishop of Chester, 62
King v. Bishop of Ely, 61–62
King v. Pasmore, 111–112, 117, 141, 170–171
King v. Vice Chancellor of Cambridge, 136
King William III, 59
Kirkland, John Thornton, 125, 127, 150

Landaff grant, 30, 34, 37, 41–42, 48, 50, 66, 68, 97, 106–107, 113, 144, 157, 167
Lang, Richard, 129
Langdon, John, 65
Lebanon, Connecticut, 7, 11, 13, 15, 18, 26, 30, 36, 83, 85, 108
Lebanon, New Hampshire, 42
Legge, William. *See* Earl of Dartmouth
L'Hommedieu, Ezra, 46
Liberty Hall Academy (later Washington College), 63–64
Literary Fund, 193–196
Livingston, Henry Brockholst, 14, 151, 154–157, 177, 197–198
Livingston, John, 198
Livingston, William, 14–15
"Livingstonians," 154–155
Locke, Francis, 75
Longfellow, Henry Wadsworth, 205
Longfellow, Stephen, 205–206
Lord, Nathan, 196
lottery, 15, 44, 64, 114, 176, 217–218
Louisville Bridge Company v. United States, 219
Lyman, Job, 129

Madison, James (President of the College of William and Mary), 45
Madison, James (President of the United States), 55, 82, 124, 159
Magdalen College, Oxford, 22, 59, 100

Maine Literary and Theological Institution (later Colby College), 183
Marsh, Charles, 44, 86, 93–96, 98–100, 125, 128, 130, 159, 179, 181, 195
Marsh, Joseph, 44
Marshall, John, vii, 3, 4; and *Bank of the United States v. Deveaux*, 118; and *Bracken v. the Visitors of William and Mary College*, 59, 61–64; and *Dartmouth v. Woodward*, 138–139, 161–171, 178–179, 205, 211, 218, 220, 222–223; death of, 214; and general support for corporate autonomy, 188; and *Martin v. Hunter's Lessee*, 73; and Joseph Story, 102, 205, 211; and *Sturgis v. Crowninshield* and *Ogden v. Saunders*, 197–201
Marsh v. Allen, 129
Martin v. Hunter's Lessee, 73
Mason, George, 55
Mason, Jeremiah, 86, 101–105, 116, 123, 126–127, 141, 143, 156, 177, 181
Massachusetts Bay Colony, 11, 22, 36, 76–77, 191, 213
Massachusetts General Hospital, 78, 196
Massachusetts Government Act, 39, 168
McFarland, Asa, 95
McGaw, Jacob, 149
McKeen, Joseph, 203
McLean, Ann (Amory), 196
McLean, John, 196–197
medical schools, 77–78, 81, 106, 153, 155
Michigan State University, 208
Middlebury College, 97, 124, 150
Miller v. State, 216
Mississippi Agricultural, Educational, and Manufacturing Aid Society, 217
Missouri Compromise, 183, 186, 203
Mohawk tribe, 15
Mohegan tribe, 15

{ *Index* }   265

monopoly, 5, 12–13, 15, 210, 214
Monroe, James, 97–98, 139, 141
Montauk tribe, 15
Moor, Joshua, 15–18, 26
Moor's Indian Charity School: conflation with Dartmouth College, 33–38, 48, 65–66, 106, 113, 142–144, 157, 162, 166–167; congressional support for, 40; early years of, 2, 7, 15–17, 85, 108; English donations to, 26, 48–49, 82–83, 108, 166–167, 172–173; discussion of charter for, 27, 30–35; invitations to relocate to New Hampshire, 18, 20–21; John Wheelock as president of, 43, 48, 66, 87, 97, 130; without Indian students, 51
Morrill, David, 195
Morrill, Justin, 195
Morrill Act (1862), 209
Moseley, Samuel, 16
municipal corporation. *See* corporation, municipal
Murdoch, Jasper, 50
Muzzy v. Wilkins, 70

Narragansett tribe, 15
natural law (also natural right), vii, 56, 104, 110, 164, 200
Neirbo Company v. Bethlehem Shipbuilding Corporation, 220
New England Mississippi Land Company, 102–103
"new facts," 157, 159–162, 164, 178, 180–181
New Hampshire College of Agriculture and the Mechanic Arts, 210
New Hampshire Gazette, 70
"New Hampshire grants," 18, 29–30, 42
New Hampshire Patriot, 84, 124, 177, 194

New Light branch of the Presbyterian Church, 13–14
New York College of Physicians and Surgeons, 155
Niles, Nathaniel, 51, 68
North American Review, 186
Northwest Ordinances (First and Second), 53, 55, 164

obligation (contractual): charter obligations, 110, 175, 211; debt obligations, 53, 56, 198–201; "obligation of contract," vii, 3, 55, 58, 102, 104, 118, 140–141, 156, 164, 170–171, 199–201, 208, 215; salary contract obligation, 205
Occom, Samson, 15–16, 26, 28–30, 39, 48–49
Ogden v. Saunders, 197–201
Olcott, Mills, 94, 161, 182, 193
Oneida tribe, 15
overseers. *See* board of overseers
Oxford University. *See* University of Oxford

Paine, Thomas, 141
Panic of 1819, 182, 192–193
Parish, Elijah, 83–84
Parker, Isaac, 149–150
Parliament, 4, 22–23, 39, 98, 104, 134, 137, 158–159, 163, 168, 200, 205
"Parnassus," 45
Parsons, Theophilus, 75–77, 85, 99, 191
partisanship, 2, 4–6, 47, 54, 75–78, 81–84, 88, 96–97, 105, 114, 116, 119–120, 124, 128, 138, 150, 153, 173, 179, 183, 185, 194
Peck, John, 102
Pendleton, Edmund, 61, 73
Pennsylvania College Cases, 216
Pennsylvania State University, 208
Perkins, Cyrus, 159–160, 178

Perrine v. Chesapeake and Delaware Canal Company, 215
personhood (corporate personhood), vii, 21, 56, 73, 118, 173, 219–222
Phillips, John, 68, 85
Phillips Academy in Andover, 68, 176
Phillips Academy in Exeter, 68, 105, 123
Phillips Professorship in Divinity, 68–69
Phillips v. Bury, 23–24, 61–62, 105
Pierce, David, 129
Pierce ex dem. Lyman v. Gilbert, 129
Pinkney, William, 149, 159–161, 178, 180
Piqua Branch of the State Bank of Ohio v. Knoop, 215
Plumer, William, 70–72, 82, 88–91, 93–95, 99, 116, 123–124, 126, 139, 157, 178, 180, 188, 194, 215
police power (as regulatory power), 201, 217–219
Pomeroy, Benjamin, 16
Powell, John, 170
Presbyterian Church, 13, 16, 67, 70, 72
Princeton (University), 14, 178
Princeton Theological Seminary, 97, 181
private corporation. *See* corporation, private
private interest, 4, 6, 83, 114, 117, 144, 178, 211–212
Providence Bank v. Billings, 201
public corporation. *See* corporation, public
public interest, 102, 211; education as, 4, 31; framed as "public benefit," 168, 212; public overseers and legislators as representatives of, 61, 63, 88, 110–111, 117, 152–153, 187–188, 201–202, 215–217, 222; served by cities, colleges, churches, and companies as corporations, 2, 4–6, 15, 23, 42, 64, 70–71, 84, 119, 153, 190, 214; served by Crown, 114, 117; served by private trustees, 87, 101–102, 188, 190, 210–212, 217
Putnam, Samuel, 196–197

Queen Elizabeth I, 21, 23, 24, 111, 159, 211
Queen Mary II, 59
Quincy, Josiah, 191

Randolph, John, 102
regulation, vii–viii, 5, 13, 24, 44, 56, 99, 133, 158, 171, 175, 201, 205, 216–219, 221–223
republican (republicanism), 5, 39, 42, 44–45, 47, 52, 54, 58, 89, 114, 119, 121, 168
Republican Party, 173; John Holmes and, 139; Thomas Jefferson, Virginia, and, 6, 73, 89, 186; Maine and, 183–186; Massachusetts and, 75–78, 82, 126–127, 190–191; New York and, 153–154; William Plumer, New Hampshire, and, 71–72, 82, 84, 88–89, 91, 97, 116, 121, 124, 177, 186, 195
reserve clause, vii, 64, 75–78, 88, 99, 111, 165, 175–176, 184–185, 191, 200, 202–206, 209, 216–220
revival (religious), 2, 12–14, 16–17, 67, 69–71, 183
revolution, 1, 92, 168, 188, 205; in Massachusetts, 76, 192; in New Hampshire, 3, 42–43, 51, 68, 70, 97, 114, 133, 142–144, 154, 157, 163; in Pennsylvania, 44; postrevolutionary, 46, 53, 57, 60, 70, 89, 98, 103, 109, 140, 152, 157, 163; prerevolutionary, 60, 140, 169, 163; in Vermont, 97, 133; in Virginia, 58–60, 72;
Richardson, William, 116–119, 126, 150
Ripley, Eleazar Wheelock, 91

Ripley, Sylvanus, 67–68
Roane, Spencer, 72

Sage v. Dillard, 208
Salem, Massachusetts, 125–127
Searle, Thomas, 182
sectarianism, 2, 6, 12, 14–15, 68–69, 82, 84, 183, 186
Shelby College, 218
Shepherd's Tent, 12–13
Sherbourne, John, 204
Shurtleff, Roswell, 68–69, 81, 83, 96, 183
Sierra Club v. Morton, 221
Six Nation tribes, 18
Smith, Jeremiah, 101, 104–107, 115–115, 123, 127–128, 141, 143, 157, 180, 182
Smith, John, 68–69
Smith, Nathan, 78
Smith, William (author of *The General Idea of the College of Mirania* and, later, president of the College of Philadelphia), 14, 57
Smith, William Sr. (attorney general of New York), 16, 27–29
Social Friends, 120–121
Society in London for the Propagation of the Gospel in Foreign Parts, 18
Society in Scotland for Propagating Christian Knowledge, 18
St. John's College v. Todington, 63
Stapleton, William, 23
Statute of Charitable Uses (1601), 21, 158, 211
Stevens, Samuel, 29
Story, Joseph, 102–104, 123, 125–129, 149, 156–160, 170–176, 177, 180–181, 190–191, 197–198, 200–202, 204–206, 211, 214–215
Stone v. Mississippi, 217–218, 220
Stetson v. Kempton, 99

Sturges, Josiah, 198
Sturges v. Crowninshield, 198–199
Sullivan, George, 101, 108–111, 115, 142, 160, 177
Superior Court of New Hampshire, 2, 65, 70, 82, 94–95, 99–101, 116, 120, 123, 128, 141, 150, 160, 177, 182, 209
Supreme Court of Massachusetts, 99, 102, 149
Supreme Court of the United States: and *Bank of the United States v. Deveaux*, 118; and *Board of Trustees of Vincennes University v. State of Indiana*, 208; and *Charles River Bridge v. Warren Bridge*, 213; and *Dartmouth v. Woodward*, vii, 1–3, 73, 116, 123–125, 127–128, 132, 135, 141, 152, 157, 159–160, 177, 197, 209; and *Fletcher v. Peck*, 102–103; and *Ogden v. Saunders*, 199–201; and *Sturgis v. Crowninshield*, 198
Supreme Court of Wisconsin, 217
Supremacy Clause, 73
Sutton's Hospital, 19, 20, 58
Swift, Zephaniah, 64
System of Laws of the State of Connecticut, 64

Takings Clause, 104
tax, 15, 39, 71, 74, 98, 103, 178, 184, 216; bank tax, 65, 160, 183, 185–186, 190, 192–193, 201, 215; church tax, 5, 11–13, 68–72, 188
Taylor, John, 58, 62–63
Taney, Roger, 214
Tennent, Gilbert, 12
Tennent, William, 12
Terrick, Richard, 59
Terrett v. Taylor, 103–104
Thompson, Benjamin, 210
Thompson, Smith, 197

Thompson, Thomas, 85
Todd, Thomas, 157, 177, 197
Tompkins, Daniel, 155
Town of Pawlet v. Clarke, 133
Treaty of Ghent, 139
Trimble, Robert, 197
Trinity Church (New York City), 14–15
trover, 94, 128
Trustees of Dartmouth College v. Woodward. See *Dartmouth v. Woodward*
Trustees of Philadelphia Baptist Association v. Hart's Executors, 220
Trustees of the University of North Carolina v. Foy, 74, 76, 208
Turpin v. Lockett, 72–73, 103
Tucker, Henry St. George, 72–73
Tuttle, Hiram, 210
Tyler, Bennett, 182, 195–196
Tyron, William, 41

Union College, 176, 183
Unitarian Church, 71, 190
United Fraternity, 120
United States v. Scophony Company of America, 219–220
University of Alabama v. Winston, 207
University of Cambridge, 11, 25, 100, 105, 134, 136, 137, 158–159
University of Edinburgh, 56
University of Florida, 208
University of Glasgow, 56
University of Iowa, 208
University of Minnesota, 208
University of Mississippi, 208
University of New Hampshire, 90, 192–193, 195, 210
University of North Carolina, 74–76
University of North Carolina v. Josiah Maultsby, 208

University of Oxford, 22–23, 25, 59, 100, 105, 134, 158–159
University of the State of New York, 46–47
University of the State of Pennsylvania, 44
University of Utah, 208
University of Vermont, 47, 182
University of Wisconsin, 208

Vermont, and statehood, 1, 41–42, 44; and college and church disputes, 68, 133, 150; and Dartmouth College bid to become state university, 43–44, 47, 51, 165; and Dartmouth College property, including "Wheelock" township, 48, 50–51, 66, 97, 107, 128–130, 182; and Dartmouth College trustees, 85–86, 93, 179; and David and Justin Morrill, 195; and eminent domain, 215
vested interests, 6, 142; vested property or privileges, 48, 54–55, 72–74, 91, 98, 103, 109–110, 118, 130, 134, 142, 156, 162, 174, 181, 191–192, 208, 220; vested rights or powers, 73, 75, 77, 85, 89, 91–92, 95, 105, 114, 118, 130, 156, 176, 184, 203
Virginia State Board of Pharmacy v. Virginia Citizens Consumer Council, 220
visitors (visitatorial rights), 13, 19, 20, 22–25, 45, 46, 58–63, 65, 77–78, 81, 83–88, 91, 95, 97–98, 105–106, 108–110, 114–115, 133–135, 137, 157–159, 168–169, 171–172, 183–184, 217–218

Wales v. Stetson, 75
Washington, Bushrod, 73, 166, 170, 198, 214
Washington, George, 64, 170
Washington Academy, 64

Washington College (Pennsylvania), 216
Washington College (Virginia; formerly Liberty Hall Academy), 63–64
Washington University v. Rouse, 216
Waterhouse, Benjamin, 77–78
W. B. Worthen Company v. Thomas, 219
Webster, Daniel, 2–3; background, 123–125; and *Charles River Bridge*, 213–214; and *Dartmouth* argument
Webster, Daniel (*cont.*)
before the US Supreme Court, 132–143, 145, 165; and defense of Harvard as private college and corporation, 190–193; legal strategies in *Dartmouth* case, 127–130, 156–161, 165, 211; legal strategies after US Supreme Court victory, 177–182; and *Ogden v. Saunders*, 199, 201; skepticism around public aid to Dartmouth College, 194; and Joseph Story, 123, 149–151, 190–194; suggests public university in New Hampshire, 90; and John Wheelock, 85
Wentworth, Benning, 17–18, 21, 63
Wentworth, John, 26, 30–41, 43, 48, 95, 97, 162, 167
Westminster College, 159
Wheaton, Henry, 199
Wheelock, Eleazar, 2–3, 7, 11, 13, 15–21, 26–43; as characterized in *Dartmouth* litigation, 106, 108–109, 113, 128, 132, 134, 136–137, 142–144, 157, 162–164, 167–168, 171–172, 179
Wheelock, John: becomes president of Dartmouth College and Moor's Indian Charity School, 43; death of, 96; dismissal from Dartmouth College presidency, 87–88, 92, 126; and disputes with Dartmouth College trustees, 49, 51, 65–69, 81–89, 93, 104; gift to Princeton Theological Seminary, 181; loans to Dartmouth College, 196; seeks to make Dartmouth College the state university of Vermont, 43–44; 47–48, 51, 133, 164–165; seeks public aid from New Hampshire, 48, 65–66
Wheelock, Ralph (seventeenth century), 11
Wheelock, Ralph (nineteenth century), 11, 29
Wheelock township (Vermont), 47–48, 51, 66, 93, 130, 182
Whitaker, Nathaniel, 26–30, 40, 48–49
White, David, 125, 127, 128
Whitefield, George, 12, 17, 26, 28–29
Wilde, Samuel, 149
Williams, Elisha, 16
Williams College, 64–65, 97, 150, 175–176, 183
Winchester College, 159
Wilson, James, 53–58, 211
Wirt, William, 140–143, 145, 149, 160, 161, 166, 180, 199–201, 213–214
Woodbury, Levi, 116
Woodward, Bezaleel, 41
Woodward, William H., 93–94, 97, 139–140, 180
writ of ejectment (or writ of entry), 130, 179

Yale College, 209; allied with Dartmouth College, 97, 124, 132, 150; charter of, 112, 192; Thomas Clap and, 19–21, 25, 59; Timothy Dwight and, 64–65; Great Awakening at, 11–14; "Parnassus" and public to, 45; Eleazar Wheelock and, 2, 11, 16, 29, 78

www.ingramcontent.com/pod-product-compliance
Lightning Source LLC
Chambersburg PA
CBHW030634250326
41837CB00015B/138